HOME OWNER'S KIT

▶ **Everything You Need To Know —
from Moving In to Moving Out**

▶ **More than 150 Ready-To-Use
Forms and Checklists**

▶ **Hundreds of Home Safety and Security Tips**

ROBERT de HEER

**Real Estate
Education Company**
a division of Dearborn Financial Publishing, Inc.

While a great deal of care has been taken to provide accurate and current information, the ideas, suggestions, general principles and conclusions presented in this text are subject to local, state and federal laws and regulations, court cases and any revisions of same. The reader is thus urged to consult legal counsel regarding any points of law—this publication should not be used as a substitute for competent legal advice.

Publisher: Anita A. Constant
Editor-in-Chief: Caroline Carney
Acquisitions Editor: Christine E. Litavsky
Senior Associate Editor: Karen A. Christensen
Managing Editor: Jack L. Kiburz
Editorial Assistant: Stephanie C. Schmidt
Interior and Cover Designs: S. Laird Jenkins Corporation

Published by Real Estate Education Company,
a division of Dearborn Financial Publishing, Inc.

Printed in the United States of America

95 96 97 10 9 8 7 6 5 4 3 2 1

Library of Congress Cataloging-in-Publication Data

De Heer, Robert, 1923–
   [Homeowners book]
   The homeowner's kit / by Robert de Heer.
     p.   cm.
   Previously published as: Homeowners book.
   Includes index.
   ISBN 0-7931-1087-4 (pbk.)
   1. Home ownership—Handbooks, manuals, etc.   I. Title.
HD7287.8.D35   1995
643'.12—dc20
                                        94-36680
                                        CIP

Contents

Preface

The Homeowner's Kit is an all-inclusive reference source of concise and practical information homeowners can refer to in solving everyday problems, including security and safety in the home, day-to-day maintenance, pest control, homeowner's insurance, refinancing, tax savings homeowners should know about, guidelines to survive natural disasters, selling a home profitably and finally great tips on moving to a new residence.

To accomplish the objective of a truly useful handbook, much of the text is in checklist format, enabling the reader to get straight to the heart of the matter.

The forms in Appendix C make the book truly a homeowner's kit. They are invaluable for recording important information about maintenance and repairs, costs of capital improvements, fixing-up expenses, computing the tax basis of your next home, exemptions for persons 55 and over, tax-deductible moving expenses, and a directory of technicians, suppliers and professional advisers.

The Homeowner's Kit is the result of in-depth research of every conceivable subject concerned with home ownership and endless consultations with numerous professionals and specialists in related fields.

May I take this opportunity to express my sincere gratitude to the many friends, experts and professionals for their invaluable contributions.

—Robert W. de Heer

CHAPTER ONE

Transfer of Ownership

Title to Real Property

Proof of Ownership

Forms of Ownership

Close of Escrow or Settlement

Closing Costs

Title to Real Property

Good Title

As applied to real estate, title indicates lawful ownership and right to property. *Good title* to real property is the owner's legal right to the peaceful possession and use of the property, free from claims of others.

Purchase agreements commonly include a provision that title is to be free of liens and encumbrances, other than the following:

- Mortgage liens set forth in the agreement
- Real estate taxes not yet due
- Covenants, conditions, restrictions, reservations and easements of record, if any, that do not materially affect the value or intended use of the property

Encumbrances

An *encumbrance* is any right or interest by a third party that affects either the title to real property or its use:

- Encumbrances affecting the title are called *liens.* A lien is a form of encumbrance that usually makes property security for the payment of a debt or fulfillment of an obligation. Examples are mortgage liens, tax liens, mechanics liens and judgments.
- Encumbrances affecting the use of property include covenants, restrictions, reservations and easements.

Restrictions, Covenants and Conditions

Restrictions, covenants and *conditions* in some way limit the free use of land by its owner. Examples include zoning laws restricting the use of a lot to a single family dwelling, minimum setback of building from the curb, architectural restrictions and restrictions affecting new subdivisions.

Reservations

Reservations are rights retained by a previous owner, usually relating to mineral rights.

Easements

Easements are rights by other parties to travel over, dig under or otherwise use a specific portion of an owner's land. Examples include access easements by neighbors; and utility easements for tclephone, telegraph or power lines, water, gas or sewer mains.

Clouds or Defects on the Title

A *cloud* or *defect on the title* is any outstanding claim by another, justified or not. If valid, it could affect the owner's title to the property, preventing him or her from conveying marketable title. Such clouds are rarely serious, but sometimes require time to be cleared and may delay the closing of the transaction. Examples include a mortgage paid off without an official recordation of the fact, or a lawsuit that has been dropped by the plaintiff but has not been removed from the record.

Proof of Ownership

In order to establish evidence, or proof, of title to real property, a qualified title examiner (from a lawyer, abstract company or title insurance company) must search the public records and prepare a title report. The report lists encumbrances, existing liens and any title defects disclosed by the examination. The title report also lists all persons having an interest in the property. In order to eliminate serious financial risk by reason of the seller not owning all of the interest in the property as claimed, it is essential for the buyer to have the title searched before the purchase is consummated.

In different parts of the country, varying methods are used to furnish evidence of title:

- Title insurance
- Certificate of title
- Abstract of title
- Certificate of registration (Torrence system)

Title Insurance

Title insurance insures against defects in the title disclosed in the public records but not listed in the title policy as exceptions and covers defense against any action, warranted or not, by reason of such defects.

The buyer or seller, depending on local custom, is generally required to pay for a lender's policy in the amount of the mortgage loan. The lender's policy, however, does not protect the owner. The buyer should therefore obtain an owner's policy for the full amount of the purchase price (not just for the amount of his equity). If the lender's and the owner's policies are purchased at the same time, usually only a nominal charge is made for the second policy.

A one-time premium is charged, payable when the policy is issued. The policy remains in force for the duration of ownership, but is not transferable to a subsequent owner.

Certificate of Title

Certificate of title is a written opinion by a title examiner as to the validity of title, based upon an examination of the public records. It offers no protection to the purchaser against hidden defects in the title that an examination of the records could not reveal, nor against any unwarranted litigation attacking the title. The issuer of the certificate of title is liable only for damages due to his or her negligence.

Abstract of Title

Abstract of title is a summary made from public records showing the continuous history of ownership, from the original governmental grant and all subsequent deeds, mortgages and other instruments and facts affecting the title. An abstract is made by an attorney or an abstract company. An abstractor does not insure the title or express an opinion as to the validity of title, although he or she may be legally responsible for errors.

Certificate of Registration (Torrens System)

Under this system, used in some states, the certificate of registration, issued by the recording authority, constitutes conclusive evidence of title.

Forms of Ownership

Tenants in Common and Joint Tenants

Homebuyers also will want to consider the best method of taking title in case two or more persons (referred to as *cotenants*) are buying the home together. Cotenants may hold title as tenants in common or as joint tenants.

Tenants in common need not have equal interests; joint tenants must have equal interests.

Upon death of a tenant in common, the decedent's share passes to the heirs or devisees as identified in his or her will. In joint tenancy, ownership automatically passes to the survivor on the death of either.

Most spouses acquire real property as joint tenants, which may or may not be desirable. It may have unplanned income, gift or inheritance tax consequences.

Only the buyer's lawyer is in a position to advise as to the best method in which title should be vested.

Close of Escrow or Settlement

Escrow is a method of ensuring that both parties have fulfilled their contractual obligations before the transaction can be completed.

An *escrow holder* is a disinterested third person (an attorney, an escrow company or the escrow department of a bank or title company) charged with the custody of funds and instruments (legal documents) received from buyer and seller. When both parties have fulfilled their contractual obligations, the escrow holder delivers the funds to which the seller is entitled and records a properly executed deed in favor of the buyer, in accordance with written instructions from both parties.

The date on which recordation of the deed takes place, referred to as *close of escrow* or *settlement date,* is the date title is conveyed or transferred.

A word of caution: A buyer should not deliver the purchase money directly to the seller. Likewise, a seller should not deliver a signed deed directly to the buyer. Delivery of a properly executed deed completes the sale. For the protection of both parties, the use of an escrow holder is absolutely essential.

Closing Costs

Closing costs or settlement costs fall into two categories:

1. *Nonrecurring costs* are one-time charges and fees incurred in transferring ownership, processing loan papers and searching and insuring the title.
2. *Recurring costs* or *prepaid items* are regular costs such as real estate taxes and insurance premiums.

Nonrecurring Closing Costs

In accordance with local custom, some of these costs are paid by either buyer or seller or divided between them. Examples of these costs follow:

❑ *Title search.* (See "Proof of Ownership.")

❑ *Title insurance.* (See "Proof of Ownership.")

❑ *Lender's legal fee.* The lending institution may charge a fee for its lawyer to handle the closing. The lender's attorney, however, cannot represent the buyer's interests.

❑ *Buyer's legal fee.* This fee is charged if the buyer retains an attorney.

❑ *Survey fee.* The lender may require a survey to determine the precise location of the house and property. Many lenders will accept an old survey the seller may have with an affidavit from the seller that no changes have been made in the structures which would overlap the boundaries.

❑ *Preparation of documents.* The deed, mortgage or deed of trust and other papers necessary to transact the sale must be prepared by a lawyer, the lender, the title company, the escrow company or some other qualified person.

❑ *Closing or escrow fee.* A charge made by the escrow holder for handling the closing of the transaction.

❑ *Credit report.* The buyer's credit report, required by the lender.

❑ *Pest control inspection report.* Required with FHA and VA loans and many conventional loans. (See Chapter 9.)

❑ *Loan origination fee.* The lender's fee for originating the loan, expressed in percent of loan amount. In FHA and VA transactions involving existing structures, the origination fee to the buyer can be no more than 1 percent.

❑ *Assumption fee.* A fee charged by the lender for consent to transfer the loan to a new owner. (See Chapter 11.)

❑ *Transfer fee.* A nominal fee charged by the lender in the event the property is taken subject to the loan. (See Chapter 11.)

❑ *Appraisal fee.* A charge made by the lender for appraising the property; often part of the loan origination fee.

❑ *Mortgage insurance premium.* A fee charged by the Federal Housing Administration (FHA) or Private Mortgage Insurance (PMI) companies for insuring the lender against loss in case the buyer defaults (see Chapter 11). This is not to be confused with mortgage life insurance policies, designed to pay off the mortgage in the event of the borrower's death.

❑ *Recording fee.* The local authority's charge for recording documents pertaining to the sale.

❑ *State or local transfer taxes.* In some localities, these taxes are levied when property changes hands.

Examples of Recurring Closing Costs

❑ *Insurance premium* for fire and extended coverage for one year. (See Chapter 6.)

❑ *Prorated taxes and special assessments.* In the event the seller has paid the property taxes for a period beyond the date title is transferred, he or she is entitled to be reimbursed by the buyer for that portion of the tax period during which the buyer shall have possession of the property. However, in the event the transaction were to close some time after the beginning of the tax year, but taxes were not due until after transfer of ownership, the buyer would have to be reimbursed by the seller for that portion of the tax period during which the seller had possession of the property. Following are two examples:

1. The closing date is December 15. The seller has paid taxes for the period from July 1 to December 31. The buyer must reimburse the seller for taxes for the period from December 16 to December 31.
2. The closing date is January 15. Taxes for the period from January 1 to June 30 are not due until April 10 in the state of California. Since the buyer will have to pay the taxes for the period from January 1 to June 30, the seller must reimburse the buyer for taxes for the period from January 1 to January 15.

❑ *Prorated interest.* In a transaction closing July 17, the first payment on a new mortgage is usually not due until September 1, including interest for the month of August. As part of the prepaid items at closing, the lender charges interest prorated for the period from July 17 to August 1.

❑ *Impound account.* Certain types of mortgages require the borrower to deposit funds into a trust fund, also referred to as impound or escrow account. From this account the lender disburses property taxes and insurance premiums when due. Many owners request such an arrangement for the sake of convenience. At close of escrow, the buyer deposits into the impound account a sum sufficient to cover the first tax payment and the first year's insurance premium. In addition to payments toward principal and interest, the monthly payments must include proportionate amounts for taxes and insurance, which are deposited into the impound account. When the property is sold, the balance left in the impound account at close of escrow must be returned to the seller. Prorations are made irrespective of the impound account.

CHAPTER TWO

Homestead Protection

What Is a Homestead?

Homestead protection is granted in many states, mainly to prevent forced sale of the family home for the payment of certain debts. It is not to be confused with homestead land grants under federal law. Because homestead laws differ from state to state, the information presented in this chapter is only of a general nature.

Following are the requirements for creating a homestead:

1. The property must be occupied as the principal residence. According to recent court decisions, the conducting of a business is not inconsistent with the right of a homestead, provided it continues to be a bona fide residence.
2. The head of the family must own the property or some interest therein.
3. A "declaration of homestead" must be filed (recorded), if required by state law. Declaration of homestead forms can usually be obtained from stationery stores.
4. Other requirements of local law must be observed.

Limitations

The following debts are not covered by homestead protection:

1. Judgments filed prior to the date the declaration of homestead is filed (recorded).
2. Mortgages given as part of the purchase price.
3. Any mortgage signed by the owners containing a proper waiver of homestead rights.
4. Mechanics' liens, issued by reason of improvements or repairs made to the property by contractors, mechanic contractors, mechanics, laborers and vendors referred to as material men.
5. Nonpayment of alimony in certain states.
6. Unpaid taxes and special assessments.

Equity Protection

Some states limit the equity protected by the homestead. For example, assume the maximum homestead protection of your equity is $20,000 in your state. Your family home is homesteaded. Its current market value is $80,000, it has a first mortgage with a $45,000 balance and a second mortgage with a $5,000 balance, leaving you an equity of $30,000. A creditor who obtains a judgment can act to have your home sold, since your equity of $30,000 exceeds the maximum $20,000 homestead protection. From the proceeds of the sale, however, the creditor must pay you the $20,000 homestead protection in cash. Assuming your home sold for only $77,000 in the forced sale, less legal and appraisal fees of $2,000, the creditor would net $5,000 in satisfaction of the judgment, after paying off the mortgages and your equity protection.

Transferring Homestead Protection to a New Home

In some states, when a homesteaded home is sold, the proceeds from the sale, not to exceed the maximum amount of equity protected by the homestead, continue to be protected for a limited number of months. That amount cannot be attached if you purchase and homestead another home within that time limit.

In the event you rent and keep your homesteaded property and move into another home, you must first file an "abandonment of homestead" before you can file a declaration of homestead on your new home.

Homestead of Widow, Widower or Minor Children

Upon the death of a spouse, the surviving spouse usually is accorded the rights in the homestead during his or her lifetime. In many states, the minor children are likewise allowed to occupy the homesteaded premises until they become of age.

CHAPTER THREE

Home Security

Security Devices for House and Contents

Burglar Alarm Systems

Security Routines

In the 1970s and 1980s, most residential burglaries were committed during daytime hours by young adult amateurs. The typical burglar might have been a clean-cut male in his early 20s, wearing ordinary clothes or the familiar uniform of a delivery or service company.

During the 1990s, the majority of burglaries are committed between 2 and 4 PM by neighborhood youth who enter the house through small open windows. They know the comings and goings of neighbors' cars and are aware of when they are not home—even for just a short time to go to the store for groceries.

If they find that a house is alarmed with other than neighborhood watch stickers, they go next door or elsewhere. The burglars are usually between the ages of 14 and 16 and in most areas can legally only be held for a very short time in juvenile hall. They are soon out doing the same thing again, even if the homeowner goes through the process of prosecuting. The main reason for many of these burglaries is to support drug habits. Victims can, in many cases, find their belongings for sale at a local flea market the following week-end. Unless there is bodily harm involved, the authorities have few resources to prevent this type of crime.

Most burglars, young or old, are not violent and are intent on stealing without being seen or confronted. Even a relatively passive person, however, will lash out when cornered. For your own safety, in the event you happen to surprise a burglar, allow him or her room to exit.

Security Devices for House and Contents

Perimeter

❑ Use timers or photocells for all outside lights.
❑ All exterior doors should have solid cores and be at least 1¾ inch thick.
❑ Door frames must be solid.
❑ Every exterior door should have some form of deadbolt.
❑ High security lock cylinders should be used in exterior door locks. Key-in-knob locks with spring latches, even those with deadlatch plungers, should not be depended on for security.
❑ Door viewers, or peepholes, in solid doors are essential for identifying persons before opening the door, provided they allow you to see 80 degrees, from the ground up.
❑ Door chains are useful as an interviewing device, that is checking credentials of tradespeople, but cannot be depended on to keep out intruders.

❑ Locks used on sliding glass doors usually provide little security. There are, however, two security devices:
  1. Bars that fold down to a horizontal position, positively blocking any movement of the door (the bar may be secured by a key-locked chain).
  2. Locking pin or bolt devices with or without key.

❑ Windows on ground floor, or those that can easily be reached, may be secured by a variety of locking devices on the market.

❑ Good locks serve little purpose if the thief can break a pane of glass and unlock the door or window from the inside. One method of foiling such action is to replace regular glass with tempered glass or laminated plastic glass. Tempered glass is said to be seven times as strong as regular glass and is required by many building codes for use in sliding patio doors. Laminated plastic glass, consisting of plastic pressed between two sheets of glass, is virtually indestructible. There is also bulletproof glass and bulletproof plastic (Lexan), though the cost may be prohibitive except in special applications.

Garage

❑ Attached garages give a burglar a secluded place from which to break into the house. If the door from the garage to the house is hollow-core, it should be replaced by a solid-core door with a deadbolt.

❑ Keep garage doors closed and locked at all times.

❑ Radio-controlled garage door openers materially reduce chances of leaving the garage door open while leaving on short errands.

Interior

❑ To help you collect every insurance dollar to which you are legally entitled due to fire, burglary or other disaster, keep an inventory of all valuable items in your house, including size, color, serial numbers and identifying marks.

❑ Take photos of every room in the house, including furniture groupings, valuable books and paintings, sterling silver, china, glassware, sporting equipment and other valuable possessions.

❑ Items of high value, such as jewelry, furs, fine arts, antiques, musical instruments, cameras, stamp and coin collections should be insured under a personal articles endorsement added to your homeowner's insurance policy. (See Chapter 6.)

❑ Check with your local police department to see if they have an "operation identification" program. An electric engraving pencil is used to mark an identification number, usually your driver's license number, on items of value. The marking of goods and posting of a window sticker furnished by the police department, which shows you are part of operation identification, accomplishes two goals. First, it has been demonstrated that houses with "operation identification" stickers suffer fewer burglaries than nonparticipating homes, possibly because the thief knows he or she will have a more difficult time disposing of the marked goods. Second, if you are burglarized, the number can help to get stolen property returned to you.

❑ Be aware of, and secure, items most likely to be stolen, which include the following:
- Money
- Firearms
- Credit cards
- Securities
- Television sets
- Stereo equipment
- Tape recorders and other electronic equipment
- Jewelry
- Furs
- Silverware
- Watches
- Liquor
- Sports equipment
- Stamp, coin and other collections
- Antiques
- Artwork
- Cameras and projectors
- Power tools
- Bicycles
- Appliances

❑ Keep the following items in a safe-deposit box:
- Inventory of household and personal property, together with receipts, photos and credit card records
- Stock and bond certificates
- Mortgages, deeds and property titles
- Birth, marriage and death certificates
- Military discharge papers
- Citizenship and adoption papers

- Income tax records
- Automobile titles
- Contracts and business agreements
- Health insurance policies
- Fire insurance policies
- Pension plans
- Life insurance policies and wills

❑ Home money safes—Any safe in which you intend to keep money or valuables should have some type of UL (Underwriters Laboratory) burglary-resistant label. A particular UL label means that the safe model has been tested to resist attacks of a specific nature for a certain number of minutes.

❑ Fire-resistant chests and files carry UL ratings that indicate an endurance to fire in minutes or hours.

❑ Consider making a security closet in your home that has bearing walls on as many sides as possible. Install heavy plywood on the inside walls. Make certain that a solid-core door, heavy-duty deadbolt, high-security strike and nonremovable hinge pins are used. If you have a burglar alarm system, trap the closet door or interior. Make a practice of keeping firearms, silver, cameras, coin collections, furs and so on in your security closet.

Burglar Alarm Systems

Studies have shown a dramatic reduction in burglaries in residences equipped with alarms. Insurance companies offer up to 15 percent reduction in premium, depending upon the alarm system's sophistication. Even with quality locks, an alarm system is a good investment, particularly if a home is vacant a good deal of the time. It also provides security against intruders while the occupants are at home.

Burglar alarm systems range from inexpensive battery-operated units that protect a single door or window to sophisticated systems that protect the entire house and alert the police or a private protective service.

Perimeter Alarms

Perimeter alarms are possibly the most common and reliable of the more sophisticated forms of residential alarm systems. They use various types of contact devices on doors, windows and at strategic locations throughout the house. The high-grade systems are of the "closed-circuit" variety, causing the alarm to be tripped when a wire is cut anywhere in the system.

When evaluating alarm systems, it is important to note three caveats:

1. The wireless or battery-operated alarm devices have proven to be very unreliable because of high false-alarm problems associated with radio frequency interference. Professional installers use the hard-wired systems to provide fault-free systems.

2. Alarms should *not* be silent (without a noise device of some kind). The main purpose of silent alarms was to apprehend the intruder in the act if the authorities received the call soon enough. This was at a time when most intruders were over the age of 21 and would require some jail time. Today, most intruders are teenagers who, after an inconvenient but short stay in juvenile hall will likely be right back at it again within a short time.

   A siren or other audible device alerts intruders that they have tripped an alarm system and, it is hoped, chases them away from your home.

3. Some alarm systems use cylindrical alarm keys to arm and disarm them. These, like other keys, can be duplicated. The best solution to eliminate the possibility of circumventing the alarm system is a digital keypad that does not use keys to arm and disarm the system.

The idea of these alarms is to frighten away an intruder and to alert occupants and neighbors.

Central Station Alarms

Central station alarms are connected to a central station through your existing telephone line (not a leased line) by a digital dialer, long-range high frequency transmitter or a simple tape dialer to the dispatch center or in some cases (although less frequent now because of false alarms) directly to the authorities.

Most police departments stop responding after a certain number of false alarms. There is generally a charge for reinstating the system after a period.

Contracting for an Alarm System

Before contracting for the installation of an alarm system, make absolutely certain you are dealing with a company that

1. is reputable and will be around for a long time to back up the system with periodic service.
2. uses reliable UL-approved equipment.
3. does neat installation work.

Locate at least two alarm companies and check their reputation with the local police department and the Better Business Bureau.

Have each firm make a survey of your house and provide the following information:

1. A listing of door and window openings to be connected to the system
2. Location of wiring and switches. (Running exposed wiring on baseboards is cheaper.)
3. Discussion of lease versus purchase of the equipment. Obtain a copy of the contract you will sign if you decide to order the system. In the event of a lease, be sure you can purchase the equipment after a given period. (In most cases, the lease is far more expensive after figuring in the installation charge and monthly fees over the term of the lease.)
4. A written proposal with the total cost

Security Routines

When You Leave Your Home

The following checklist is included in Appendix D.

During the Day

❏ Check all your windows and doors before you leave. Someone in the family probably left a window open.

❏ Lock the door from the garage to the kitchen or house. An intruder can simply pry open the garage door or enter the garage through a side door or window and have free access to the house.

❏ Bring in the morning newspaper if it is still outside.

❏ Lock your deadbolt lock. Don't get lazy and revert to using only the key-in-knob lock.

❏ Turn on your burglar alarm, if you have one. Remember, daytime burglaries are increasing faster than nighttime burglaries.

❏ Try to arrange with a neighbor to pick up your mail (if you don't have a mail slot in the door). Mail in the box is one of the best clues to an empty house. Burglars know that the average person scoops up the mail just after it arrives.

❏ Make absolutely certain that you have closed and locked your garage door.

❏ Don't leave notes telling anyone you are not at home.

❑ As a fire safety measure, make certain all burners and heating elements not thermostatically controlled are turned off (stove, oven, broiler, hot plate, portable heater, etc.).

❑ When valet-parking your car at a concert, dance, charity event, etc., remove the registration materials from the car, so the attendant cannot find out where the occupants live. A dishonest attendant could easily read the registration address and pass it on to a burglar who could be robbing the household while the owners are at the function.

At Night

❑ Try to leave as many "at home" signs as you can think of.

❑ Use your timers to come on first in the living areas, then in the sleeping areas. Don't leave the bedroom lights on all night. Use a timer so your bedroom light goes off at your usual bedtime.

❑ Leave a radio playing, put it on the same timer. Don't leave a television set on, as this can create a fire hazard.

❑ Double-check your windows and door deadbolts to see that they are secure.

❑ Turn on your yard and porch lights, or let them come on with timers or photo cells.

❑ Set your burglar alarm.

❑ Make sure your garage is locked.

Vacations

❑ Try to have your house maintain a "lived-in" look during your vacation.

❑ Have your inside lights on timers; lights left on all day will stand out.

❑ Have a radio on a timer.

❑ If you have a burglar alarm, see that a trusted neighbor, your private patrol or the police have a key to the alarm, if the shut-off is outside. If the shut-off is inside, provide the same person with a house key, so he or she can enter in case of an alarm. Make sure your neighbor has a key or the combination to the alarm locker, the phone number of the central station and the security code, to avoid having authorities respond if not necessary.

❑ Put as many valuables as possible in safekeeping, in your safe deposit box, with a friend, at the office and so on.

❑ Cancel deliveries of newspapers, milk and so on.

❑ Ask a neighbor to put rubbish and advertising materials in your trash container each collection day. This takes a really good friend!

❑ Ask the post office to hold your mail, submit a temporary change of address or ask a neighbor to pick up your mail each day.

❏ Make arrangements to have your lawn mowed and have walks and drives shoveled in case of snow. A few footprints in the snow would help too.

❏ Notify the police department or private police patrol of the dates of your departure and return. Give them a description and the license numbers of all cars that will be parked near the house or have reason to be there for short periods.

❏ If you have a second car, leave it parked in the driveway. If neighbors are going to be looking after your house, ask them to vary the position of your car from day to day.

❏ Do not leave house keys outside, no matter how well you have hidden them.

❏ If possible, avoid loading your car for a vacation in daylight in plain view.

❏ Discuss your vacation plans as little as possible in public. Don't publicize your plans in local newspapers.

Precautions with Strangers

You may have become familiar with the delivery persons, meter readers, tradespeople, and so on who make regular visits to your home and you know them to be reputable and trustworthy employees. The turnover of personnel is so rapid today, however, that it may be difficult to identify these persons or know when an imposter may be calling. Install an optical viewer and a good door chain on front and back doors, as well as an intercom system, so you can identify callers before opening the door. Should you happen to meet an unfamiliar face at the door, be sure to check the person's credentials before letting him or her come into the house. Call the employer if you must, especially if the work to be done involves removing television sets or other appliances from the house for repair.

Children should be told never to give information to strangers on the street or over the phone.

Advice Concerning Babysitters

❏ Instruct the sitter to lock all doors after you have left.

❏ Instruct the sitter never to allow a stranger to enter, even if the caller insists he or she is a friend, relative or neighbor. Giving an explanation or apology to the injured party the following day is far more desirable than taking the chance of letting a potential criminal into your home.

❏ Leave a list of emergency phone numbers (doctor, hospital, poison control center, fire department and police) beside the telephone. Include the address and phone number of your place of destination and the phone numbers of neighbors who could help in an emergency. Make sure the sitter's parents know your home address and telephone number.

❏ Instruct the sitter to keep the telephone line free in case you need to call home. If the sitter receives phone calls from unidentified callers, he or she should not give out information of any kind, especially that they are alone in the house.

❏ Be sure the sitter knows the full name and the age of each child. Leave instructions as to special medical needs.

❏ When you return, escort the sitter home.

See "Babysitter Information and Safety Checklist," in Appendix D.

Steps To Take after Your Home Has Been Burglarized

Since most burglaries are committed in unoccupied houses, it is unlikely that you will ever come face to face with a burglar in your home. In the off chance that you do, there is one basic rule to follow—do not confront him or her. The burglar could be armed, and your intrusion could frighten or anger him or her while attempting to escape. Simply retreat, if you have gone unnoticed, and call the police. Be sure to furnish complete information over the phone—your full name and exact address.

If the thief has already left by the time you arrive home, call the police immediately, then your insurance agent. Do not clean up the ransacked area or alter it in any way. Before the police arrive, however, you should itemize the stolen property as well as you can at that time. Check the household inventory you prepared in advance to make sure you haven't missed any items. If later you should discover still more property is missing, report the loss to the police and your insurance agent, no matter how much time has elapsed since the burglary.

If you find the lock on your door has been forcibly bypassed, take a picture of the damaged area. Do not repair the damage until the police and insurance agent have made their inspections. If you suspect that no force was used to gain entry, call a locksmith right away and have all your locks changed. The burglar may have a duplicate of your key.

Burglars are the hardest of criminals to catch and convict. If a burglar who has ransacked your home is apprehended, your fullest cooperation with the police will be needed. Do not hesitate to identify the person and press charges. Your unwillingness to carry the matter through would only convince the burglar to continue his or her illegal activities with impunity. (See Chapter 6, under the heading "Processing a Claim.")

CHAPTER FOUR

Home Safety

Poor safety habits and unsafe conditions can make a house a death trap. Many deaths and injuries could be avoided if proper care were taken to prevent the three most common household hazards: falls, fire and poisoning.

Basic Safety Precautions

Preparation Is Key

❏ Affix stickers with emergency telephone numbers to each telephone in the house:
- 911 instructions
- Doctor
- Hospital
- Poison control center
- Ambulance
- Fire department rescue squad
- Police
- Gas company
- Electric company
- Taxi service

Emergency Procedures

❏ When making an emergency phone call, remember these four points:
1. *Tell where it happened.* Give exact location and repeat.
2. *Tell what has happened.* Is your home on fire? Is someone trapped inside? Is someone bleeding badly? Has someone had a heart attack? Has someone swallowed a poison? What kind of poison?
3. *Tell who you are.*
4. *Tell what kind of help is needed.* What kind of equipment is needed?

❏ In case of *poisoning,* do the following:
1. Read the label of the substance swallowed.
2. Telephone your doctor, emergency room of nearest hospital or poison control center.
3. Check the label for an antidote and follow instructions carefully.
4. If you go to the doctor or hospital, take the poison container with you.
5. Small children, one through four years old, are generally the victims of home poisonings. To prevent them, the key word is *up!: lock up!, high up!*

In the Kitchen

❏ With small children in the house, move all poisons from under the sink and other low storage areas to high shelves, storing canned goods and dry foods in the low areas instead. The following chemicals are all killers: detergent, drain cleaners, scouring powder, oven cleaners, furniture polish, floor wax, metal polish, wax remover, wall cleaner, carpet cleaner, floor cleaner, ammonia, toilet bowl cleaner and food extracts (vanilla, almond, maple and so on).

❏ If hazardous materials must be stored in low cabinets in homes with small children, be sure to install childproof cabinet door latches, available in most hardware stores.

❏ Keep chemicals in their original containers to avoid mistakes in their use.

❏ Use nonskid wax on kitchen floor.

❏ Wipe up spills immediately.

❏ Have stove and sink areas well lighted.

❏ Turn pot handles away from stove front, but not over another hot burner.

❏ Keep sharp knives in their storage bins.

❏ Use a step stool when reaching into high cupboards.

In the Bathroom

❏ With small children in the house, don't keep drugs in medicine cabinets where children can climb. All medicines should be kept in a place that can be locked.

❏ Close childproof packages immediately after use.

❏ *Never* make the mistake of telling a child that aspirin—or any other medicine—is candy.

❏ Always read and double-check the label for proper dosage. Never take medicine in the dark.

❏ Check with your doctor before taking any combination of medicines.

❏ Never take medicine prescribed for someone else.

❏ Flush away old prescriptions and don't save the empty containers.

❏ Tubs and showers should have textured surfaces or nonskid mats.

❏ With elderly or disabled people in the household, tubs and showers must have sturdy grab bars (not towel bars), mounted on a firm backing, strong enough to support 250 pounds (minimum HUD requirement).

❏ Use skid-resistant floor tile or nonskid rugs or mats.

❏ Dry your hands and don't stand on a wet floor before using electrical appliances.

❏ Ground-fault circuit interrupters can be installed in an individual outlet, to protect against a fatal electric shock. (See "Electrical Safety Checklist" later in this chapter.)

❏ Never touch an electric switch or operate an electrical appliance when you are in the bathtub or shower.

❏ Avoid using hair sprays near open flame or when smoking.

In Bedrooms

❏ Keep cosmetics where children cannot get into them.

❏ Keep purses away from children; they usually contain poison perils such as aspirin, medicines, perfume, lotions and so on.

❏ *Never* keep medicines, especially sleeping pills, on bedside nightstands.

❏ Make sure crib carries label stating it meets federal safety standards.

❏ Buy only children's sleepwear made of flame-retardant material.

❏ *Never smoke in bed!*

❏ Make sure draperies, rugs, bedding, toys and so on are a safe distance from electric baseboard heaters.

❏ Make sure closet light bulbs do not touch clothing.

❏ Provide cabinets for storage of toys to prevent falls.

❏ Make sure all closet doors can be opened from inside.

❏ Threshholds and sliding door tracks protruding above floor level should never be used in traffic areas.

❏ Minimum height of upstairs window sills should be 36 inches or should have protective bars.

❏ Use nonskid pads, tape or backing under small rugs.

In Utility Areas

❏ Laundry area, workshop, garage and garden shed commonly hold numerous poisons. Keep them out of reach of children and keep children away. If possible, keep poisonous products in locked cabinets.

❏ Keep all harmful substances in their original containers to avoid mistakes in their use.

❏ Rinse out empty containers and discard them.

❏ Store flammable liquids in their original metal containers, a safe distance away from pilot lights of water heaters or furnace.

❏ Store oily rags in air-tight metal cans.

❏ Keep power tools disconnected and keep them and hand tools out of reach of children.

On Stairways

❏ All stairways should have sturdy handrails, at least on one side.
❏ Banisters must be sturdy and balusters (upright supports) should be spaced so that a child cannot get his or her head caught between them.
❏ All stairways should be well lighted with three-way switches at top and bottom, including attic stairs.
❏ Keep treads and carpeting in good repair.
❏ Never have a throw rug near a stairway.
❏ Keep stairways clear of toys and other articles.

Outside the Home

❏ Never have walkways adjacent to ground floor windows that open outward.
❏ Have clotheslines high enough to clear pedestrian traffic.
❏ Keep walkways and driveways well lighted.
❏ Repair broken walkways, stairs and driveways.
❏ Keep areas under porches and stairways and around fences free of weeds and leaves.
❏ Return garden tools to their storage racks after use.
❏ Keep walkways and driveways free of snow and ice.
❏ Keep play equipment, such as swings and slides, firmly anchored. Keep protruding bolts and pipe ends protected by caps.
❏ Swimming pool decks, diving boards and ladders must have nonslip surfaces.
❏ Pools must be surrounded by six-foot fences with locked gates to keep out unsupervised children.

General Safety

❏ Nonskid pads, tape or backing should be used under small rugs.
❏ Apply tape or decals to sliding glass doors and other floor to ceiling glass areas, to keep people from mistaking them for door openings.
❏ Many falls can be prevented by good lighting, indoors and out, with switches you can locate before entering, as well as night lights.
❏ Never use makeshift substitutes for a solid, firm-footed climbing stool with steps or a good stepladder.

Hazardous Toys

The toys that amuse your children could also hurt them. Following are age-based toy hazards, and suggested precautions.

Under One Year: Awareness Age

Hazards: Avoid toxic, heavy breakable toys; sharp edges that might cut or scratch; small attachments that might become loose and be put into ears, nose or mouth.

Suggestions: Brightly colored objects hung in view; squeak toys; sturdy, nonflammable rattles; washable stuffed dolls with embroidered eyes; colored balls; cups or smooth nonbreakable objects to chew on.

One to Two Years: Investigative Age

Hazards: Avoid small toys that may be swallowed; flammable objects; toys with small removable parts; poisonous paint on any object; stuffed animals with glass or button eyes.

Suggestions: Rubber or washable squeak toys and soft stuffed dolls or animals; blocks with rounded corners, push-and-pull toys with strings or rounded handles; nests of blocks.

Two to Three Years: Explorative Age

Hazards: Avoid anything with sharp or rough edges that will cut or scratch; objects with small removable parts; poisonous paint or decoration; marbles, beads, coins; flammable toys.

Suggestions: Sandbox with bucket, shovel and spoon; large pegboards; wooden animals; cars and wagons to push around; tip-proof kiddie cars and tricycles; large crayons; low rocking horse; small chair and table; simple musical instruments.

Three to Four Years: Imitative Age

Hazards: Avoid toys that are too heavy for child's strength; poorly made objects that may come apart, break or splinter; sharp or cutting toys; highly flammable costumes; electrical toys.

Suggestions: Small broom and carpet sweeper; toy telephone; dolls with simple wraparound clothing; doll buggies and furniture; dishes; miniature garden tools; trucks and tractors; nonelectrical trains; drums; clothes; building blocks.

Four to Six Years: Beginning of Creative Age

Hazards: Avoid shooting or target toys that will endanger eyes; ill-balanced mobile toys that may topple easily; poisonous painting sets; pinching or cutting objects.

Suggestions: Blackboard and dustless chalk; simple construction sets; nontoxic paints and paint books; doll house and furniture; small sports equipment; jump rope; washtub and washboard; paper doll sets with blunt-end scissors; flame-retardant costumes; modeling clay.

Six to Eight Years: Beginning of Dexterity Age

Hazards: Avoid nonapproved electrical toys; anything too large or complicated for child's strength and ability; sharp-edged tools; poorly made skates; shooting toys.

Suggestions: Carpenter bench and well-constructed, lightweight usable tools; sled; construction sets; roller skates; approved electrical toys; kites; equipment for playing store, bank, filling station, etc.; playground equipment; puzzles and games; sewing materials; dolls and doll equipment.

Eight to Twelve Years: Specialization of Tastes and Skills

Hazards: Avoid air rifles, chemistry sets, dart games, bows and arrows, dangerous tools and electrical toys *unless* used under parental supervision.

Suggestions: Hobby materials; arts and crafts; photography; coin and stamp collections; puppet shows; musical instruments; gym and sports equipment; model and construction building sets; electrical train with underwriters' laboratories (UL) approval; bicycle.

More Than Toys

Proper selection of safe toys is not enough. Many accidents involving toys occur from the misuse of toys. Consider these other factors relating to toy safety:

- *Space.* Children need adequate space in which to use their toys and playthings. Shooting toys meant to be used outdoors can certainly become more dangerous when used inside or in a crowded play area. A safer place, free from interferences, is needed both indoors and outdoors for play activities.

- *Storage.* Each child needs adequate and accessible places to store toys and playthings. Children should be taught the importance of putting their toys away, since playthings littering the floor can be hazardous to others. Proper storage might help prevent misuse of toys by another child.
- *Repair.* One of the responsibilities of parents and adults is to keep toys safe after they are in use. Toys and equipment should be checked periodically for broken or worn parts. If a toy can't be safely repaired it should be thrown away. Electric toys should be examined frequently for any damaged or frayed cords. Nontoxic paint should be used to repaint any toys.
- *Adults.* All children need supervision, guidance and instruction regarding play activities. Supervision is necessary for toddlers using backyard play equipment. Instruction and guidance should be present when a child first uses a hammer, bicycle, chemistry set, electric train, archery set and similar playthings. Parents must also provide for meaningful safety training through play activities of children.

Selecting Playthings for Children

Consider the following tips, provided courtesy of the National Safety Council:

- Pick toys that fit a child's age, development, interests and ability. Choose a variety of toys for purposeful play that will help children develop physically, mentally and emotionally.
- Look for smooth, rolled edges and materials that won't splinter or shatter easily. Look for infant playthings that can be washed or sterilized.
- Ask to see "nontoxic" labels on children's art supplies and painted toys.
- Your choice or preference of toys may not be suitable for a child. Adults sometimes tend to select noncreative toys that can only be used for one type of play activity. A child will not benefit from toys that are too complicated or too advanced for his or her ability.
- Try to determine whether certain toys are flammable or filled with hazardous substances. If unable to do so, it is best not to purchase them.
- Handle toys to determine if they are too heavy for a child's strength and too difficult to manage.
- Insist that electrical toys carry the Underwriters Laboratory mark on the toy, the cord and the plug.

- Note stability of riding toys and larger play equipment.
- Get toys that can't be swallowed and that have no small, removable parts for infants and young children.
- Select well-built, good quality toys and equipment from reputable manufacturers or dealers. Quality toys will hold up longer, require less repair and are usually safer.

Electricity

Shock and fire are two electrical hazards caused by unsafe conditions and safety hazards.

Electrical Shock

Electrical shock occurs when you become part of an electrical circuit. A 120-volt household circuit usually has two wires—a *hot* (black or red) wire that carries current to the outlets and a *neutral* (white) wire that carries current back to the earth or *ground.* You become part of the circuit if you touch a hot wire or a conductor connected to it (such as a plugged in electrical appliance), while you are connected to the ground by standing on earth or on a damp floor or while you are touching any plumbing or metal object connected to the ground.

Ground-fault circuit interrupters can be installed in individual outlets or in entire circuits to protect against fatal electrical shock. While they will not prevent a shock, they will sense a shorted condition and turn off the power quickly enough to avoid a fatality.

Electrical Fires

Electrical fires are caused by overheated wires that ignite adjacent combustible materials. The electrical wiring in a house is divided at the main power supply into several circuits, each designed to carry a safe part of the electrical load. Each circuit is protected against overloading by a *fuse* or *circuit breaker,* acting as a safety valve. For illustrations of both systems, see Figure 4.1. If an overload gets the wires hot enough, or a short circuit occurs, it shuts off the power to the circuit.

When a fuse blows, find the cause. It is usually an overload from too many things plugged into the same circuit or a motor under too much strain. If the window in the center of the fuse is clear and you can see the melted metal strip through the window, the cause is an overload. If the window is

FIGURE 4.1   Fuse Box and Circuit Breaker Systems

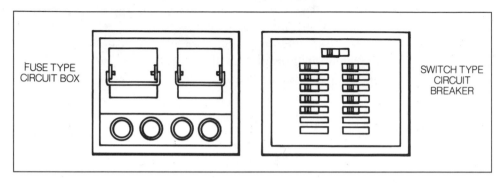

blackened, the cause is probably a short circuit. (See Figure 4.2.) If the cause is an overload, correct it by turning off one of your appliances to reduce the load.

Turn off the power at the fuse box and replace the blown fuse with another one of the same rating. Never use a fuse with a higher ampere rating; it may hold the load but may cause a fire later.

Be sure your feet are on a dry surface and keep your other hand at your side or in a pocket. Keep extra fuses and a flashlight handy.

Ordinary household circuits are protected by 15 or 20 amp fuses or circuit breakers. Any major appliances—such as kitchen range, washer, dryer, electric water heater or boiler, dishwasher, air conditioner and the like—should have its own heavy duty circuit, using 30 to 50 amp fuses or circuit breakers. Amps are marked on fuses and on circuit breaker switches.

A circuit breaker does the same job as a fuse, but it simply trips instead of burning out. All you do is flip the switch back to the *on* position.

If the fuse blows or the circuit breaker trips again, recheck for the cause. If you still cannot find it, call an electrician.

FIGURE 4.2   Reasons for Blown Fuses

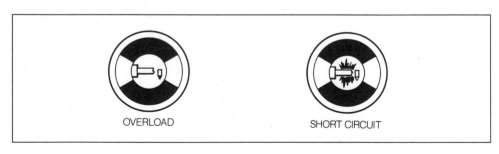

To determine whether the circuits in your home are being overloaded, add up the wattage of all lights and appliances on each circuit. If the total wattage of the appliances used at the same time exceeds 1800 watts for a 15 amp circuit or 2400 watts for a 20 amp circuit, the circuit is overloaded. Wattages are shown on the name plate of all appliances or can be estimated from the following table.

Appliance	Typical Wattage
Television, stereo, mixer, blender	250–350
Refrigerator, freezer, sump pump, vacuum cleaner	300–400 (High momentary starting current may require two-element fuses.)
Coffee pot, disposal	600–900
Toaster, waffle iron, griddle, electric frying pan, deep fryer, hand iron	1,000–1,500
Electric heater, hot plate, rotisserie grill, dishwasher	1,500–1,650

Any of the following telltale signs may be warning of an overloaded circuit or improper wiring. If the total wattage on the circuit is within the maximum amperage marked on the fuse or circuit breaker, have a qualified electrician check your wiring:

- Lights flicker or stay dim when a major appliance goes on.
- A motor slows down.
- Toasters or irons take a long time to heat.
- TV picture shrinks.
- Fuse blows or circuit breaker opens.

Electrical Safety Checklist

❏ Label fuses or circuit breakers to identify equipment and appliances they protect, in particular those that could be hazardous (stove, oven, TV sets, basement circuits in case of flooding). When an electric appliance emits smoke or flames, turn it off and pull the plug or shut off power to the circuit.

❏ In case of power failure, the full surge of current that occurs when the power comes back on may damage large current-consuming appliances, such as air conditioners, television sets, kitchen ranges, dishwashers, washing machines, dryers and other appliances with heating elements. You can prevent such possible damage by turning them off.

❏ Keep appliance cords and extension cords in good condition. Replace cord if frayed or brittle. Don't pull plugs by yanking on cord. Don't tack extension cords to walls as substitutes for permanent wiring and don't lay them under rugs or carpets. Replace outlets and switches that are damaged or hot to the touch.

❏ If you need to use an extension cord for any appliance using more than 600 watts or 5 amperes (toaster, iron, heater or room air conditioner), you must use heavy-duty cords of proper length. If the wire is too thin, too long or both, the current will overheat and damage the cord—and may even start a fire. Select a cord with wire thick enough for its length and the current consumption marked on the appliance nameplate in watts or amperes. The following chart matches wire sizes to length of cord and appliance ratings in watts and amperes.

Appliance		Length of Cord	Wire Size
Watts	*Amps*	*Feet*	*Gauge No.*
600 to 1,000	5 to 8	Up to 25	18
		50	16
		100	14
1,200	10	Up to 25	16
		50	14
		100	12
1,800	15	Up to 25	14
		50	12
		100	10

❏ Water near electricity is extremely dangerous because it is one of the best conductors of electricity. Keep electric appliances and cords away from water and keep water away from outlets and switches.

❏ Don't touch a plugged-in appliance while touching a metal object connected to the ground, such as a faucet.

❏ No electric switch or outlet should be within reach of a bathtub, shower, lavatory or sink.

❏ Never throw water on an electrical fire, unless you pull the plug first.

❏ Never enter a flooded basement; you may be electrocuted. Shut off power to all circuits in the basement at the fuse or circuit breaker box. The basement circuits should be well identified at the box.

❏ All major electric appliances—such as kitchen ranges, washers, clothes dryers, water heaters, and dishwashers—should be grounded with a three-wire plug.

❏ All appliances should bear the UL label.

❏ Turn off any appliance that sparks, stalls or overheats. Have it repaired immediately.

❏ Keep appliances with hot surfaces away from things that can be ignited.

❏ Use a heat-resistant tray under fondue or chafing dishes.

❏ Keep paper and cloth away from light bulbs.

❏ Provide a ground connection for the outside TV antenna.

❏ When raising any antenna—either CB or TV—make certain that the antenna and its support cables or guy wires cannot fall into or contact power lines.

❏ Never place your ladder next to electric wires leading to your home.

❏ If you are installing a rotor, make sure it won't turn the antenna around into nearby power lines. Make sure the power lead is grounded.

❏ Support cables should be well secured at both ends and should be insulated according to manufacturer's instructions.

❏ Never leave a television set on while no one is watching.

❏ Never leave unattended a plugged-in heating device that does not have its own thermostatic control.

❏ Never leave appliances running while you are away.

❏ If you leave your ironing board for any length of time, disconnect the iron and place it on its stand.

❏ Use only UL-labeled Christmas tree lights. Check cords for frayed or bare wire and bad connections. Turn off the lights when you leave or retire.

❏ To protect small children from electric burns or shocks, use snap-in plastic covers on unused openings of wall outlets. Wrap unused taps on extension cords with electrician's tape or use plastic covers.

Fire

Smoke Alarms

Smoke—not heat—is the first symptom of fire and usually spreads throughout the house long before heat can be detected. Thus a smoke detector can sound an alarm long before a heat-sensing device can, giving occupants early warning of a menacing fire, so they may safely evacuate the premises. No home should be without this inexpensive, essential protection. Insist on a product that carries the UL label.

Smoke detectors sound an alarm loud enough to be heard through a closed bedroom door. They are mounted on the ceiling or on the wall 6 to 12 inches below the ceiling. Some models plug into an electric outlet, some are permanently wired and others are battery powered. Models running on house current should have a battery back-up power source in case of power failure.

In one-story homes, the smoke detector should be located in the hallway outside the bedroom area. In multi-story homes, a smoke alarm should be installed on each level in the hall adjoining the bedrooms.

For homes requiring more than one alarm, multi-station smoke detectors are available. They are inter-connected, so that alarms on the upper floors would sound if the detector in the basement were to sense smoke.

Proper maintenance and regular testing of smoke detectors in accordance with manufacturers' recommendations are of the utmost importance for continuity of protection. Battery-powered smoke detectors need new batteries once or twice a year. Upon return from vacation, check control lights to make sure batteries arc functioning properly.

Fire Extinguishers

If a fire breaks out in your home, the first and most important thing you should do is to get all the people out of the house as quickly as possible. Then, if you have a clear exit way and if the fire is not spreading too quickly, you may be able to put out the flames yourself. Portable fire extinguishers are designed to fight small or beginning fires and to prevent excess damage to property. *Never attempt to use extinguishers on large fires or if your escape route is in danger of being blocked by flames or smoke.*

Location Extinguishers should be installed near exits, within easy reach and simple to remove, in locations throughout the house where a fire is most likely to break out. They are labeled A, B or C, depending on the types of fires they can extinguish (Figure 4.3).

Multipurpose extinguishers, such as A-B-C dry chemical, are the wisest choice for general use in the home.

If you have extinguishers labeled B and C, they should be installed near the kitchen, garage, workshop or storage area, where grease, flammable liquids, gases or electrical equipment and appliances are potential fire hazards. *Never use a water-type extinguisher on burning liquids, grease, or live electrical equipment.*

Class A fires, likely to occur in living room, dining room and bedroom areas, are best extinguished with water. Have garden hoses connected that can reach every room in the house.

FIGURE 4.3   Extinguishers for Three Classes of Fire

Extinguishing agents → suitable ↓ for	⟁A Water-base agent	B C Regular dry chemical	⟁A B C Multi-purpose dry chemical	B C Carbon dioxide (CO$_2$) gas	⟁A B C Halon* 1211 gas
Class fires A (Paper, wood, cloth, plastics, rubber, etc.)	Yes	No	Yes	No	Yes
Class fires B (Oil, gasoline, solvents, paint, thinner, grease)	No	Yes	Yes	Yes	Yes
Class fires C (Live electrical equipment, appliances, motors, switches, wiring)	No	Yes	Yes	Yes	Yes
Characteristics	Leaves yellowish deposit. Needs protection from freezing.	Leaves residue. Nonfreezing.	Leaves residue. Nonfreezing.	No residue. Nonfreezing.	No residue. Nonfreezing.

*Note: Halon extinguishers are being phased out for ecological reasons.

Fighting a Fire For any type of fire extinguisher, read the operating instructions on the label and in the owner's manual at the time of installation, before the event of fire.

The following are steps to take when fighting a fire with a portable extinguisher:

1. Stay as far from the fire as possible. Keep your back to drafts or strong currents of air.

2. Grasp the extinguisher firmly and direct the nozzle at the base of the flames.
   - *Class A fires.* Move the nozzle back and forth across the burning area. *Never use water on burning liquids, gases, grease or live electrical equipment.*
   - *Class B fires.* Stand at least eight feet from the fire to protect yourself from splashes of burning droplets. Move the nozzle from side to side across the base of the flame.
   - *Class C fires.* Shut off the power and pull the plug of the burning appliance, if possible. If necessary, shut off the power at the fuse or circuit breaker box. Aim the chemical discharge at the base of the flame.
3. Carefully observe the area around you for flying embers or small pockets of flame while you are fighting the fire and for several minutes after you have extinguished it.
4. Many extinguishers leave residues that could be harmful to the burned materials and surrounding area. Clean up this deposit as soon as you are able to touch the material or equipment. Avoid breathing the irritating vapors from dry chemical extinguishers and never handle the foam left by carbon dioxide (CO_2) discharges.

Maintenance and Inspection Regular monthly inspections by the homeowner should include examining the pressure gauge and checking for rust spots and nozzle obstructions.

Immediately after each use (even if extinguisher has been partially or accidentally discharged for only a moment), have the extinguisher recharged by an authorized fire extinguisher service agency. Even a small loss of pressure can make the extinguisher inoperable.

Once a year, have an authorized fire extinguisher service agency inspect your extinguishers.

Common Household Fires and What To Do about Them

Type of Fire	What To Do
Food in oven	Close oven door. Turn off heat.
Smoke from electric motor or appliance	Pull the plug or otherwise turn off the electricity. If flaming, use water *after* electricity is off. *Never use water on live electrical equipment.*
Smoke from TV set	*Keep clear!* The picture tube may burst. Shut off power to circuit. Call the fire department.

Small pan fire on stove	Cover with a lid or plate. Turn off heat. *Never pour water on it.* Use baking soda as a substitute for a fire extinguisher.
Deep-fat fryer	Cover with metal lid if you can approach it. Turn off heat. *Don't* attempt to move the appliance. *Don't fight the fire.* Evacuate, then call the fire department.
Clothing	If you are wearing the clothing, *don't run!* It fans the flames. Lie down and roll over and over. Remove the clothing if you can do so without pulling it over your head. Act fast! If it's someone else's clothing, don't let the person run. Get the victim on the ground; grab and push if necessary. Roll the victim over and over. Use anything handy to smother the flames (a rug, coat or jacket, blanket, drapes, towel or bedspread). If outside, use sand, dirt, snow or anything else handy. Don't wrap the victim's face, only the body. Try to remove the burning clothing, but don't pull it over the victim's head.

Clothing Fires

Clothing fires are dangerous and frightening. The victims can be scarred for life. Knowing in advance how to deal with a clothing fire can save you or a loved one from a lifetime of disfigurement and pain. Children and the elderly in particular suffer the agony of clothing fires. Young children are unfamiliar with the danger of fire, while the elderly may have poor eyesight, slow reflexes and physical infirmities.

Women and girls suffer more often from clothing fires than men and boys. Women's clothing can be loose-fitting, flowing or frilly, catch fire easily and burn quickly.

Clothing fires start in the following circumstances:

- From children climbing on the kitchen range
- By reaching or leaning over the kitchen range
- When children play with matches
- Because someone was careless with smoking materials
- Because someone was careless in lighting a stove, oven, fireplace or barbecue
- From standing too close to a heater, stove or fireplace

To avoid clothing fires, practice the following precautions:

❑ Avoid getting close to open flames and red-hot surfaces with sleeves and loose clothing.
❑ Keep curtains and potholders away from burners.
❑ Teach children the danger of playing with matches and lighted candles.
❑ Buy flame-retardant sleepwear. Manufacturers are required to make infants' and children's sleepwear flame retardant through size 14. While still combustible, clothing that has a flame-retardant treatment or is made of special fabrics does not ignite as easily as clothing that has not been so treated. Check for a flame-retardant label on children's clothes, shown in Figure 4.4.

Escaping a Fire

Most fire casualties are caused not by flames but by intake of smoke, poisonous gases and superheated air (up to 1,000°F). If a fire breaks out in your home, do the following:

❑ Stay low to the floor. This will give you the best chance of getting out of smoke-filled rooms and hallways. Hot gases and smoke collect near the ceiling first, then move toward the floor as the smoke layer gets thicker. *The best air is near the floor.*
❑ Never rise straight up from bed. You may thrust your head into a layer of toxic gases or superheated air, which could kill you with one breath. Always roll out of bed.
❑ Sleep with your bedroom doors closed. This prevents rapid movement of gases and shuts off potential drafts of air currents, which could spread the fire more rapidly throughout the house.
❑ As you approach a door, feel it first. If the door is hot, don't open it! If the door is not hot to the touch, brace your feet against the door and

FIGURE 4.4 Symbol Indicating Fire-Retardant Clothing

open it just an inch or so. If warm air comes through the crack, don't go out the door. While no flames may be present, toxic gases, often under pressure, could engulf you as soon as you open the door.

❏ Always close the door before opening a window. This prevents smoke and fire from being drawn into the room.

❏ Stuff blankets or wet towels against the bottom of the door to keep out smoke while awaiting rescue.

Escape Plans   Most fires spread by 100 percent every 60 seconds so that survival may depend upon rapid evacuation. For your best chance at a rapid evacuation, practice the following:

❏ Conduct fire drills at regular intervals, first using regular escape routes, then alternate routes. Since most fires occur after people have retired for the night, it is best to accustom your family to holding fire drills after dark.

❏ Make sure that everyone in your household recognizes the importance of getting out immediately if they even suspect the existence of a fire.

❏ Work out a way to communicate in case of fire (banging on walls, shouting, using an intercom system, fire alarm system and so on), and make sure everyone knows it.

❏ Make sure everyone knows that life safety is the first consideration and that no actions (even calling the fire department) should be taken until after everyone has been alerted of the fire's presence.

❏ Make sure every person in your household knows the ways to get out in case of fire. There should be more than one way out. Use folding escape ladders for second-floor windows.

❏ Make sure all windows and doors needed for emergency escape can be opened easily from the inside.

❏ Designate a meeting place outside the house, so nobody will go back inside looking for someone who is safe outside. Watch your children; don't let them reenter the house to rescue a pet or stuffed animal.

❏ Make sure everyone in your household knows the location of a nearby telephone or street fire alarm box, which fire department to call and to tell the firemen if anyone is trapped inside the building.

❏ Ensure that everyone in your household knows the four points of information to give in an emergency phone call.
  1. Tell exactly where it happened, then repeat it.
  2. Tell what has happened.
  3. Tell who you are.
  4. Tell what kind of help is needed.

❏ Make special plans to evacuate elderly and disabled persons.

❏ Teach small children to first close their bedroom doors in case of fire and then wait by an open window until someone can reach them from outside.

❏ Make it a regular practice to let babysitters know what to do in case of fire. (See the babysitter instruction form in Appendix D.)

Fire Prevention Checklist

Hazardous Materials

❏ Gasoline, if it must be stored at all, should be kept in UL-approved safety cans a safe distance from pilot lights of water heater and furnace. Gasoline must only be poured and used outdoors.

❏ Keep only a minimum of fuel in gasoline-powered equipment.

❏ Other flammable and combustible liquids should be kept in their original containers.

❏ Keep oily rags in metal containers.

❏ Never "freshen" any barbecue or other fire with a combustible liquid.

Location of Shut-Off Valves and Switches
The location of the following should be well known to all adult members of the household and should be marked where necessary:

❏ Electrical fuse or switch-type circuit box containing an itemized list of all electrical systems and major appliances, as well as light fixtures and receptacles connected to each circuit

❏ Switches at the major electrical systems

❏ Main water supply valve

❏ Water supply valve for each plumbing fixture

❏ Main gas supply valve, next to the meter on the inlet pipe (Use a wrench and give it a quarter-turn so that it runs crosswise to the pipe; The main gas supply is now shut off.)

❏ Gas supply valve and pilot light on each gas appliance

❏ Main fuel oil supply valve

Heating Equipment

❏ If you smell leaking utility gas, open windows. Don't switch on lights or strike a match to avoid an explosion. Shut off main gas supply valve at the meter. Vacate the house at once and call fire department and local gas company from a neighbor's house.

❏ Know how to light the pilot light on your furnace and water heater.

❏ Make sure your water heater is equipped with a temperature relief valve.

❏ All heating equipment should carry a UL or American Gas Association (AGA) label.

❏ Furnace room must be adequately ventilated.

❏ Furnaces, boilers and water heaters must be properly vented to the outside.

❏ Heating system should be cleaned, lubricated and serviced periodically.

❏ Fireplace chimneys should be cleaned and checked for cracks periodically.

(See Chapter 8, "House and Equipment Maintenance.")

Safe Housekeeping Rules

Kitchen

❏ Have a fire extinguisher close to the stove.

❏ Install a smoke detector in the kitchen and test battery regularly.

❏ Keep baking soda on hand to extinguish stovetop fires.

❏ Store matches and lighters out of reach of children.

❏ Keep flammable liquids in approved containers away from burners and pilot lights.

❏ Keep potholders and other flammable materials at a safe distance from burners.

❏ Make sure kitchen curtains cannot blow over flames or glowing burners.

❏ Avoid getting close to burners with loose sleeves or clothing. Spilled grease left on top of the range, under burners or in the oven is a fire hazard and should be wiped up at once.

❏ Keep exhaust fan free of dust and grease buildup.

❏ Keep stove in good working condition.

Fireplaces and Barbecues

❏ Keep a fire extinguisher near the fireplace.

❏ Use screens or glass doors in front of all fireplaces. Glass doors can shut off air to quench fire before retiring.

❏ Always make sure the damper is open *before* lighting a fire.

❏ For gas fireplaces, place a twist of paper near the gas outlet and light the paper with a match before turning on the gas valve. Or, use a long fireplace match or special fire starter tool, readily available in grocery or specialty stores. *Never* turn on the gas valve before striking a match. Igniting accumulated gas causes an explosion.

❑ Quench fire in fireplace or barbecue before retiring by shutting off air supply.

Garage or Basement

❑ Have a fire extinguisher easily accessible.

❑ Have tools such as a shovel, rake, hoe and bucket readily available.

❑ Install a solid door with self-closing hinges between living areas and the garage.

❑ Dispose of oily rags by putting them in a fireproof container.

❑ Store all combustibles away from ignition sources such as water heaters.

❑ Disconnect electrical tools and appliances when not in use.

❑ Allow hot tools such as glue guns and soldering irons to cool before storing.

General Precautions Inside the Home

❑ *Absolutely do not smoke in bed or if there is a possibility of dozing in a chair.*

❑ Where smoking is allowed, keep plenty of large, clean ashtrays on solid surfaces, not on the arms of upholstered furniture.

❑ Empty ashtrays into toilets or metal containers or sprinkle smoking ashes and butts with water before emptying into trash containers.

❑ Keep storage areas clear of accumulated papers and other combustible materials.

❑ Empty waste baskets regularly.

❑ Choose fire-resistant fabrics for draperies, curtains, carpets and upholstery.

❑ *Insist on* fire retardant sleepwear for children.

❑ Use only cleaning products that are flame proof.

❑ Draperies, shag rugs, toys, electrical cords etc., should be a safe distance from electric baseboard heaters.

❑ Never leave candles burning unattended.

❑ Be especially careful at holiday seasons such as Christmas. Never use real candles on a Christmas tree and use only fireproof decorations. The smaller the tree, the safer it is. Place it in a water-filled stand and keep adding water daily throughout the season. Place the tree where it will not obstruct a doorway. Do not place the tree near a radiator, television set or other source of heat.

❑ Keep the exhaust pipe of the clothes dryer free of lint.

❑ Each telephone in the house should have stickers with **911** instructions and/or the telephone numbers of fire and police departments.

❑ Make fire safety a part of your family training. Never leave matches or lighters where young children may find them. Teach children the danger of playing with matches and candles. Do not leave small children alone!

Exterior of Your Home

❑ Class A fire-resistant roofing materials are highly recommended.

❑ Gutters and eaves should be swept and cleaned regularly.

❑ A minimum space of 30 feet around the house should be maintained as a defensible fire barrier. All shrubs should be pruned to a height of three feet or less and spaced so fire cannot jump from one to the other.

❑ When planting new trees, keep them at least 15 feet away from the house. Refrain from using those high in oils and resins, including pines, junipers and eucalyptus.

❑ Remove flammable debris such as scrub growth at the base of older trees and dead tree branches lower than eight feet from the ground.

❑ Climbing plants and trees close to buildings and fences are fire hazards.

❑ Remove all tree limbs within ten feet of a chimney and trim dead limbs hanging over a house or garage. Place screens over all chimneys and air ducts.

❑ Install wire screens under decks and porches, over vents around the house and over attic vents to protect support timbers in basements, crawl spaces and attics against flames and sparks.

❑ When building patios and walls, consider stone, brick or concrete rather than wood.

CHAPTER FIVE

Natural Disasters and First Aid

Disaster Preparation Guidelines

Earthquakes

Tornadoes

Hurricanes

Floods

Electrical Storms

Disaster Survival Guide

While it is never possible to forecast the future, you can attempt to prepare for possible natural disasters. Following are general guidelines that can help you and your family survive the event of an earthquake, tornado, hurricane, flood or electrical storm.

Disaster Preparation Guidelines

❏ Have the following basic emergency supplies in a designated place:
  • Portable radio (with extra batteries)
  • Several flashlights (with extra batteries)
  • First aid kit
  • Medications used by family members
  • Water (several gallons for each family member)
  • Small bottle of chlorine bleach to purify drinking water
  • Food (canned foods and powdered milk for at least one week's meals)
  • Alternate means of cooking, like barbecue or camp stove
  • Clothing, sleeping bags and blankets
❏ Keep valuable documents in bank safety deposit.
❏ Have fire extinguishers in operating condition.
❏ Tie water heater with metal straps.
❏ Know the location of your electric circuit breaker or fuse box. Practice turning off the power to make sure you can do it in an emergency.
❏ Know the location of the main water shut-off valve.
❏ Have pipe wrenches and crescent wrenches on hand (for turning off water; and—if necessary—gas.)
❏ Know where gas, electric and water main shutoffs are. If in doubt, ask your water, power and gas companies. The main gas shut-off valve is located next to your gas meter on the inlet pipe. Use a wrench and give it a quarter-turn in either direction so that it runs crosswise on the pipe (Figure 5.1). The line is now closed. *Note:* Turn off gas only if there is a hiss that sounds like escaping gas or if there is a smell of rotten eggs, or you see evidence of pipe damage. *Do not relight gas pilot!* Call the utility company to turn gas back on.

Earthquakes

The earthquake experience is commonplace in California and other Western states, but unbeknownst to many, earthquakes have occurred throughout the country and every region has some risk of mild earthquake activity. Quakes in the West, although frequent and often violent, are confined mainly

FIGURE 5.1   How To Shut Off the Main Gas Line

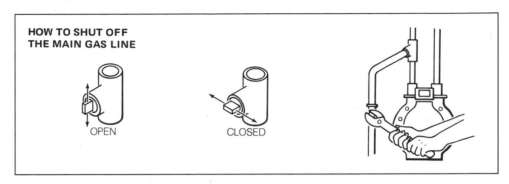

to fault areas. In the East, however, shaking is felt over much larger areas, because seismic waves travel greater distances before they dissipate, so the potential for damage is often greater.

The following checklist is included in Appendix D.

Preparing the Home for Quakes

❏ Bolt existing sill plates to the concrete foundation to prevent house from slipping off its foundation. Drill hole through sill plate and into concrete, insert and set ⅝″ steel expansion bolt; secure bolt with washer and nut.

❏ Reinforce frame walls in basement or crawl space to prevent walls from collapsing. Nail ½″ exterior structural grade plywood to studs, using eight-penny nails every 3″ around edges.

❏ Secure water heater to wall to prevent fire and water damage from broken gas line caused by falling water heater. Appropriate straps are available at most hardware stores. Make sure to use flexible gas pipe connection between gas pipe and water heater.

❏ Secure bookshelves and heavy furniture to walls.

❏ Store heavy objects on lower shelves.

❏ Keep fire extinguishers near appliances.

❏ Place beds away from windows and heavy objects.

During an Earthquake

Keep calm. Panic kills. The motion is frightening, but unless it shakes something down on top of you, it is harmless.

❏ If you are indoors, stay there. Get under a desk or a table, or in a doorway. Stay clear of windows, glass doors and mirrors. The greatest hazard from falling objects is just outside doorways and close to outer walls. Stay inside!

❏ If you are outside, get into the open, away from buildings and power lines. Stay there until the shaking stops.

❏ If you are driving a car, pull over to side of road, stop the car, but stay inside. Avoid overpasses, bridges and power lines.

After an Earthquake

Injuries

❏ Check for injuries. If anyone has stopped breathing, give mouth-to-mouth rescue breathing. (See "Rescue Breathing" below.)

❏ Stop any bleeding injury by applying direct pressure over the site of the wound.

❏ Do not attempt to move seriously injured persons unless they are in immediate danger of further injury.

❏ Cover injured persons with blankets to keep them warm. Be reassuring and calm.

Safety Check

❏ Check for safety. Check your home for fire or fire hazards.

❏ Check utility lines and appliances for damage.

❏ If a gas leak exists, open windows and shut off the main gas valve. Leave building and report leakage to authorities. Do not search for a leak with a match. Do not turn on the gas again; let the gas company restore service.

❏ Shut off electrical power at the control box if there is any damage to your house wiring.

❏ Do not use lighters or open flame appliances until you are certain that no gas leak exists.

❏ Do not operate electrical switches or appliances if gas leaks are suspected. Sparks can ignite gas from broken lines.

❏ Do not touch downed power lines or objects touched by them, or by electrical wiring of any kind.

❏ Check to see that sewage lines are intact before using your toilet. *Note:* The toilet tank (not the bowl) can be a source of emergency water supply if water is cut off. Don't waste it.

❏ Check your chimney for cracks and damage. Approach chimneys with caution. They may topple. *Caution:* Using a damaged chimney invites fire. When in doubt, don't use it.

❏ Check closets and cupboards. Open doors cautiously. Beware of falling objects tumbling off shelves.

Food and Water

❏ Check your food supply. If the water supply is shut off, emergency water supplies may be all around you, in water heaters, toilet tanks (again, not the bowl), melted ice cubes and in canned vegetables.

❏ Do not eat or drink anything from open containers near shattered glass. Liquids may be strained through a clean handkerchief or cloth if danger of glass contamination exists. Water may be disinfected with household chlorine bleach. Use the following proportions:

Clear Water	Chlorine Bleach
1 quart	2 drops
1 gallon	8 drops
5 gallons	½ teaspoon

Mix thoroughly and let stand 30 minutes.

❏ If the power is off, check your freezer and plan meals to use up food that will spoil quickly.

❏ Use outdoor charcoal broilers for emergency cooking.

Cooperate with Public Safety Efforts

❏ *Do not:* Use lighters, candles, open flame appliances or smoke until you are sure there are no gas leaks.

❏ *Do not:* Operate electrical switches or appliances, including telephones, if you suspect a gas leak. The appliances may create a spark that could ignite the leaking gas.

❏ *Do not:* Use your telephone except to report medical, fire or violent crime emergencies. If lines are blocked, it may be easier to call out of the disaster area during emergencies.

❏ Turn on your portable radio for instructions and news reports.

❏ *Do not:* Go sightseeing immediately afterwards, especially in beach and waterfront areas where seismic waves could strike.

❏ Keep streets clear for emergency vehicles.

❏ Be prepared for aftershocks. Most of these are smaller than the main quake, but some may be large enough to do additional damage.

❏ Cooperate with public safety officials. Don't go into damaged areas unless your help is requested.

❏ Informed and cooperative citizens can help minimize damage and injury.

❏ Stay calm and lend a hand to others.

Tornadoes

Tornadoes, the most violent storms produced by nature, come on much faster than other forms of extreme weather. Destruction is caused by winds of up to 300 miles per hour, which uproot trees, destroy buildings and create a serious hazard from objects blown through the air. Further destruction is caused by differences in air pressure, which can lift people and automobiles and can cause buildings to collapse.

Tornadoes can occur anyplace at any time of the year, but most frequently in the midwestern, southern and central states from March through September, usually between 3 and 7 PM. Tornado winds are generally 25 to 40 m.p.h. and in most cases travel from the southwest.

Tornadoes usually occur in conjunction with dark, thick thunderstorm clouds, heavy rain or hail. An hour or two before a tornado, topsy-turvy clouds sometimes appear, bulging down instead of up. Clouds often have a greenish-black color.

A tornado is a funnel-shaped cloud, spinning rapidly and extending toward the earth from the base of a thundercloud. When close by, it sounds like the roar of hundreds of jet airplanes.

A *tornado watch* means there is a possibility of a tornado developing; a *tornado warning* means that a tornado has been sighted or spotted by radar. In these types of circumstances, the National Weather Service issues regular bulletins via local radio and television stations. Have a battery-powered radio on hand and keep listening to the latest bulletins.

When a Tornado Has Been Sited

In Homes Open windows to equalize air pressure, but stay away from them. Take shelter immediately. The corner of the basement toward the tornado usually offers the greatest safety. In a house with no basement, take cover under heavy furniture in the center area of the house.

In Mobile Homes Evacuate when strong winds are forecast. Securing mobile homes and trailers with cables anchored in concrete minimizes danger from overturning. Do not take shelter in a parked car.

In Schools, Office Buildings and Factories Move quickly to designated shelter areas or to an interior hallway on the lowest floor. Stay away from windows. Avoid auditoriums and gymnasiums with large, poorly supported roofs.

In Open Country Try to escape at a right angle to the tornado's path. If there is no time, lie flat in the nearest depression, such as a ditch or a ravine, with your hands shielding your head. Be alert for flash floods. Do not take shelter in a parked car.

After the Storm

Beware of live wires. Report broken wires to the proper authorities. Broken or dangling wires may be hazardous; stay away from them.

Hurricanes

Hurricanes are tropical storms originating over water areas near the equator, where the air is warm and moist. They usually commence in the West Indian region, but belong to the same family as cyclones and typhoons in other parts of the world.

As a hurricane begins to develop, the air gradually assumes a counter-clockwise circular motion around a center of lowest pressure (the "eye"). The system then begins to move forward and usually travels at speeds of 10 to 15 miles per hour. As the storm progresses, the circular motion becomes more and more violent, often reaching speeds in excess of 100 miles per hour. The highest speeds run around the eye of the storm and extend 20 miles or more. Hurricanes may leave a path of destruction 25 to 500 miles wide. Follow disaster preparation guidelines at the beginning of this chapter.

During a Hurricane

Most areas where hurricanes are likely to strike have some type of pre-arranged warning system. If a hurricane strikes in your area, the National Weather Service advises you to do the following:

❑ Keep a battery-powered radio on and act only on official advice. Pay no attention to rumors.
❑ Leave low-lying beaches and flood areas early. Don't risk being stranded.
❑ Stay in your house if it is well built and out of danger of high water.
❑ Board up windows or close storm shutters. Use good lumber, securely fastened (makeshift boarding may result in severe damage). Brace the outside doors strongly.
❑ Stock extra foods, especially items that need no refrigeration and little preparation. Electric power and gas may be interrupted.

❏ Sterilize several large containers and fill them with water, because water service may also be interrupted. The toilet tank (not the bowl), water heaters and melted ice cubes can be a source of emergency water supply if water is cut off. Don't waste it. Boil drinking water after service has been restored unless you are sure the regular supply is safe.

❏ Have a flashlight handy.

❏ Store all lawn furniture and other movable objects inside, if possible.

❏ Stay in a safe place for a time after the storm has apparently passed. If the center or the eye of the storm is directly over you, there will be a lull in the wind lasting from a few minutes to half an hour or more. Then the wind will return suddenly from the opposite direction, frequently with even greater force.

❏ After the hurricane passes, seek medical care for injured persons. This can be obtained from Red Cross disaster stations or hospitals.

❏ When the storm is over, beware of live wires. Report broken wires to the proper authorities. Broken or dangling wires may be hazardous; stay away from them.

❏ Stay away from disaster areas unless you are qualified to render first aid or other disaster services.

❏ Be on the alert to prevent fires. Hurricane winds could spread fires very fast and cause great devastation.

❏ Report any broken sewer or water mains.

❏ Don't empty your stored water until the regular water service has been resumed. Watch out for spoiled food in refrigerators if the power has been off for any length of time.

Floods

Follow disaster preparation guidelines outlined at the beginning of this chapter.

During a Flood

❏ Fire is a major danger during or following a flood. All gas stoves and electrical appliances should be turned off or disconnected if flood waters are likely to reach the house. Learn now where gas and electricity can be shut off at the point where they enter the house.

❏ Don't use matches or open flames even after the flood has receded, until gas lines are checked for breakage and escaping gas.

❏ Have all electric appliances checked before connecting them again if they have been submerged.

❏ Flood waters often contain backed-up sewage and other contamination. Destroy anything, such as medicines, fruit, vegetables and any other product that has been under flood water.

❏ Even hermetically sealed cans should be thoroughly washed before opening.

❏ Put on serviceable, warm clothing, if time permits. Have blankets available in case the heating system breaks down.

❏ After the flood waters recede, remember that any objects covered by the water are likely to be coated with muck or some other kind of contaminated residue. Anyone cut or scratched by such an object should get immediate medical attention. Keep a good first aid kit handy, in addition to blankets, food and other emergency equipment.

❏ To be completely safe, act before a flood reaches the danger stage. Leave the area. Know alternate routes out of the area in case roads are blocked.

❏ If it is too late to leave the area, go to the nearest community flood shelter.

❏ If you are trapped in a building, go to the highest place in the building and wait for help to arrive. Don't attempt to swim or use makeshift rafts, except as a final resort.

Electrical Storms

Lightning bolts have a frightening force of about 15 million volts. The distance of an approaching electrical storm can be quickly estimated by counting the seconds between the lightning and the sound of thunder. Sound travels at five seconds per mile. So if the time lapse between lightning and thunder were 20 seconds, the storm would be about four miles away.

During an Electrical Storm

❏ A professionally installed lightning protection system (lightning rods, connectors and grounds) will conduct a lightning bolt harmlessly to the ground. If installed by a qualified company, Underwriters Laboratory will issue a "master label," indicating the system meets its requirements. Such a system is not inexpensive, but is well worth the cost in regions where electrical storms occur frequently, or in locations which cannot be reached quickly or easily by firemen.

❏ Lightning can charge electrical equipment and metal pipes with a sudden surge of high voltage. Therefore, stay out of the bathrooms, kitchen, laundry room, workshop and basement. Do not touch sinks or any kind of electrical equipment or appliances.

❏ To avoid damage to electrical appliances, disconnect them from the electrical outlets, especially television sets, stereo equipment and outside antennas. Better yet, have an electrician install a lightning surge arrestor. Should lightning strike, this inexpensive device will momentarily interrupt power to the entire electrical system while the sudden surge of current is conducted safely to the ground.

❏ Remain in the center of the house. Stay away from windows and outside doors.

❏ Avoid using the telephone; lightning may cause a deafening blast through the receiver.

Disaster Survival Guide*

In an emergency, seconds can be the difference between life and death. When calling for emergency help, let the emergency person end the conversation. DO NOT HANG UP!

The following pages describe what to do until medical help arrives.

Medical authorities suggest that you become familiar with the following procedures and also take a first aid course from the American Red Cross.

Urgent care is first aid given in life-threatening situations. These situations include stopped breathing, heart attack and stroke, heavy bleeding, poisoning and shock.

Take care of life-threatening situations first, then seek help. If several people are available, one can go for help while others help you give first aid. DO NOT LEAVE people who need urgent care—not even to call for help.

See your telephone directory for the number of your local Poison Control Center. Keep it near your phone.

Medic Alert Foundation International provides 24-hour medical emergency protection to members with special medical conditions. In an emergency, medical and emergency personnel are directed to look for the Medic Alert or similar emblem worn as a bracelet or necklace and to take appro-

*Information in this Survival Guide is reprinted with the permission of the copyright owner, © Pacific Bell, 1991. This information was provided by medical and emergency service authorities and published as a public service. While every reasonable effort was made to ensure its accuracy, Pacific Bell is not responsible and assumes no liability for any action undertaken by any person in utilizing such information. Any person relying upon such information does so at his or her own risk.

priate action when necessary. Additional information on Medic Alert can be obtained by calling (toll free) 800-432-5378.

Calling for Help—9-1-1

1. If the victim is NOT breathing, phone 9-1-1 at once or get someone else to call for emergency help. Then begin rescue breathing.
2. If the victim is in distress—but breathing, phone 9-1-1 at once.
3. What to say:
   - Give the phone number from which you are calling.
   - Give the address and any special directions of how to find the victim.
   - Describe the victim's condition—burned, bleeding, broken bones, etc.
   - Describe what happened, how many are injured or what help is being given.
   - Give your name.
   - DO NOT HANG UP! Let the emergency persons end the conversation. They may have questions to ask and/or special information to give you about what you should do until help arrives.

Breathing

Unconscious Person Many medical authorities agree that everyone 13 years of age and older should learn rescue breathing. Courses are offered by the American Heart Association and the American Red Cross.

Be careful approaching an unconscious person. He or she may be in contact with electrical current. If that is the case, turn off the electricity before you touch the victim. There are many possible causes of unconsciousness, but the first thing you must check for is breathing.

1. Try to awaken the person. Tap or shake the victim's shoulder gently. Shout: "Are you all right?"
2. If there is no response, check for signs of breathing. Have someone call for emergency medical help immediately.
   - Be sure the victim is lying flat on his or her back. If you have to, roll the victim over. To avoid possible neck injury, turn his or her head with the body as one unit.
   - Loosen tight clothing around the neck and chest.

FIGURE 5.2

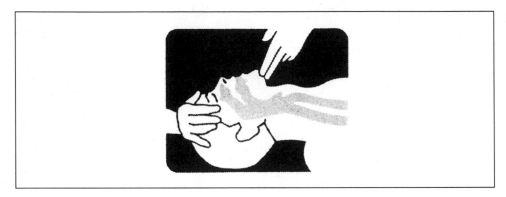

3. Open the airway (see Figure 5.2).
   - If there are no signs of head or neck injury, place one hand on the victim's forehead and apply firm, backward pressure with the palm to tilt the head back.
   - Place the fingers of the other hand under the bony part of the lower jaw near the chin and lift to bring the chin forward, thus supporting the jaw and helping to tilt the head back.
   - Place your ear close to the victim's mouth. Listen for breathing. Watch for chest and stomach movement for at least 5 seconds.
   - If there is any question in your mind, or if breathing is so faint that you are unsure—assume they are not breathing.
   - Give rescue breathing immediately.

Rescue Breathing for Adults

1. Put your hand on the victim's forehead. While holding the forehead back gently pinch the nose shut with your fingers.
2. To open the airway, put your other hand under the victim's jaw and lift the chin until it points straight up.
3. Take a deep breath. Open your mouth wide. Place it over the victim's mouth. (For neck breathers, pinch nose and mouth and breath into neck opening.) Blow air into the victim until you see the victim's chest rise. (See Figure 5.3.)
4. Remove your mouth from the victim's. Turn your head to the side and watch the chest fall while listening for air escaping from the victim's mouth. Give another breath.
5. If you hear air escaping and see the chest fall, rescue breathing is working. Continue until help arrives.

FIGURE 5.3

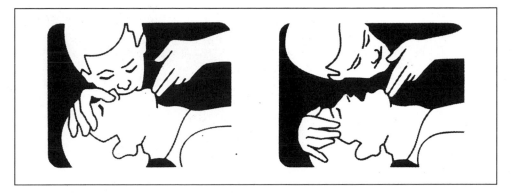

6. Check the victim's pulse (see "Heart Attack").
7. Repeat a single breath every 5 seconds (12 breaths per minute). Wait for chest deflation after each breath.
8. If you don't hear air escaping, airway is blocked (see "Choking").

Rescue Breathing for Infants and Small Children

1. Check for breathing by carefully tilting the child's head back to open the airway. It should not be tilted as far back as an adult's, even less for infants. Look, listen and feel for breathing. If tilted back too far, it will make the obstruction worse.
2. If not breathing, cover the child's mouth AND nose with your mouth (see Figure 5.4). Initially give 2 full, slow breaths in succession. Allow 1 to 1½ seconds per breath. *For infants, give 2 slow, gentle breaths at 1 to 1½ seconds per breath.*

FIGURE 5.4

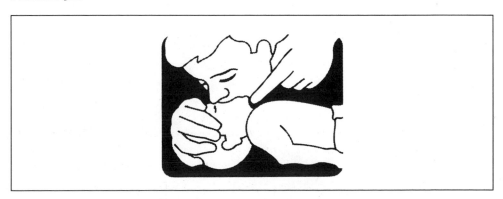

3. Blow air in with less pressure than for an adult. Give small puffs. A child needs less air.
4. Feel the chest inflate as you blow.
5. Listen for air escaping.
6. Repeat once every 3 seconds (20 breaths per minute).

Please Note: Keep up rescue breathing until help arrives to relieve you. Remember, you are doing the breathing for the victim. If you stop, the victim could die in about 4 to 6 minutes. Even if the victim should begin to breathe on his or her own, call for professional help.

Choking

Warning Sign: The universal distress signal indicates an airway obstruction.

For a choking victim who *can* speak, cough or breathe, do *NOT* interfere. If the choking continues without lessening, call for emergency medical help.

For a choking victim who *cannot* speak, cough or breathe, have someone call for emergency medical help and take the following action.

For a Conscious Victim

1. Stand behind the victim, who can be standing or sitting.
2. Wrap your arms around his or her middle, just above the navel.
3. For adults, clasp your hands together in a doubled fist and press in and up in quick thrusts. Be careful not to exert pressure against the victim's rib cage with your forearms (see Figure 5.5).

FIGURE 5.5

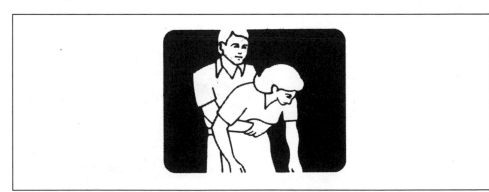

For infants, position along the inside length of the rescuer's arm. Apply firm, controlled blows with the other hand to the infant's back between the shoulder blades.

Repeat procedure until the victim is no longer choking or becomes unconscious.

For an Unconscious Victim

1. Place the victim on the floor or ground and give rescue breathing (see "Rescue Breathing"). If the victim does not start breathing and it appears that your air is not going into the victim's lungs, try giving 2 more breaths.

2. With the victim remaining on his or her back, try giving manual thrusts (see Figure 5.6). To give the thrusts to adults, place one of your hands on top of the other with the heel of the bottom hand in the middle of the abdomen, slightly above the navel and below the rib cage. Press into the victim's abdomen with a quick upward thrust. Repeat 6 to 10 times if needed. Do not press to either side.

   For infants, give 4 back blows. Then give 4 chest thrusts by placing two fingertips over the center of the chest and depressing 1 inch.

3. Clear the airway (see Figure 5.7).
   - Hold the victim's mouth open with one hand using your thumb to depress the tongue.
   - Make a hook with the pointer finger of your other hand and in a gentle sweeping motion reach into the victim's throat and feel for a swallowed foreign object that may be blocking the air passage.

     For infants and small children, look first. Sweep mouth only if you see the object.

FIGURE 5.6

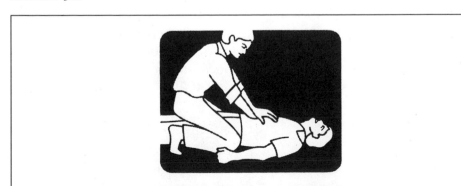

FIGURE 5.7

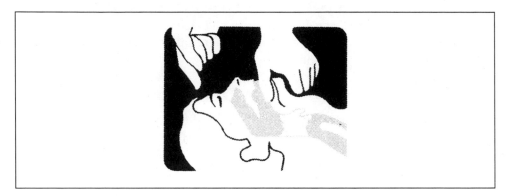

- If object comes out and victim is not breathing, start rescue breathing immediately.

Please Note: In any event of severe choking, take the victim to the hospital. This is especially critical if the swallowed object is a fish bone, chicken bone or other jagged object that could do internal damage as it passes through the victim's system.

Drowning

Get the victim out of the water at once being careful to support the neck. A panicked victim may accidentally drown the rescuer as well, so use extreme caution to avoid direct contact with the victim.

If the victim is conscious, push a floating object to him or her or let the victim grasp a long branch, pole or object. Rescuers should not place themselves in danger. Go or swim to the victim as a last resort.

If the victim is unconscious, take a flotation device with you if possible. Approach the victim with caution. Once ashore or on the deck of a pool, the victim should be placed on his or her back.

If the victim is not breathing, check for airway clearance and open the airway. If after a few seconds the victim is still not breathing, immediately begin rescue breathing (see "Rescue Breathing").

Electric Shock

1. Do not touch a person who has been in contact with electrical current until you are certain that the electricity is turned off. Shut off the power at the plug, circuit breaker or fuse box.

2. If the victim is in contact with a wire or a downed power line, use a dry stick to move it away. If the ground is wet, do not approach.
3. Check for breathing. If the victim's breathing is weak or has stopped, open the airway. If after a few seconds the victim is still not breathing, immediately begin rescue breathing (see "Rescue Breathing").
4. Call for emergency help or get someone to call for help immediately. While you wait for help to arrive:
   - Keep the victim warm (cover with a blanket, coat, etc.) and lying down.
   - Give the victim nothing to drink or eat until he or she is seen by a doctor.

Heart Attack

Warning Signs:

- Severe squeezing pains, crushing pains or heavy pressure in the chest.
- Pain that radiates from the chest into either arm, the neck or jaw.
- Shortness of breath.
- Sweating and weakness, nausea or vomiting.

1. If the victim is experiencing any of these sensations—take no chances. Call for emergency help at once.
2. *If the victim is not breathing,* give rescue breathing immediately (see "Rescue Breathing"). Get someone else to call for emergency help.
3. If you cannot detect a heartbeat by taking a pulse at the carotid artery (the carotid artery can be felt on either side of the neck slightly below and forward of the base of the jaw; see Figure 5.8): Apply CPR.

FIGURE 5.8

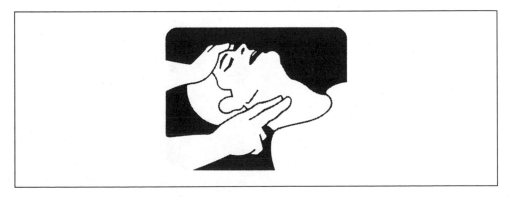

Cardiopulmonary resuscitation (CPR) should be given to the victim along with rescue breathing only by a person properly trained and certified.

Please note: You are urged to learn CPR. CPR is a way of forcing the heart to continue pumping blood (carrying oxygen) through the lungs and out to the rest of the body where it is needed. Courses are offered by the American Heart Association and the American Red Cross.

Bleeding

Wounds The best way to control bleeding is with direct pressure over the site of the wound (see Figure 5.9). Do not attempt to apply a tourniquet yourself; leave to a professional.

1. Use a pad of sterile gauze, if available.
2. A sanitary napkin, clean handkerchief or even your bare hand, if necessary, will do.
3. Apply firm, steady direct pressure for 5 to 15 minutes. Most bleeding will stop within a few minutes.
4. If bleeding is from a foot, hand, leg or arm use gravity to help slow the flow of blood. If there are no broken bones, elevate the limb so that it is above the victim's heart.
5. Severe nose bleeding can often be controlled by leaning forward or lying down and applying direct pressure such as by pinching the nose with the fingers. Apply pressure 10 minutes without interruption.

FIGURE 5.9

Head Injuries If there is bleeding from an ear, it can mean that there is a skull fracture.

1. Call for emergency help. Let a professional medical person attend the wound.
2. Special care must be taken when trying to stop any scalp bleeding when there is a suspected skull fracture. Bleeding from the scalp can be very heavy even when the injury is not too serious.
3. Always suspect a neck injury when there is a serious head injury. Keep the neck and head still.
4. Keep the airway open (see "Rescue Breathing").
5. When stopping the bleeding, don't press too hard. Be very careful when applying pressure over the wound so that bone chips from a possible fracture will not be pressed into the brain.
6. DO **NOT** give the victim any fluids, cigarettes or other drugs. They may mask important symptoms.

Internal *Warning Signs:*

- Coughing or vomiting blood or passing blood in urine or stool.
- Cold, clammy pale skin; rapid, weak pulse, dizziness.

1. Get emergency medical help immediately.
2. Have the victim lie down and relax. Stay calm and keep the victim warm.
3. Do not let the victim take any medication or fluids by mouth until seen by a doctor who permits it.

Broken Bones

1. Call for emergency help or get someone to call for emergency medical help immediately.
2. DO **NOT** move the victim unless the victim is in immediate danger of further injury.
3. Check for the following:
   - Breathing. Give rescue breathing if needed (see "Rescue Breathing").
   - Bleeding. Apply direct pressure over the site.
   - Shock symptoms like pale or bluish, cold, clammy skin, rapid weak pulse, overall weakness, and rapid, shallow breathing. Keep the victim calm and comfortable.
4. DO **NOT** try to push the broken bone back into place if it is sticking out of the skin. Do apply a moist dressing to prevent the bone from drying out.

5. DO **NOT** try to straighten out a fracture. Let a doctor or trained person do that. If you must move or transport the victim, immobilize or stabilize the fracture as best as possible.

Seizure

Warning Signs:

- Limbs may jerk violently.
- Eyes may roll upward.
- Breathing may become heavy with dribbling or frothing at the mouth.
- Breathing may even stop in some cases.
- The victim may bite his or her tongue so severely that it may bleed and cause an airway obstruction.

1. During the seizure:
   - Call for emergency medical help at once.
   - Let the seizure run its course.
   - DO **NOT** attempt to force anything into the victim's mouth. You may injure yourself and/or the victim.
   - There is little you can do to stop the seizure.
   - Help the victim lie down and keep from falling and injuring himself or herself.
   - Loosen restrictive clothing.
   - DO **NOT** use force or attempt to restrain a seizure victim.
   - Move objects out of the way which may injure the victim (like chairs, desks, tables, etc.)
   - If an object endangers the victim and cannot be moved, put clothing or soft material between the seizure victim and the object.
2. After the seizure:
   - Check to see if the victim is breathing. If not, give rescue breathing at once (see "Rescue Breathing").
   - Check to see if the victim is wearing a Medic Alert, or similar bracelet or necklace (see Figure 5.10). It describes emergency medical requirements.
   - Check to see if the victim has any burns around the mouth. This would indicate poison.
3. The victim of a seizure or convulsion may be conscious but confused and not talkative when the intense movement stops. Stay with the victim. Watch the victim to make sure breathing continues. Then, when the victim seems able to move, get medical attention.

FIGURE 5.10

Poisoning

Small children are most often the victims of accidental poisoning. Poisons are all around them. Keep cosmetics, detergents, bleach, cleaning solutions, glue, lye, paint, turpentine, kerosene, gasoline and other petroleum products, alcoholic beverages, aspirin and other medications out of their reach. If a child has swallowed or is suspected to have swallowed any substance that might be poisonous, assume they have indeed swallowed it and call for help.

Check to see if the victim has any burns around the mouth. This could indicate poison had been ingested.

Locate and keep the suspected substance and container.

If the Victim Is Conscious

1. Call the Poison Control Center.
2. DO **NOT** give counteragents unless directed by the Poison Control Center or a physician.
3. DO **NOT** follow directions for neutralizing poisons found on the container.
4. Dilute poison by giving victim moderate amounts of water if directed by the Poison Control Center.

If the Victim Is Unconscious

1. Call **9-1-1.**
2. Check to see if victim is breathing. If not, tilt victim's head back and perform *mouth-to-nose* rescue breathing. DO **NOT** GIVE MOUTH-TO-MOUTH RESCUE BREATHING.
3. DO **NOT** attempt to stimulate victim.

If the Victim Is Vomiting

1. Roll the victim over onto his or her side. This helps ensure the victim will not choke on what is brought up.

Drug Overdose

A drug overdose is a poisoning. And don't take drunkenness lightly. Alcohol is as much a poison as stimulants, tranquilizers, narcotics, hallucinogens or inhalants. Remember: Alcohol alone or in combination with certain other drugs can kill.

1. Call for emergency medical help at once.
2. Check the victim's breathing and pulse. If breathing has stopped or is very weak, open the airway. If after a few seconds, the victim is still not breathing, immediately begin rescue breathing (see "Rescue Breathing"). *CAUTION: People under the influence of alcohol or drugs can become violent. Be careful.*
3. While waiting for help:
   • Watch breathing.
   • Keep the victim warm with a blanket or coat.
   • DO **NOT** throw water in the victim's face.
   • DO **NOT** give the victim liquor or a stimulant.

Burns

1. Fire burns:
   • Cool the burn with running water to stop the burning process.
   • Remove garments and jewelry. Cover the victim with clean sheets or towels.
   • Call for emergency help immediately.
2. Chemical burns:
   • Remove victim's affected clothing.
   • Wash burned areas with cool water for at least 20 minutes.
   • Call for emergency medical help immediately.
   • *For chemical burns of the eye:* Flush eye with water for 20 minutes.

CHAPTER SIX

Homeowner's Insurance

Replacement Cost Coverage

Secondary Dwellings

Condominium Insurance

Standard Types of Homeowner's Policies

Additional Living Expenses or "Extra Expense"

Earthquake Coverage

Flood Insurance

Premium Savings

Liability Coverage

Workers' Compensation for Household Employees

Material Misrepresentation

Processing a Claim

Insurance companies can be divided into two major categories: the direct writers and the independent agency companies. Allstate, State Farm and Farmer's Insurance are examples of direct writers. The agents of direct writers are employees of the insurance company, whereas the independent agent or broker represents several insurance companies, such as Hartford, Fireman's Fund or Traveler's.

The insurance agent or broker should determine the replacement cost of your home, recommend the proper amount of insurance and answer your particular questions. As is the case in every profession, it stands to reason that there are varying degrees of competency among insurance brokers and agents. Homeowners would be well advised to take the same precautions in selecting an insurance broker or agent as they would be in selecting a doctor, lawyer or any other professional.

Homeowner's insurance coverage can vary depending on the state in which they are offered and the company that offers them. These are somewhat reflected in the cost.

Competition has resulted in discounts for newer homes and those with fire and burglar alarms. Insurance companies offer a wide variety of payment plans including quarterly and monthly billings for a minimum service charge.

Homeowner's insurance offers the homeowner a package of multiperil coverages at substantial premium savings. Insurance companies make available several homeowner's policy forms. All of these cover the dwelling, outbuildings and contents against loss by fire and a number of extended perils; they further provide protection against loss by theft of personal property on the premises as well as away from the premises. Standard homeowner's policies also cover additional living expenses and personal liability coverage, including liability coverage for household help.

Policies only insure losses caused by perils named specifically in the policy with the exception of "all risk" policies, which cover all perils except those specifically excluded.

Replacement Cost Coverage

For Homes

Standard homeowner's policies provide that compensation for loss or damage to buildings is based upon the "replacement cost" concept. Replacement cost covers the cost to rebuild your home even if it is more than the insured amount of your policy. Remember that only the value of the improvements (buildings, not the land) are insured.

Most insurance companies limit the amount they will pay in excess of the insured amount (for example, 150 percent of insured amount or 200 percent of insured amount). To be eligible for replacement cost coverage, most companies require that the home be insured for 100 percent of the company's estimate of replacement cost when the policy is issued. The importance of this coverage is based on the premise that no one can accurately predict the actual cost to rebuild your home until it is actually destroyed. Most insurance companies will use anywhere from $100 to $200 per square foot to determine replacement cost, depending on locality and construction. Replacement cost coverage could result in a savings of thousands of dollars in the event your home is totally destroyed.

The two following examples show payments of claims in case of total loss of the insured dwelling, *with* and *without* replacement cost coverage. Note that without replacement cost coverage the insurance company will only pay up to the insured amount of the policy.

Total Loss with Replacement Cost Coverage

Replacement cost	$ 100,000
Insured amount	$ 100,000
Cost to rebuild home	$ 120,000
Insurance company pays	**$120,000**

Total Loss Without Replacement Cost Coverage

Replacement cost	$100,000
Insured amount	$ 90,000
Cost to rebuild home	$120,000
Insurance company pays	**$ 90,000**

The following example shows a partial loss of the dwelling. The company pays the cost of replacement, provided the insured amount equals at least 90 percent of replacement cost of the dwelling at the time of the loss. This is true whether or not the policy provides for replacement cost coverage.

Partial Loss with or Without Replacement Cost Coverage

Replacement cost	$100,000
Insured amount	$ 90,000
Amount of damage	$ 40,000
Insurance company pays	**$ 40,000**

Most insurance companies offer *ordinance upgrade* replacement cost coverage for an additional cost. Some companies limit such coverage to a certain percent of the insured amount; some include it automatically. As shown in the following example, this coverage pays for the additional cost of rebuilding caused by building code requirements enacted since the home was built.

Total Loss with Ordinance Upgrade Replacement Cost Coverage

Replacement cost	$ 100,000
Insured amount	$ 100,000
Cost to rebuild home	$ 120,000
Additional cost to upgrade to code	$ 30,000
Insurance company pays	**$ 150,000**

For Contents

Replacement cost can be defined as replacement or repair of damaged property without making allowance for depreciation, whereas under the "actual cash value" concept, compensation is the cost to replace the damaged or lost personal property minus depreciation.

If, for example, a fire were to destroy a sofa purchased for $900 five years ago, the amount recovered would be $900 minus the effect of five years of wear and tear, so that under actual cash value coverage, compensation could be as low as $400.

A sofa identical to the one purchased for $900 five years ago will likely cost $1,500 to replace today. Under replacement cost coverage, compensation would be $1,500.

Most companies offer replacement cost coverage for contents. The maximum amount companies will pay to replace an item of personal property under the replacement cost endorsement varies among companies. It may be four times the actual cash value of the item at the time of the loss but could be as low as 2½ times, while some have no maximum limit at all.

The best way to determine the value of your contents is to maintain an inventory of your household possessions and other personal property. Estimate the cost to replace these items at today's prices. The inventory should be updated periodically and kept in a safe place away from the home, as it will be helpful in the event of loss. For this reason, all receipts of major purchases should be kept. Most insurance companies will provide inventory forms for this purpose. Color photographs can be very beneficial in reconstructing the contents of each room. They can effectively serve as evidence of loss and—together with photographs taken after the casualty—can help establish the extent of the damage.

It should be remembered that most carriers provide a maximum coverage of $1,000 for unscheduled valuable items, including jewelry, gold, silver, furs and securities, with a $100 limit on cash, and are subject to deductibles. Such items, scheduled under a *personal articles floater,* are not subject to any deductible amount.

Standard homeowner's policies automatically cover contents for one-half the amount of the insurance on the home. This amount can be increased at an additional premium.

Coverage of contents includes most of the items you have around the house, whether they belong to you, your family, relatives living with you, guests, household employees or minors staying with you.

Standard homeowner's policies automatically cover contents away from the premises, for 10 percent of the home's insured value or $10,000, whichever is the greater, subject to deductibles. This coverage includes unlocked, unattended automobiles.

Secondary Dwellings

Secondary dwellings, whether owner occupied or rented by the insured, or personal property at a secondary location, can be added to the homeowner's policy by endorsement or by a supplementary homeowner's or fire policy. Often, this coverage is not as broad as a primary homeowner's policy.

Condominium Insurance

A condominium is a form of ownership that consists of fee simple (absolute) title to a unit in a multiple development, with joint ownership of common areas used by all occupants. The building is usually insured under a separate policy purchased by the owners' association.

The condominium owner can insure personal property and all interior walls, fixtures and appliances under the standard HO-6 policy form, specifically designed for condominium owners.

Theft of personal property and liability coverages are provided subject to the limits of the policy, deductibles and exclusions. The basic form provides $1,000 of coverage for additions and alterations, such as cabinets and custom fixtures. In the event of a loss by a covered peril, the company would pay the cost of replacement or repair without deduction for depreciation.

The amount for additions and alterations coverage can be increased for an additional premium.

The breadth of coverage can be changed from a named peril to an all-risk basis for an additional premium.

Also available is a *loss assessment* coverage. This indemnifies the insured for his or her share of the assessment levied by the condominium owners' association against owners for certain losses not covered by the insurance of the association.

Standard Types of Homeowner's Policies

Perils Key:

1. Fire and lightning
2. Damage to property removed from premises endangered by fire
3. Windstorm and hail
4. Explosion
5. Riots or civil commotion
6. Damage by aircraft
7. Damage by vehicles not owned or operated by people covered by the policy
8. Damage from smoke
9. Vandalism and malicious mischief
10. Theft
11. Window breakage (including storm doors)
12. Falling objects
13. Weight of ice, snow, sleet
14. Collapse of building or any part of building
15. Bursting, cracking, burning or bulging of a steam or water heating system, or of appliances for heating water
16. Leakage or overflow of water or steam from a plumbing, heating or air-conditioning system
17. Freezing of plumbing, heating or air-conditioning systems and domestic appliances
18. Injury to electrical appliances, devices, fixtures and wiring (excluding TV, radio tubes and resistors) from short circuits or other accidentally generated currents

	HO 3 Standard	HO 5 Deluxe	HO 6 Condominiums
Perils Covered	Perils 1–18 on personal property. All risks on buildings except perils excluded in policy.	All risks on building and personal property, except perils excluded in policy.	Perils 1–18 except 11
Standard Amount of Insurance			
Dwelling and attached structures	Based on value of property. Minimum $20,000	Based on value of property. Minimum $25,000	Building insured under separate policy.
Detached structures	10% of insurance	10% of insurance	Fixtures, installations or additions to interior surfaces of unit. Maximum $1,000
Trees, shrubs, plants	5% of insurance 250 per tree	5% of insurance 250 per tree	
Personal property on premises	50% of insurance	50% of insurance	Minimum $10,000
Personal property away from premises	10% of personal property	50% of insurance	10% of personal property. Minimum $1,000
Additional living expense	20% of insurance	20% of insurance	20% of personal property
Comprehensive Personal Liability	$50,000	$50,000	$25,000
Medical payments	$1,000 per person. $25,000 per accident	$5,000 per person. $25,000 per accident	$1,000 per person. $25,000 per accident
Unscheduled securities, precious metals, cash	$250	$250	$250

Additional Living Expenses or "Extra Expense"

If your premises become uninhabitable due to a disaster, your insurance company will reimburse you for any additional living expenses over and above your normal living expenses. The standard homeowner's policy covers an additional 20 percent of the homeowner's insured value, in order for you to continue your normal standard of living as nearly as possible.

Policies may contain several exclusions and limitations, such as the length of time needed to repair or replace destroyed property, or the amount of time for you to become settled in new permanent quarters. Most companies limit the period of recovery to one year from date of loss.

Earthquake Coverage

The standard homeowner's policy does not include coverage for earth movement or earthquake damage to your home. This protection can be purchased for an additional premium.

There are three separate deductibles of 10 to 15 percent in most homeowner's policies. The basic quake policy covers damage to the structure of the home only. A separate deductible is applied against the damage to the contents of the home, such as furnishings, artwork, clothing or electronic equipment. A third deductible is then applied against the value of "other" structures outside the home, such as a garage, swimming pool or fence. There is no deductible on additional living expense.

The cost of this coverage varies from region to region depending upon the seismic activity of the area. In addition, earthquake coverage is several times more expensive for masonry than frame homes, as frame homes have greater resiliency.

Flood Insurance

Under the National Flood Insurance Program, certain areas have been designated as *flood prone* on maps that are usually available at local city or county building departments, lending institutions and insurance agencies.

A buyer of real property located in such a flood-prone area is required to purchase flood insurance in order to obtain a loan secured by the property from any federally regulated financial institution, or a loan insured or guaranteed by an agency of the U.S. government.

Flood insurance policies covering such properties are issued by private insurance carriers at rates set by the National Flood Insurance Program.

Premium Savings

The maximum credits are reserved for *central station* reporting systems. A homeowner can elect to significantly reduce premiums by choosing a higher deductible. The $250 deductible is the most common, but deductibles of $500 or $1,000 can result in substantial savings. Higher deductibles should always be considered if the amount of the deductible would not present financial hardship.

Liability Coverage

Coverage for *comprehensive personal liability and damage to property of others* is automatically included in standard homeowner's policies.

In addition to the liability limits provided in the homeowner's policy, insurance companies write *umbrella* policies that extend liability coverage over and above the limits provided in the homeowner's policy.

Workers' Compensation for Household Employees

Most states require homeowner's insurance policies to cover workers' compensation for household employees automatically. Household employees include babysitters, gardeners, maids and others you hire to provide personal services in your home. Not included are such people as plumbers and electricians who are in business for themselves, people working for a business or independent contractors.

Workers' compensation coverage is only required if you hire employees on a regular and systematic basis. The laws vary by state but generally apply only if the employee works a specific minimum number of hours per week or month.

Failure to meet your responsibility as an employer can result in a large judgment against you if an eligible household employee is injured while working in your home.

The cost of such coverage is usually included automatically in your premium. It varies by state and insurance company, depending on the number of employees, how often they work and the total annual payroll. You would be well advised to discuss your individual situation with your insurance agent.

Material Misrepresentation

Any material misrepresentation made by an applicant for insurance, even though made innocently, whether verbal or written, renders the insurance contract voidable. A misrepresentation is *material* where the insurance company would not have entered the contract had the complete facts been known at the time the policy was issued. The company has the legal right to rescind or cancel the policy in such an event.

Processing a Claim

1. In case of burglary, notify the police at once. The insurance company will require a copy of the police report as proof of the loss.
2. In case of a casualty, safeguard the remaining property.
3. Check your insurance coverage.
4. Notify your insurance agent of the loss as soon as possible.
5. File a claim form furnished by your agent, accompanied by a list of articles lost, together with:
   • Description of article
   • Date of purchase
   • Original cost
   • Present value
   • Serial numbers
   • Identification marks
   • Canceled checks, receipts, bills, vouchers (Merchants usually cooperate in providing copies of receipts if lost)
   • Photographs before and after the casualty can serve effectively to substantiate a loss, as well as the extent of the damage.
   • Do not forget to claim sales taxes; they are part of the cost of an article.
   • Other pertinent information

(See also Chapter 10, "Tax Information for Homeowners" under the heading "Casualty Losses.")

CHAPTER
SEVEN

Energy Conservation

Energy-Saving Tips

Insulation

Solar Energy

Energy conservation is an increasingly important national issue. Every homeowner can contribute to this effort and reap important dividends by understanding the importance of proper conservation habits, insulation and application of new technology.

Energy-Saving Tips

General

The following are some tips for general energy conservation:

- ❑ *Illumination.* Turn off lights when room is not occupied.
- ❑ *Hot water.* Use hot water conservatively and at lowest practical temperature.
- ❑ *Cooking.* The oven is more efficient than surface units when cooking several dishes at a time.
- ❑ *Warmer clothes and down comforters or electric blankets.* These enable people to be more comfortable at reduced room temperatures.
- ❑ *Thermostat settings.* In winter, reduction of 1°F can save 2 percent to 3 percent in fuel. Night setbacks of 10°F generally are most efficient. Larger night setbacks during extremely cold nights are not recommended because recovery periods may be too long. Vacation settings should not be below 50°F. Changing the setting from 70° to 75°F in summer can save as much as 15 percent of the cooling costs.
- ❑ *Water heater thermostat setting.* Try to reduce the thermostat setting to a lower temperature. Check water temperature before and a few hours after, by holding a thermometer under tap when water is hottest.
- ❑ *Spare rooms.* Keep unoccupied spare rooms closed in summer and winter, with heat and cool-air registers partially closed.
- ❑ *Fans and space heaters.* Use of these can keep individual rooms comfortable for much less than it costs to heat or cool the entire house.
- ❑ *Basement.* Keep heat and cool-air registers closed. Close door of stairway to basement.
- ❑ *Smoke and odors.* Cutting down on smoking and cooking odors reduces need for use of exhaust fans.
- ❑ *Windows.* Reduce air leakage by only opening windows to clear smoke and odors.
- ❑ *Draperies, shades and blinds.* These items keep solar heat out in summer and keep heat in during winter.

❏ *Low power demand periods.* Defer operation of dishwasher, self-cleaning feature of oven, clothes washer, dryer and iron to low-power demand periods: early morning or late at night.

❏ *Damp-drying clothes.* Doing this rather than overdrying eliminates need for sprinkling before ironing.

❏ *Fireplace damper.* Always close the damper when not in use.

❏ *Crawl space vents.* These vents should be open in summer and closed in winter, unless there is a heating unit in the crawl space or a moisture problem.

❏ *Attic vents.* Keep these open at all times. Adequate insulation is therefore necessary.

❏ *Storm windows and doors.* Leaving these on during cooling season can cut your cooling load by as much as 20 percent.

❏ *Energy efficiency rates (EERs).* When purchasing major appliances, check and compare their EERs to be sure you are getting the one with the best operating performance for the least amount of dollars.

❏ *Meter reading.* This is the best way to gauge and compare energy use to previous months. Most types of gas and electric meters have a series of four or five dials (Figure 7.1). Read the leftmost dial first, then proceed to the right. When a pointer is between two digits, always read the lower number. If a pointer is directly on a number, read the next lower number only if the pointer on the dial to the right has not yet passed the zero. The example of the gas meter reading in Figure 7.1 shows the pointer of the third dial exactly on four; since the pointer on the dial to the right has not yet passed the zero mark, however, the reading is recorded as 5-2-3-9. If the pointer on the last dial were between zero and one, the reading would be 5-2-4-0.

Energy-Saving Maintenance and Installation

One of the best ways to save energy is to keep appliances in proper working order. Following are some tips for appliance maintenance:

❏ *Heating equipment.* Replace or clean filters, dust around furnace, air grille and ducts every two or three months during winter. Oil the fan and motor bearings and inspect fan belt tension before start of the cold season. Necessary adjustments should be made by a service professional. With hot water or steam systems, check radiator shut-off valve for leakage. Check oil storage tank for leakage.

❏ *Air-conditioning equipment.* Replace or clean air filters every two or three months during summer. Lubricate fan and motor bearings and

FIGURE 7.1 Types of Utility Meters

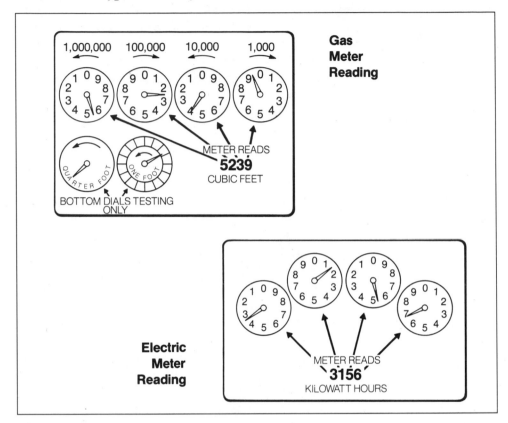

inspect fan belt tension before the start of summer. A service professional should check the cooling surfaces and make necessary adjustments every two years.

❏ *Air flow.* This should be unobstructed by draperies and furniture deflecting cold air back into the unit, causing it to shut off without cooling the room adequately.

❏ *Air-conditioning compressors.* Keep these shaded by structure or plantings, but without impeding air flow.

❏ *Refrigerator and freezer door seals.* Ensure that these are airtight and condensing coils should be kept clean.

❏ *Air leaks.* Caulk around doors and window frames. If necessary, caulk around baseboards on ground floor. Seal off all air leaks around electrical, plumbing and heating ducts penetrating the floor system over basement or crawl space, underneath the kitchen sink, and in ceiling between upper floor and attic. Seal area around window air conditioners.

☐ *Ducts and hot water pipes.* Insulate pipes in the basement, crawl space and attic to prevent heat loss. Repair disconnected or crushed ducts.

☐ *Attic insulation.* Attic vents must remain open at all times. Use fiberglass ductwrap with an insulation rating of R-6 or higher.

☐ *Attic exhaust fan.* These should be thermostatically controlled to operate at about 100°F to keep upper floors cooler.

☐ *Sun control film or double glazing.* This material, applied to windows and glass doors, conserves energy by rejecting a large portion of the sun's heat in summer and by reducing heat loss during winter months. The film also makes glass resistant to shattering, practically eliminates fading of furnishings and drastically reduces glare. A range of shades and tints are available commercially. Darker shades usually provide more insulation but may darken the room to a degree unacceptable to you.

☐ *Insulating glass.* If it is time to replace some windows, check the white energy labels found on many windows for sale. Look for windows with "U-values" of below 0.65. Windows with this rating won't let much heat escape from your home.

☐ *Trees.* Planting these for wind break and shade can lower your utility consumption.

☐ *Air-lock entrance way.* Installing a small foyer-type entrance way, about four by four feet, stops inrush of cold wind into the house. The outer door should open out to ensure that in a fire no one can block the exit door.

☐ *Weatherstripping.* Use of this material on exterior doors and doors leading to basement and garage can save energy.

☐ *Water heater insulation blankets.* These items, which are easy to install and inexpensive, save a great deal of energy. Touch your water heater; if you feel any heat, you are losing energy.

☐ *Shower flow limiters.* These items, available at most hardware stores, save water and conserve water heat.

Insulation

Insulation is usually a good investment in geographic areas that require a great deal of air conditioning, even if heating requirements are low. How much you should invest in energy conservation improvements depends equally upon climate and energy prices. Spending your improvement dollar efficiently also means a balanced combination of energy conservation techniques. For instance, you may not be making the best use of your money if you invest only in attic insulation while neglecting the use of storm windows or insulation in floors over unheated areas, where these are economical.

Most insulation material used in homes is made of Fiberglas and comes in two forms:

1. Blanket (slab-like bats or rolls)
2. Loose fill, sold by the bag, to be poured or blown into place

R-Value

R stands for resistance (to the flow of heat.) The R-value of a material is simply a measure of how good an insulator the material is. The higher the R-value, the better the insulator. It's R-values, not inches, that count. For example, 6 inches of Fiberglas have the same R-value as 15 inches of wood or 7 feet of brick.

Most Important Places To Insulate

1. *The attic.* This is where most of the heat is wasted in winter, and where the sun seeps in to run up air-conditioning bills in summer.
2. *Exterior walls.*
3. *Crawl spaces and basements.*

Make sure you have enough insulation: at least R-30 in ceilings, R-11 in exterior walls and R-19 in floors.

Other Energy-Saving Methods

Insulation works best in combination with other ways to save energy, such as caulking and sealing around doors and chimneys, double-glazed windows (in certain geographical areas), weather-stripping around doors and windows, and good attic ventilation to expel hot air and moisture.

Insulation Requirements in Different Geographical Areas

There are five geographical winter heating zones and five cooling zones, shown in Figure 7.2. It stands to reason that requirements for R-values vary from zone to zone.

FIGURE 7.2   Heating and Cooling Zone Maps

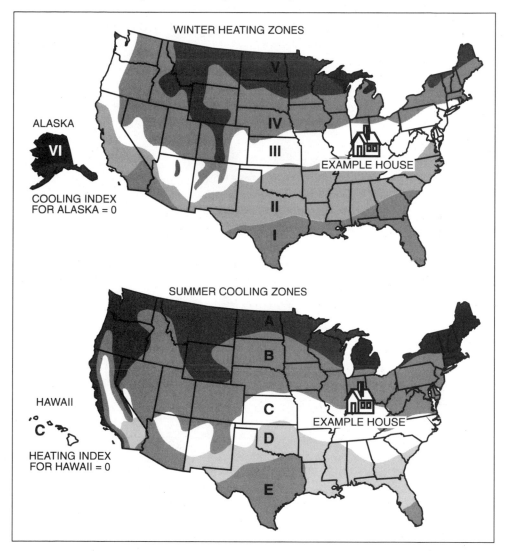

Solar Energy

Numerous designs and techniques for capturing solar heat and storing it for residential use have evolved and new ones are being developed at a rapid rate. Because this subject is far too complex for a detailed discussion within the scope of this book, the following is no more than a very basic introduction to solar heating. For detailed information about solar home design, space heating and water heating, contact your local library. Consult your architect about the cost and efficiency of solar energy.

Site Planning, Design and Conservation

Conception of a solar home begins with site selection and site planning for solar energy utilization, taking maximum advantage of wind shelter and sun exposure.

Most solar houses are designed with large window areas in walls, the roof, or both, to allow maximum penetration of sun rays into the living space. Roof overhangs, louvres and other devices are incorporated into designs to shade occupants from excessive heat.

All such efforts to capture the sun's rays would be in vain, however, without measures to prevent unnecessary heat loss in winter and heat gain in summer, including insulation, weatherstripping, caulking, storm windows and so on.

Solar Heating Systems

Any solar heating system consists of three basic components, as shown in Figure 7.3:

1. Collector
2. Storage
3. Distribution

The sun's heat rays are captured through a variety of heat traps or collectors mounted on the roof or elsewhere. Heat thus collected is transferred to storage units. When needed, the stored heat is conducted to occupied living spaces via one of several distribution systems.

A storage unit could, for instance, be a masonry wall designed to absorb and store heat, or it could be water stored in receptacles. Another type of heat storage could be an insulated container under the floor holding pebbles or rocks that absorb heat transferred from the collectors via a forced air duct system.

Generally speaking, there are four methods, illustrated in Figure 7.4, by which heat from a storage unit can be distributed to occupied spaces:

1. Naturally circulating air flow caused by the rising of hot air and replaced by cooler air moving in

FIGURE 7.3   Solar Heating System

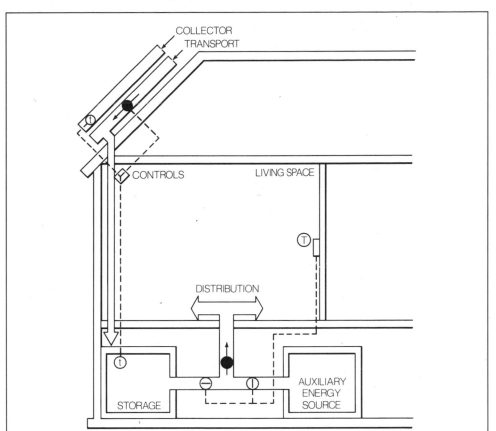

2. A forced air duct system using an electric blower, much as a conventional forced air heating system
3. Forced radiation piping hot water to convectors in the occupied spaces
4. Natural radiation, the transfer of heat by electromagnetic waves without the assistance of mechanical devices

The manner in which solar radiation is collected and stored will usually determine the means of distribution.

Check with the local office of the Internal Revenue Service on tax credits applicable to energy conservation, which may be available at the time you plan to proceed. (See Chapter 10 under the heading "Residential Energy Credit.")

FIGURE 7.4   Thermal Energy Distribution

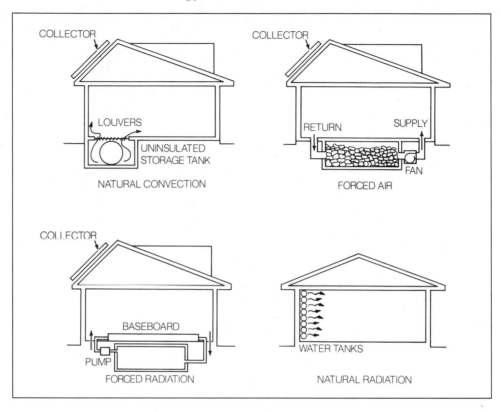

CHAPTER
EIGHT

House and Equipment Maintenance

Importance of Regular Inspections

Building Maintenance

Grounds and Yard Maintenance

Mechanical Systems Maintenance

Just as the human body needs a balanced diet, exercise and regular checkups to stay healthy, the home needs basic care to run efficiently. Here are some tips on how to give your home its annual checkup. Use the maintenance checklist in Appendix D.

Importance of Regular Inspections

Regular preventive maintenance will extend the life of the house and its equipment and can keep the cost of operating a house under control. Spring and fall are good times for making thorough maintenance inspections.

Many household maintenance and repair jobs can be done by the homeowner at considerable savings. For more information on home repairs and maintenance, contact your local library. Unless you feel fully qualified to undertake the job, however, get professional help from local contractors or technicians.

Select contractors carefully; use those who have satisfied your neighbors. Make a written agreement with the contractor in advance, including your specific requirements of the work to be done and the price you have both agreed to.

The benefit of periodic inspections by a professional pest control operator cannot be overemphasized, especially in the warmer southern and western regions of the United States. (See Chapter 9.)

Building Maintenance

Permanent Maintenance Record

A record of all maintenance and repairs to the house and its equipment should include the following information:

1. The date on which each job was done
2. The frequency of work to be done
3. The cost of each job, thereby allowing the homeowner to budget for future maintenance
4. Who did the job, which provides the homeowner with a list of service and technical providers to call (or not to call) in the future
5. If the job was done by the homeowner, what materials were used and where they were purchased

When moving to a new house, it is a good idea to obtain from the builder extra floor tile, ceiling tile, wall covering, interior and exterior paint and similar materials for repairs. Appendix C contains record forms for house and equipment maintenance.

Maintenance of the Building

Water is the leading cause of premature failure and deterioration of building materials. The penetration of water (whether it be as a vapor, a liquid or as ice) into the structure can cause paint failure, discoloration, decay, foundation failure, masonry cracking and many other problems. Water can come from the exterior as rain or snow, from below the house as either liquid or vapor, or from within the house as vapor produced by family activities. It is most important that the house be checked thoroughly for all symptoms of moisture damage.

Look for the "red flags" discussed in some detail on the following pages. They are also summarized in the home and equipment maintenance checklist in Appendix D.

Foundation and Exterior Walls

❏ Check for large cracks and crumbling mortar joints in exterior walls and fireplace chimneys, and have them repaired immediately. Check with your local building supply stores for proper sealing materials.

❏ Watch for paint failure. Check for cracking, peeling, blistering or bare spots. The most important function of exterior paint is to seal out moisture and protect structural wood members in the walls. The length of time between repainting varies with the type of paint, method of application, exposure of the surfaces and climate. Often only a portion of the exterior needs repainting; in fact, excessive paint build-up can cause peeling.

❏ On wood surfaces, check for nails loosened by normal expansion and contraction, as they must be reset.

❏ Earth-filled structures (patios, porches, planters, steps and the like) in contact with and extending above foundation walls can cause serious damage to structural wood members. Consult a qualified contractor or pest control operator.

❏ Patios and porches should slope away from the house. Check by using a marble.

Roof, Gutters and Downspouts
For diagrams of a roof and a gutter system, see Figures 8.1 and 8.2.

Asphalt shingle roofs: Check for missing shingles and shingles with broken tabs or curled-up corners. Do not use nails; curled-up corners can be cemented down with special asphalt shingle adhesive. Replace bad shingles by reaching under the old shingle with a screwdriver, lifting it off the old roofing nail. Apply cement to back of new shingle and slide it underneath.

FIGURE 8.1 Basic Roof Parts

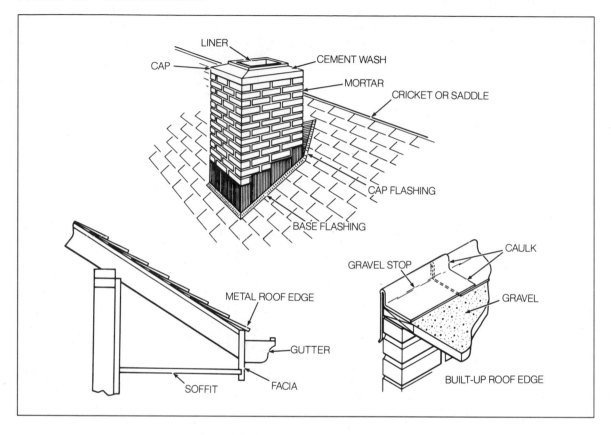

Wood shingle roofs: Check for missing, bowed, split or rotted shingles, especially under overhanging branches and replace them as soon as possible. Pull out or cut old nails. Use galvanized shingle nails to fasten new shingles.

Cement and adobe tile roofs: Check for broken or missing tiles that should be replaced. Otherwise, such roofs are fairly permanent.

Flat roofs: A tar-and-gravel flat roof consists of several overlapping layers of tar paper, coated with hot tar. Check for delaminated spots, cracks and large blisters. Be careful not to step on blisters. Cracks develop over a period of time and should be filled. Use a nonfibered asphalt coating for all those fine cracks and a fibered coating for wide cracks and wide open seams. If any wood shows through, the roof definitely should be replaced. At the edge of flat roofs are gravel stops made of sheet metal. The joints between lengths of these gravel stops are quite vulnerable to leakage due to expansion and contraction of the metal. These joints must be resealed periodically.

FIGURE 8.2   Roof Drainage System

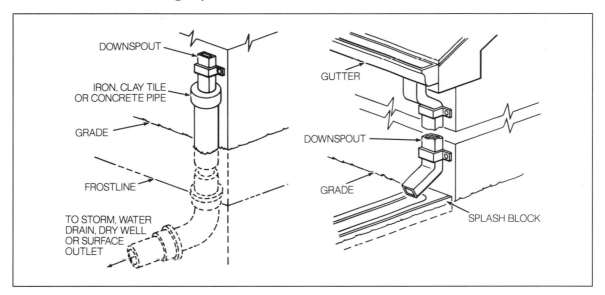

Check all roof penetrations for water-tight seals at the juncture of roof and vertical surfaces (chimneys, plumbing vents, flues, ventilators, air-conditioning equipment, TV antenna, skylights and so on). Seal openings with asphalt coating.

❏ Check for rust holes in metal flashings. Check painted metal flashings for deterioration, especially on older buildings.

❏ Periodically clean gutters, gutter strainers and downspouts of leaves and silt. When gutters become clogged, overflowing water finds its way to joints in soffits and fascias, causing paint failure and decay. Wire cages keep leaves from clogging downspouts.

❏ Gutters receive severe exposure and are likely to require annual painting or spot painting. Replace those with holes or excessive rust.

❏ Refasten sagging gutters to provide proper run-off.

❏ Check downspouts for loose connections, loose mounting brackets and rust holes.

❏ On level lots and in areas that become icy and slippery during the winter, make sure that downspouts empty directly into a drainage system, rather than onto cement splash blocks.

Foundations, Basement, Crawlspace, Garage For illustrations of basic foundations, see Figures 8.3–8.5.

FIGURE 8.3 Crawl Space Construction

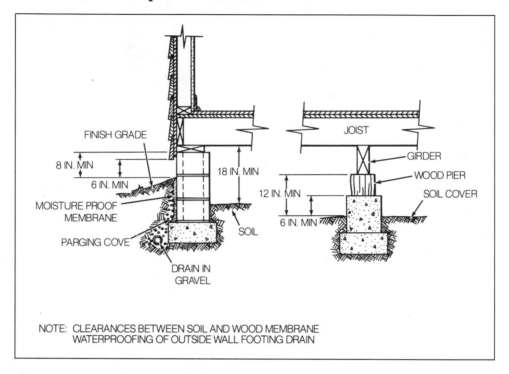

FINISH GRADE

8 IN. MIN

6 IN. MIN

18 IN. MIN

MOISTURE PROOF
MEMBRANE

PARGING COVE

DRAIN IN
GRAVEL

SOIL

JOIST

GIRDER

WOOD PIER

SOIL COVER

12 IN. MIN

6 IN. MIN

NOTE: CLEARANCES BETWEEN SOIL AND WOOD MEMBRANE
WATERPROOFING OF OUTSIDE WALL FOOTING DRAIN

FIGURE 8.4 Slab Floor Construction

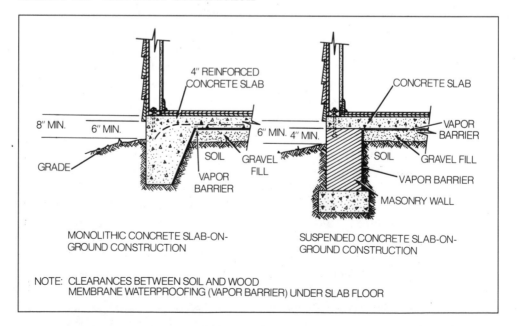

4" REINFORCED
CONCRETE SLAB

CONCRETE SLAB

8" MIN.

6" MIN.

VAPOR
BARRIER

GRADE

SOIL

GRAVEL
FILL

VAPOR
BARRIER

6" MIN. 4" MIN.

SOIL

GRAVEL FILL

VAPOR BARRIER

MASONRY WALL

MONOLITHIC CONCRETE SLAB-ON-
GROUND CONSTRUCTION

SUSPENDED CONCRETE SLAB-ON-
GROUND CONSTRUCTION

NOTE: CLEARANCES BETWEEN SOIL AND WOOD
MEMBRANE WATERPROOFING (VAPOR BARRIER) UNDER SLAB FLOOR

FIGURE 8.5   Basement Construction

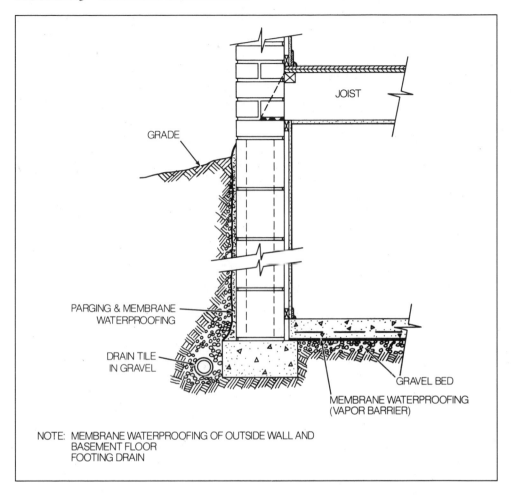

JOIST

GRADE

PARGING & MEMBRANE
WATERPROOFING

DRAIN TILE
IN GRAVEL

GRAVEL BED

MEMBRANE WATERPROOFING
(VAPOR BARRIER)

NOTE: MEMBRANE WATERPROOFING OF OUTSIDE WALL AND
BASEMENT FLOOR
FOOTING DRAIN

❑ Check for termite shelter tubes on foundation walls, concrete footings
or pipes, a sign of subterranean termite infestation. Also watch for small
holes in wood members with piles of wood dust and pellets of partly
digested wood resembling sawdust. (Also see Chapter 9.)

❑ Watch for signs of excessive moisture and high water stains along walls
and foundations. Some materials on the market can be used to make
minor repairs of basement walls from the inside; any serious water
penetration, however, must be repaired from the outside. This may be a
major undertaking and should be done by a qualified waterproofing
company.

❑ Puddles against foundations after heavy rains indicate a drainage
problem that should be corrected.

Windows and Doors

❏ Replace, don't just caulk over, badly cracked caulking around windows and doors. When the bottom layer breaks up, it will take the new caulking with it.

❏ On storm windows, check for condensation inside the glass. Drill angled holes to outside, to allow water to run off.

❏ Replace loose or missing putty to avoid water entering and causing decay of wood sash. Use modern glazing compound rather than white lead putty.

❏ Check for free functioning of all door locks and catches, including sliding glass doors. Adjust and lubricate as required.

❏ Check for proper fitting of weatherstripping, storm windows and screens. Warped or sagging doors and decayed door frames should be repaired.

Grounds and Yard Maintenance

Depending on the severity of the winter, outside hosebibbs (if they are not freezeproof) and water lines should be drained each fall. For examples of standard and freezeproof hosebibbs, see Figure 8.6. Water should also be drained from garden hoses and they should be cleaned and stored in a protected location. Storage on a reel provides protection from damage. Some plastic hoses become brittle in cold weather, and cannot be used during the winter.

Areaways, window wells, storm drains, and their outlets should be cleaned and damaged items repaired. During the fall, particularly, areaways and window wells should be checked frequently, since drains in these area-

FIGURE 8.6   Hosebibbs

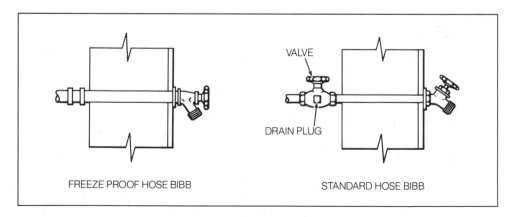

FREEZE PROOF HOSE BIBB   STANDARD HOSE BIBB

ways can be clogged by only a few leaves. Windblown leaves will collect quite rapidly in such locations.

All gasoline-powered equipment that will be out of service for a season should have fuel drained from the system and be serviced in accordance with the manufacturer's directions. In the fall, all snow handling or snow melting equipment should be checked and readied for service. Snow removal is made easier by coating the snow shovel with wax or silicone.

The winter is a good time to clean and repair all garden tools and equipment. All dirt and rust should be removed and surfaces coated with oil, silicone or wax. Splintered, or rough wood surfaces, such as handles, should be sanded and refinished.

Spray guns can become clogged and useless due to the chemical residue from pesticides and weed killer. Fertilizer left in a spreader can be extremely corrosive. All such equipment should be thoroughly cleaned after each use. Leftover chemicals should be checked for expiration dates and those which are to be saved should be stored in a cool, dry, locked cabinet.

All paved areas (covered with concrete, asphalt, etc.) should be checked for adjacent cracks, settlement and soil erosion. Asphalt surfaces are quite susceptible to deterioration from water if adequate drainage from these surfaces is not provided. Also, asphalt is subject to deterioration from petroleum products, such as gasoline and oil drippings. If you are contracting for this sealing operation, be sure to choose a reputable contractor. Cracks in concrete surfaces should be thoroughly cleaned and repaired with patching compounds that will bond to existing concrete.

All wood structures such as fences and gates should be inspected for termite attack and decay. When replacement becomes necessary, use a more durable species of wood (redwood, cypress or black locust). Wood that is to be imbedded in the ground or in concrete should be pressure-treated.

Mechanical Systems Maintenance

This chapter is concerned with the maintenance of mechanical systems in the home. The scope of this book does not permit inclusion of how to repair equipment and appliances. A variety of such manuals are available in local libraries.

Main Shut-off Valves and Switches

The location of the following items should be well known to all adult members of the household and should be marked where necessary:

❏ The electrical fuse-type or switch-type circuit box, which should contain an itemized list of all electrical systems and major appliances, as well as light fixtures and receptacles connected to each circuit
❏ Switches at the major electrical systems
❏ Main water supply valve
❏ Water supply valve for each plumbing fixture
❏ Clean-out plugs in sanitary waste lines
❏ Septic tank distribution box and leaching field
❏ Main gas supply valve, which is located next to the meter on the inlet pipe; to close, use a wrench and give it a quarter turn, so that it runs crosswise on the pipe
❏ Gas supply valve and pilot light on each gas appliance

The Plumbing System

Water Supply Check water pressure by turning on water in bathtub and lavatory while flushing toilet. If the water supply diminishes to a trickle, the source of the trouble could be either insufficient pressure in the main water supply to the property or clogged water pipes inside the house. Call the water department to determine whether pressure in the water main is normal (between 50 and 70 lbs). If the pressure is normal, odds are that the pipe system in the house, and/or the supply line from the water meter to the house, are in need of replacement. Galvanized pipe, often found in older homes, is susceptible to corrosion by certain minerals found in water and should be replaced by a copper pipe system. This is an expensive project.

Stains in tubs, lavatories and sinks are indications of rust inside the pipes or high iron content in the water. Probe further by filling the tub to see how rusty the water is. If discoloration is excessive, have a plumber check the pipe system for corrosion. Rust in the hot water line may indicate trouble in the water heater. Light discoloration may be cleared by installing purifying filters at the faucets.

Check for leaks and drips by opening and closing each faucet a few times. This is easily corrected by replacing washers.

Check for leaking flush valves in toilets by adding blue food coloring into the toilet tank without flushing. If water in bowl turns blue, the flush valve leaks. Repair or replacement is inexpensive.

There should be enough water hose connections around the outside of the house to reach all garden areas with a 75-foot hose.

Before turning on the lawn sprinkler system, walk around the lawn to check for water running from or standing around any of the sprinkler heads, especially the one at the lowest level. This indicates a faulty or leaky sprinkler valve. Turn on lawn sprinklers to check for sufficient water coverage and for any broken or clogged sprinkler heads.

If the water source is a private well, taste the water for palatability and have the nearest water district check water samples for safety from time to time. Rusty color in well water is often a sign of high iron content, which can be cleared by installing filters at faucets.

Listen for the following unusual sounds. They may be signals of trouble.

- A high-pitched whistling sound when the toilet is flushed indicates the toilet valve needs adjustment. A plumber can easily eliminate this problem.
- A sucking sound when water runs out of a fixture is caused by improper venting. A plumber may be able to eliminate this noise by unclogging the vent system; otherwise, a major change in the vent system may be involved.
- A hammering noise in water pipes when water is turned off is caused by a sharp build-up of water pressure in the pipes and may result in broken or leaking pipes.
- Clicking sounds usually are caused by faulty water meters, which is the responsibility of the water department.

When the sound of running water can be heard throughout the building, it can usually be traced to one of three causes:

1. Excessive water pressure, which can be corrected by installing a pressure regulator
2. Faulty faucet washers
3. Improperly isolated pipes, which may be remedied by installing felt spacers between pipes and structure

Winter Water Tips

❏ Turn off your irrigation system for the winter and drain any exposed pipes.

❏ If below-freezing temperatures are predicted, insulate in advance any sections of pipe exposed to the weather (the pipe leading from your water meter service line into your house). You may also need to insulate pipes in your attic and basement, depending on how well those areas of your home are insulated.

❏ Foam insulation to protect your pipes may be purchased from your local hardware store. Use either electrical tape or copper wire to secure the insulation. (See Figure 8.7.)

FIGURE 8.7   Foam Insulation of Underground Service Line

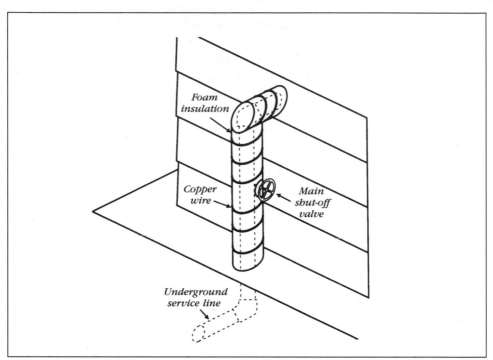

❏ If your pipes freeze, pour lukewarm water on them so they thaw slowly. (If they thaw too fast, they may break.) Once they are thawed, insulate them to prevent further freezing.

Water Heater Look for signs of leaks, including rust and water spots at and around the base of the water heater. Leaks sometimes seal themselves with mineral deposits from the water and can begin to leak again at any time.

To test for excessive mineral deposits, close the cold water inlet valve at the top of water heater, then open any nearby hot water faucet. A crackling, popping and sometimes rumbling noise from the water heater is an indication of excessive mineral deposits, a sign the water heater will soon need to be replaced.

Make sure the water heater is equipped with a temperature-pressure relief valve. The relief valve usually is located on top of the heater. When the temperature reaches 210°F, the relief valve is activated and water is discharged via a pipe directed downward toward the floor. A lever manually operates the valve for testing. The pressure relief valve should be opened periodically to see that it is in operating condition. In the event the heater is not equipped with this necessary and required safety device, it can be installed easily.

If the gas connection to the water heater is copper pipe, it should be replaced with rigid pipe or a flexible brass connector as soon as possible. Gas forms scale in copper, clogging and fouling the thermostat. This can cause dangerous overheating.

Make sure gas water heaters are properly vented, that vent pipes are tightly connected to chimneys and not rusted through or sagging.

See Figure 8.8 for illustrations of types of water heaters.

Septic Tank The frequency with which you clean the septic tank depends on the size of the tank, the flow of sewage to it and the method and conditions of disposal of the tank overflow. As long as the active working space between the scum and sludge is adequate to decompose sewage by bacterial action, the tank does not have to be cleaned. A tank does not need to be pumped when it is filled; the tank is always full.

The tank should be inspected every year or two. When the space between the scum and the sludge becomes one-half the total depth of the tank, cleaning is advisable. If inspection shows raw sewage at the outlet, the tank should be cleaned. If the tank is allowed to fill to the point that sludge is discharged into the disposal field, the disposal field may become plugged and have to be replaced.

Keep a record of inspection and cleanings. It also is a good idea to plot the location of the septic tank and its inspection tiles, and the disposal lines.

Detailed step by step instructions on checking scum and sludge level in septic tanks can be found in Time-Life's *How Things Work in Your Home.*

Figure 8.9 illustrates disposal systems.

The Electrical System

In order to discuss your home's electrical system, we must first review the terminology:

Volt. This is the unit used to measure electrical force or pressure between two points on a circuit. The current at most receptacles and light fixtures in the United States and Canada is approximately 120 volts. As the current moves from the hot supply wire (black or red) through the load presented by an appliance or light, it loses voltage. When the current leaves the load and enters the return circuit provided by a neutral wire (white), it has lost all voltage and is at zero pressure, the same as the earth or ground.

Ampere (generally referred to as amps). This unit is used to measure the amount of current that flows past a given point on a circuit each second.

FIGURE 8.8   Types of Water Heaters

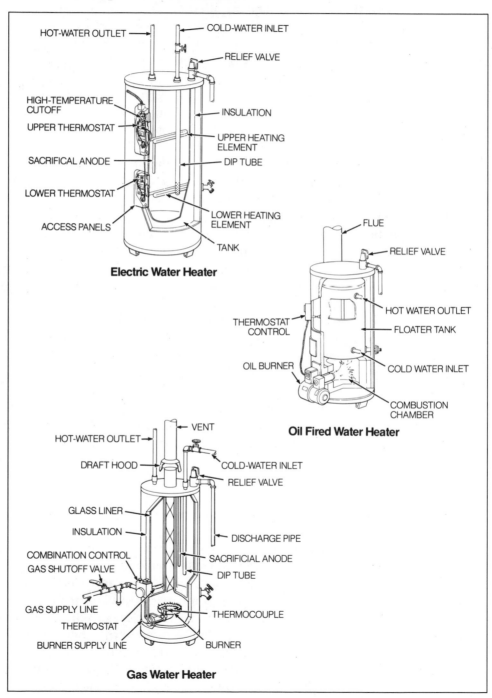

HOT-WATER OUTLET
COLD-WATER INLET
RELIEF VALVE
HIGH-TEMPERATURE CUTOFF
INSULATION
UPPER THERMOSTAT
UPPER HEATING ELEMENT
SACRIFICAL ANODE
DIP TUBE
LOWER THERMOSTAT
ACCESS PANELS
LOWER HEATING ELEMENT
TANK

Electric Water Heater

FLUE
RELIEF VALVE
THERMOSTAT CONTROL
HOT WATER OUTLET
FLOATER TANK
OIL BURNER
COLD WATER INLET
COMBUSTION CHAMBER

Oil Fired Water Heater

VENT
HOT-WATER OUTLET
DRAFT HOOD
COLD-WATER INLET
RELIEF VALVE
GLASS LINER
INSULATION
DISCHARGE PIPE
COMBINATION CONTROL
GAS SHUTOFF VALVE
SACRIFICIAL ANODE
DIP TUBE
GAS SUPPLY LINE
THERMOSTAT
THERMOCOUPLE
BURNER SUPPLY LINE
BURNER

Gas Water Heater

FIGURE 8.9   Disposal Systems

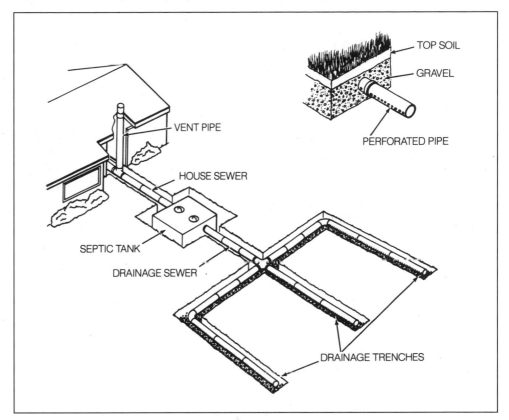

Devices such as fuses and motors are rated by amperes, their current-carrying capacity.

Watt. This unit is used when measuring the rate at which a device consumes electric power. The power consumption of many devices, such as lamps and irons, is marked on them in watts.

Kilowatt hour. This unit measures the total amount of electric power that is consumed. A 1,000-watt iron used for one hour will consume exactly one kilowatt hour, which is tallied as such on the electric meter.

The relationship between volts, amperes and watts is expressed in a simple equation: volts × amperes = watts. If the current is 120 volts and a device requires 4 amperes of current, the equation will read: 120 volts × 4 amperes = 480 watts. To figure the current needed for a device rated in watts, turn the equation around: watts ÷ volts = amperes. If at a current of 120 volts, an appliance such as a toaster uses 120 watts, the equation reads: 1200 ÷ 120 = 10 amperes.

Fuse and Circuit-Breaker Panels The electric wiring in a house is divided at the main power supply into several circuits, each designed to carry a safe part of the electrical load. Each circuit is protected against overloading by a fuse or circuit breaker acting as a safety valve. If an overload gets the wires hot enough or a short circuit occurs, it shuts off the power to the circuit.

If the cause is an overload, it can be corrected by turning off one of the appliances on the circuit to reduce the load. If the fuse blows or the circuit breaker trips again, call an electrician to determine the cause.

To determine whether the circuits in your home are being overloaded, add up the wattage of all lights and appliances on each circuit. If the total wattage of the appliances used at the same time exceeds 1,800 watts for a 15-amp circuit, or 2,400 watts for a 20-amp circuit, the circuit is overloaded. Wattages are listed on the nameplate of all appliances, or they can be estimated from the following table:

Appliance	Typical wattage
Television, stereo, mixer, blender	250–350
Refrigerator, freezer, sump pump, vacuum cleaner	300–400
Coffee pot, disposal, microwave ovens	600–1,000
Toaster, waffle iron, griddle, frying pan, deep fryer, hand iron	1,000–1,500
Room heater, hot plate, rotisserie, grill, dishwasher	1,500–1,650

Label fuses or circuit breakers to identify equipment and appliances they protect, particularly those that could be hazardous, such as the stove, oven, television sets or basement circuits, in case of flooding.

Electrical Safety Precautions Electricity, when improperly used, can cause fires, electrocution and, in both cases, death. It is important to heed the following precautions:

❑ Use heavy-duty cords with 16- or 18-gauge wire if you need to use an extension cord for an appliance using more than 600 watts, such as a toaster, iron, heater or air conditioner. Unplug the cord when not in use.

❑ Remove extension cords tacked to walls or baseboards as substitutes for permanent wiring. Have an electrician install additional outlets where needed. Do not lay cords under rugs or carpets.

❑ Replace switches and receptacles that are damaged, hot to the touch, or show the least sign of malfunction. Never work on switches or outlets without first turning off the power at the fuse or circuit breaker panel.

❏ Immediately disconnect any appliance that sparks, stalls, overheats or causes a slight tingling shock. Have it repaired as soon as possible.

❏ Check Christmas or other holiday exterior and tree lights before the holidays for frayed or bare wire and bad connections.

❏ Water near electricity is extremely dangerous, because it is one of the best conductors of electric current. Keep electric appliances and cords away from water and keep water away from electric outlets and switches.

❏ With small children in the house, make sure unused openings of wall outlets and extension cords have plastic snap-on covers.

Heating and Cooling Systems

Central Heating Systems Central heating systems consist of four basic elements: the heat producer, heat exchanger, heat distribution system and heat controls.

1. The heat producer or burner may be fueled by natural gas, propane, oil, electricity or coal. It delivers heated combustion gases to the heat exchanger.

2. The heat exchanger, called the "furnace" in warm-air systems, or "boiler" in hot-water or steam systems, is a compartment containing metal conduits. The hot combustion gases from the burner pass through these conduits before they are expelled via a flue or chimney. Air, water or steam, as the case may be, flow past the hot conduits in the heat exchanger, entirely separated from the combustion gases. Heat is thus transferred to the air, water or steam which continues to circulate through the house via the heat distribution system.

3. The heat distribution system consists of a series of ducts or pipes through which the heated air, water or steam flows to warm air registers, radiators or convectors located throughout the house.

   • In steam systems the steam rises naturally to radiators where it condenses to water and returns to the boiler.

   • In hot-water systems the water is pumped through the boiler and continues on via pipes to convectors or to a system of pipes looped under floors or embedded in concrete slabs.

   • In warm-air systems the air is blown through the furnace by a large fan and sent via ducts to warm air registers and into the rooms. Cold air registers return the air to the furnace where it is filtered and reheated.

   • Gravity warm-air systems were installed in many older homes, causing air circulation by the fact that warm air rises and cool air flows downward. Gravity systems may be updated by installation of blower units.

4. Heat controls, or thermostats, are temperature sensitive switches which automatically turn the heating (or cooling) system on and off, to maintain an even temperature.

Central Cooling Systems Most central air-conditioning systems are combined with or can be added to warm-air heating systems, using common air distribution ducts and common thermostatic controls (Figure 8.10).

The cooling units are generally made in two separate parts:

1. The evaporator coil, which is mounted at the air discharge outlet of the furnace
2. The condensing unit, usually located outside the house because of its noisy machinery

FIGURE 8.10 Forced-Air Heating/Cooling System

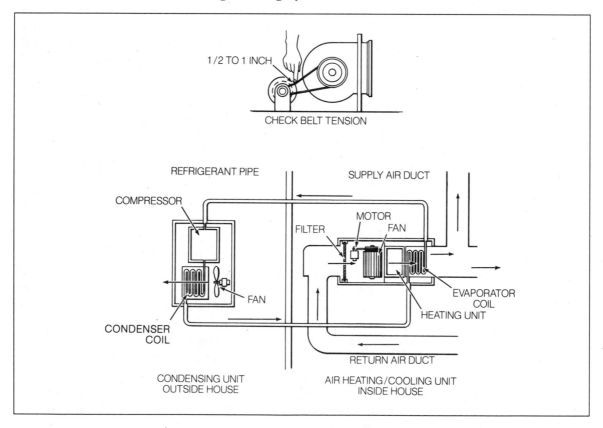

The evaporator and condenser are connected by two lines of copper tubing. In the less expensive air conditioners, the evaporator and condenser are contained in one single unit.

The evaporator coil receives cold liquid refrigerant from the condenser. As the refrigerant absorbs heat from the hot air being forced across the coil, it evaporates into gas. The warm refrigerant gas is returned to the condenser unit outside the house, where it goes through a compressor. The pressurized gas is then pumped through the condenser. Air blown across the condenser coil cools the gas and causes it to condense again into liquid refrigerant, which is recirculated to the evaporator.

Hot, moist air coming from the rooms is cooled as it is forced across the evaporator coil. In the cooling process, the moisture in the air condenses on the coil, trickles down to a pan and flows off through a drain pipe. Thus cooled and dehumidified, the air is then blown via the duct system to the registers and into the rooms.

Heating and Cooling System Maintenance It is desirable to have the heating system checked in the fall and the cooling system checked in the spring by a qualified service contractor. Compressors, pumps, motors, and adjusting of pilot lights, bonnet thermostats and other devices within the system should be checked only by a qualified service professional.

It also is important to clean the furnace room, supply and return grilles, and ducts with a vacuum cleaner in so far as possible. The air-conditioning condensing unit (usually located outside the house) should also be cleaned. The grille and coils will collect insects, dirt and trash, and should be brushed and hosed as needed.

In a forced-air heating or cooling system, the blower and motor must be protected from dirt and dust. For this reason, filters are located in the return-air side of the blower unit. The filters must be changed or cleaned at least twice a year and perhaps as frequently as once a month, depending on the amount of usage and the amount of dirt and dust in the air. Clogged filters will not allow a sufficient amount of air to pass across the heat exchanger or the cooling coil, thereby causing inefficiency of operation and inadequate heating or cooling. The homeowner should check filters monthly to determine their condition. The maintenance record will then establish an anticipated frequency for change.

The blower bearings, blower motor or hot water circulating pump motor should be oiled unless they are sealed. Manufacturer's recommendations should be checked for amount and frequency of oiling. (Unless specified otherwise, bearings on electric motors should receive 2 or 3 *drops* of oil once or twice per year.) Check fan belts and pulleys for wear and proper tension.

Fan blades should be kept clean of lint. Turn off power to the blower unit and use a small brush.

The evaporator coil (usually located within the house in the heating and cooling unit) functions as a dehumidifier as well as a cooling element. Therefore, it condenses water which collects in a pan beneath the coil and is conducted to a drain. This drain line can easily become obstructed and may require periodic cleaning to remove dust and algae. Overflowing water during cooling is a symptom of this condition.

If air conditioners are installed in windows, they should be removed and stored for the winter season for the following reasons:

- They leak cold air both around and through the unit, thereby creating drafts and discomfort.
- Window and sill decay can occur unnoticed around the unit if it is left in place permanently.
- Maintenance of unit is more convenient when the unit is not in the window.

The window air-conditioning unit should be cleaned thoroughly, motor and blower lubricated as required, and checked for rusting of metal parts (spot-paint as required). Window air conditioners also have filters that should be checked frequently. Plastic foam filters can be washed in warm water and detergent. Metallic filters should be washed and recoated with a product available for that purpose. Fiberglass filters are disposable and should be replaced.

Most manufacturers recommend against covering outdoor portions of air-conditioning units during the off-season, since the units are designed to be weather-resistant, and a watertight cover can trap moisture within the unit.

If a humidifier or dehumidifier is used, clean and dry it thoroughly, oil as required, and check for rusting. Spot-paint all rusted areas as required. Check humidifiers for calcium deposits and check dehumidifiers for algae growth. Algae can be removed with household chlorine bleach.

Do not allow the furnace or boiler room to become a storeroom for flammable materials.

CHAPTER NINE

Pest Control

Causes of Excessive Moisture

Wood Decay

Wood Destroying Insects

Checking for Damage and Infestation

To detect and control wood destroying organisms, specialized skills are required. Therefore, as a homebuyer, you would be well advised to have the house you are about to purchase inspected by a professional pest control operator. Such an inspection is required before certain types of mortgages can be obtained, including FHA and VA loans.

Many buyers who would carefully inspect an old house for evidence of pests and decay, fail to consider these wood destroyers when choosing a new house. Lumber in new homes not properly protected against moisture by correct construction methods is highly susceptible to decay and insects, and damage is likely to occur within a few years.

A good protection against infestation is a contract for regular periodic inspections including treatment when necessary, offered by most pest control companies.

Causes of Excessive Moisture

Excessive moisture is the primary cause of wood decay and wood destroying insects. Listed below are the most common sources of excessive moisture in and around the home:

- Paint deterioration on exterior walls
- Leaking or clogged gutters and downspouts and inadequate flashing
- Insufficient roof overhang at gables and eaves
- Improper drainage around the house, causing water standing against foundation walls to seep into basements and crawl spaces (Patio and porch surfaces should slope away from the house. The soil level of crawlspaces beneath the house should always be higher than that of the surrounding area.)
- Earth-filled structures, such as planters, porches, patios, steps, in contact with the foundation and extending above the sill plates (see Figure 9.1) (Sill plates, also called mud sills, are the lowest wood members of the house framing, resting on top of the foundation walls.)
- Improper ventilation (Crawlspaces and attics should have at least four vents located near the corners; attic vents must always remain open, while crawl space vents can be closed during the winter; clothes dryers should be vented to the outside of the house, not into the crawlspace, garage or attic.)
- No vapor-resistant ground cover (Uncovered ground in crawlspaces should be covered with a vapor-resistant ground cover, such as four or six mil polyethylene film, to stop the rise of water vapor from the ground.)
- Plumbing leaks (toilets, showers, bathtubs and sinks)

FIGURE 9.1   Earth-Filled Porches

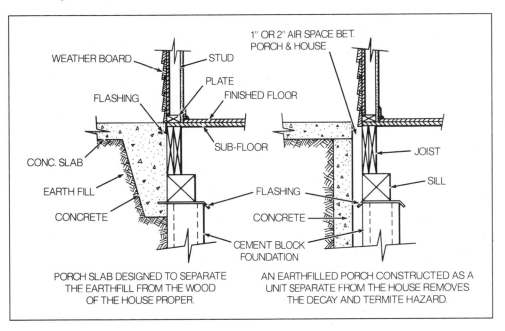

PORCH SLAB DESIGNED TO SEPARATE THE EARTHFILL FROM THE WOOD OF THE HOUSE PROPER.

AN EARTHFILLED PORCH CONSTRUCTED AS A UNIT SEPARATE FROM THE HOUSE REMOVES THE DECAY AND TERMITE HAZARD.

- Condensation within the walls, usually caused by large temperature differences between the inside and the outside of the house

Wood Decay

Wood decay is caused by airborne spores that produce minute plantlike growth called fungi. These organisms cannot decay wood with a moisture content of less than 30 percent. It is therefore essential to keep wood dry.

Fungi are present throughout the United States. Since wood decays very slowly at temperatures below 40°F, deterioration is more rapid in warmer regions.

Wood Destroying Insects

The skill and techniques of a professional pest control operator are essential for a thorough inspection and effective control of pests. The homeowner should, however, learn to recognize the damage caused by wood destroying insects and the proper methods of controlling them.

The danger of attack by most wood destroying insects and the speed at which destruction occurs increase with the average temperature. They are, therefore, of graver concern in the southern United States, as well as in California, Hawaii and Puerto Rico.

Subterranean Termites

These are the most destructive of all wood destroying insects in the United States. They require high humidity, either from the soil or from moisture in wood under attack.

When subterranean termites cannot gain direct access from the soil to wood, they build shelter tubes of earth and partially digested wood, about a quarter-inch to half-inch wide, crossing such obstacles as concrete or brick foundation walls, concrete footings, pipes and even termite shields provided by some builders (Figure 9.2).

FIGURE 9.2   Termite Damage

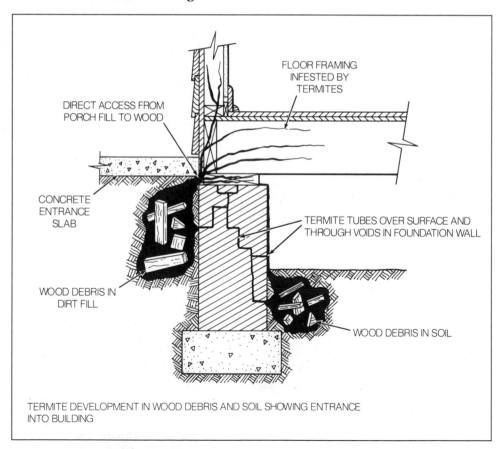

FLOOR FRAMING INFESTED BY TERMITES

DIRECT ACCESS FROM PORCH FILL TO WOOD

CONCRETE ENTRANCE SLAB

TERMITE TUBES OVER SURFACE AND THROUGH VOIDS IN FOUNDATION WALL

WOOD DEBRIS IN DIRT FILL

WOOD DEBRIS IN SOIL

TERMITE DEVELOPMENT IN WOOD DEBRIS AND SOIL SHOWING ENTRANCE INTO BUILDING

Subterranean termites produce winged adults (Figure 9.3). On warm, humid spring or summer days they swarm toward windows and other light sources and shed their wings, the first sign of termite infestation.

The only practical way to control and eliminate infestation of subterranean termites is to deny them a source of moisture. Without moisture, a colony in a house will die. Therefore, keeping wood dry is just as important for termite prevention as it is for decay prevention.

Chemical soil poisoning has proved to be a highly effective way to control termite activity in buildings, both for preventing infestation prior to construction of new houses and for controlling it in older ones. Such chemicals are highly poisonous and are apt to contaminate surrounding soil and water sources and endanger animals if not used with proper precautions. Use of these chemicals by other than licensed professional pest control operators is, therefore, not recommended.

FIGURE 9.3   Ant and Termite

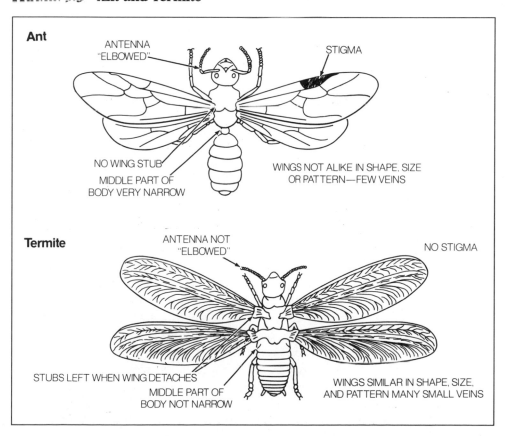

Dry Wood Termites and Beetles

These insects do not have ground connections. They can be recognized by piles of slightly compressed pellets of partially digested wood resembling coarse wood or sawdust. Such piles accumulate underneath tiny round or oval push-out holes in unfinished wood members.

Wood Nesting Insects

Unlike other wood destroying insects, carpenter ants and carpenter bees do not eat wood; they nest in it. In making their nests, they can cause considerable damage.

Carpenter ants are reddish-brown to black, about a quarter-inch to half-an inch long (see Figure 9.3). They feed on sweets and other foodstuffs. Their nests may be adjacent to the house, in a stump or hollow tree or inside the house in supporting timbers, sills, girders, joists, studs and window or door trim.

To find carpenter ants, probe suspected wood with an icepick or other sharp object. If wood gives way and ants come tumbling out, the nest has been found. Great effort should be made to locate the nest, since insecticide applied to it will eliminate the entire colony.

Carpenter bees look like bumblebees, except for their bare, shiny abdomens. They prefer soft, unpainted wood when nesting, typically in sheltered places, such as porch ceilings, window sills, door frames, headers, sidings and so on. Carpenter bees cut an entrance hole of about five-eighths of an inch in diameter, which is easily located. Insecticide applied to the nest galleries is all that is necessary.

Checking for Damage and Infestation

The pest control inspector uses a small hammer to sound walls, window sills and wood frames for damage. A dead sound indicates decay; a hollow sound indicates possible termite infestation.

The inspector uses an icepick to probe exposed wood posts, landings, stairways, entrance door frames and thresholds, garage sills and studs and any area where wood structural elements are close to the ground.

Damage may not be noticeable on wood surfaces, because most termites avoid exposure to air by constructing galleries within the material they attack. When the exterior surface of timber is stripped away, tunnels and specks of greyish excrement can be seen along the grain of the wood.

Often the wood is completely honeycombed, leaving little more than hard thin shells with the soft wood in between eaten away.

Termite shelter tubes, about one-quarter to one-half of an inch wide, on exterior foundation walls, concrete footings in crawlspaces and on pipes, are a sure sign of subterranean termite infestation.

Indications of termite damage include small push-out holes in wood members and piles of wood dust and pellets of partially digested wood resembling coarse sand or sawdust. Discarded whitish translucent wings beneath doors and windows and around light fixtures are also signs of termite infestation.

In basements where pests are attracted by furnace warmth, the inspector checks joints between floor slabs, foundations, chimneys and all penetrations of pipe through foundation and slab floors, in particular under and around furnaces. The attic is another area that requires thorough inspection.

The pest control operator will check bathroom partitions and flooring around toilets, showers, bathtubs and sinks, where plumbing leaks may have caused decay and attracted termites.

CHAPTER
TEN

Tax Information for Homeowners

The homeowner who pays careful attention to the tax advantages presented here in easily understood language cannot help but save significant sums of money. The task is greatly simplified by the forms provided in Appendix C. While the importance of professional tax counsel cannot be overemphasized when selling a home, your accurate records are the key to keeping large sums of money out of Uncle Sam's pockets.

Federal law provides homeowners with special tax advantages that basically fall into two categories:

1. Expenses deductible against ordinary income
2. Adjustments to taxable profit realized on the sale of a home

Deductible Expenses

- Residence interest on primary and secondary homes, including pre-payment penalties
- Noncompensated casualty losses in excess of $100
- In the event a portion of the home is used for rental or business, the homeowner may deduct all other expenses applicable to the portion of the home devoted to such use, including depreciation (depreciation deductions must also reduce the basis).
- Discount points, to be deductible, must:
  1. show on the settlement statement as "loan origination," "loan discount" or "discount points."
  2. be computed as a percentage of the loan amount.
  3. conform to an established business practice with respect to home financing in the area in which the residence is located and must not exceed the amount generally charged in that market area.
  4. be paid for financing a principal residence.
  5. be paid in cash from funds other than the loan proceeds.
- Points paid in the following situations are never deductible:
  - Points paid for refinancings or lines of credit
  - Points paid for home improvement loans where the amount borrowed has no connection with an acquisition of a principal residence
  - Points paid for loans on second or vacation homes, business or investment properties
  - Points paid in connection with purchases of a principal residence that are allocable to a loan amount exceeding the $1 million dollar limit

Tax Basis upon Purchase of a Home

Basis or *Tax Basis* is the book value of property for income tax purposes. Ordinarily, the basis of property is its acquisition cost, which is the purchase price plus certain acquisition expenses. Acquisition expenses may not be deducted against ordinary income, but are added to the basis. Examples are appraisal fees, credit reports, inspection fees, title or abstract fees, attorney fees, escrow fees and mortgage insurance premiums.

Costs Incurred During Ownership of a Home

During ownership of the home, the basis is further adjusted by adding the cost of any capital improvements the owner may have made and by subtracting any noncompensated casualty losses in excess of $100. In the event a portion of the home is used for rental or business, depreciation deductions taken must also be deducted from the basis.

Tax Liability upon Sale of a Home

Profit realized from the sale of a home is taxable. If a personal residence is held for more than 24 months and is sold or exchanged, any resulting profit is treated as a *capital gain.* This means that only a portion of the capital gain is to be reported as ordinary income. Losses incurred when a personal residence is disposed of cannot be deducted against ordinary income.

Taxable gain on sale of a home is calculated as in the following example:

Sale Price	$200,000
Minus Selling Expenses	−14,000
Amount Realized on Sale	186,000
Minus Adjusted Basis	−70,000
Taxable Gain on Sale	116,000

Examples of *Selling Expenses* are broker's commission, title or abstract fees, legal fees, escrow fees, notary fees, appraisal fees, reconveyance fees, forwarding fees, statement fees, processing fees, wire fees, document preparation fees, underwriting fees, warehouse fees, rate lock fees, credit report fees, inspection fees and other names of settlement fees that have not yet been coined.

Capital Improvements and Repairs

Capital improvements are added to the tax basis and in the event the home is used for rental or business purposes, capital improvements are subject to annual depreciation deductions.

To qualify, an improvement must materially add to the value of the home, appreciably prolong its useful life or adapt it to new uses. Examples of capital improvements include the addition of a room, construction of a fireplace, installation of a fence, addition of storage area, installation of security systems, insulation, installation of a new roof and so on. When an existing component of the home (for example, a water heater, dishwasher, garbage disposal or carpets) is replaced with another of better quality, utility or durability, the difference in cost between the old and the new component may be added to the basis as a capital improvement.

Repairs, as opposed to capital improvements, are a recurring type of expenditure to maintain the home in good condition; they do not add to the value of the home. Such expenses may not be added to the basis, nor are they deductible unless they are applicable to a portion of the home used for rental or business. An exception is made where a resale home is purchased and expenditures, otherwise considered repairs, are made to bring the property up to standard. Such expenditures may be accepted as capital improvements if they are made within a reasonable time after the purchase.

Another exception is "fixing-up expenses," defined as the cost of work to assist the sale of a home, if performed within 90 days prior to the agreement to sell and paid within 30 days after closing of the transaction. While fixing-up expenses are not deductible and have no effect on the tax basis of the home, they do reduce the recognized (taxable) gain upon sale of the home. Examples of fixing-up expenses include repairs, painting, cleaning and servicing of lawn and trees. (Any major improvements made before the sale should be added to the basis as capital improvements.)

Accurate records should be kept of all capital improvement costs, as well as of those repair and maintenance expenses which are deductible. Forms for this purpose are included in Appendix C.

The chart in Figure 10.1 shows expenditures the Internal Revenue Service considers to be capital improvements and others that are designated as repair and maintenance expenses.

Noncompensated Casualty Losses

A tax deduction is allowed to a person who has sustained a casualty or theft loss of property, to the extent that the loss is not compensated by

FIGURE 10.1   Capital Improvements versus Repairs

Type of Expenditure	Capital Improvements	Repairs or Maintenance
Foundation—new	x	
Foundation—repair		x
Pest control		x
New front	x	
Painting—outside		x
Painting—inside		x
Papering		x
Plastering		x
Floors—new	x	
Floors—resurfacing and patching		x
Floors—replacing with tile	x	
Roof—replacement	x	
Roof—reshingling	x	
Roof—repair broken portions		x
Ratproofing	x	
Fire escapes—new	x	
Fire escapes—rails replaced	x	
Stairway—new supports		x
Electric wiring—new	x	
Electric wiring—replacing defective wiring		x
Iron water pipes replaced by copper	x	
Plumbing—replacing defective system		x
Plumbing leaks—stopping		x
Heating—permanent conversion	x	
Furnace—relining	x	
Furnace—enameling		x
Insulating	x	
Air conditioning—compressor replaced		x
Wells—cleaning and repairing		x
Maintenance of property		x
Casualties—repairs resulting from		x
Damaged property restored to normal		x
Damaged property restored to something better and different	x	
Restoration of property purchased in run down condition	x	
Alterations to suit taxpayer's use	x	
Repairs and improvements as part of a general plan of remodeling	x	
Alteration of building	x	
Architect's fee—addition	x	
Assessments for improvements	x	
Enlarging and adding bathrooms	x	
Office layout—nonpermanent change		x
Residence—converting upper floor for rental	x	
Keeping building in safe condition		x
Shoring up building to prevent collapse		x
Installation of a swimming pool or landscaping	x	

insurance and exceeds $100. A separate $100 exclusion applies to each individual casualty or theft. Suppose, for example, that during a tax year you sustained two noncompensated losses: a sofa that cost you $1,000 was lost in a fire and a camera was stolen, for which you paid $500. Your deduction would be the sum of $900 and $400, totalling $1,300. Had the sofa been insured and you recovered $500 for its loss, your deduction for the sofa would be $400.

In the event a deduction is taken for a noncompensated casualty loss as a result of damage to the home, the tax basis will also have to be reduced by that amount.

Casualty losses include the following:

- Damage caused by hurricane, tornado, storm, flood, shipwreck, fire, earthquake or accident.
- Damage to your automobile from an accident caused by faulty driving of either driver, or by your willful act or negligence.
- Mine cave-in damage to your property.
- Sonic boom damage from jet aircraft.
- Loss from vandalism caused by agencies beyond your control, if the damage is sudden or unexpected.
- Damage to ornamental trees and shrubs on residential property. You must establish that the damage resulted in a decrease in the total value of the real property.

When To Deduct a Loss

Casualty losses generally are deductible only in the tax year in which the casualty occurred, even though the damaged property may not have been repaired or replaced during that year.

Theft and embezzlement losses generally are deductible only in the year of discovery. You must prove that there was a theft and establish the year in which it occurred.

Proof of Loss   To prove that you actually sustained a casualty or theft loss and the deductible portion of the loss, you must be able to establish the following:

- The nature of the casualty and when it occurred (or in case of theft, when it was discovered)
- That the loss was a direct result of the casualty (or in case of theft, that the property was actually stolen)
- That you were the owner of the property, or were contractually liable to the owner for damage to the property leased by you
- The cost or other basis of the property, evidenced by purchase contract, checks, invoices, receipts and so on

- Depreciation allowed or allowable, if any
- The value before and after the casualty
- The amount of insurance or other compensation received or recoverable, including the value of repairs, restoration and clean-up provided without cost by disaster relief agencies

Photographs of property taken prior to the casualty or theft can be very beneficial in establishing the condition of the property before the loss. Photographs of the property after the casualty will help establish the extent of the damage.

(See also Chapter 6, under the headings "Inventory of Personal Property" and "Checklist for Processing a Claim.")

Rental Use of a Home

If a homeowner converts his or her home, or part of it, to rental property, maintenance expenses become deductible nonbusiness expenses and depreciation deductions may be taken while the property is held for the production of income.

If the conversion is made at any time other than the beginning of the tax year, annual expenses (insurance, depreciation and the like) must be prorated.

In the event only a portion of the home is used as rental property, all otherwise nondeductible expenses (insurance, depreciation, maintenance, etc.) must be allocated to the portion of the home used for rental purposes.

For more information, refer to IRS Publication 551, *Property Converted to Business or Rental Income* or IRS Publication 534, *Tax Information on Depreciation.*

Business Use of a Home

A taxpayer is entitled to deduct certain business expenses attributable to a portion of the home used exclusively and regularly as his or her principal place of business or as a place of business that is used by patients, clients or customers in meeting or dealing with the taxpayer in the ordinary course of business.

In addition, employees must establish that they are required, for the convenience of their employer, to provide their own space and facilities for the performance of their duties, and not merely appropriate and helpful in their employment.

Deductible expenses include those made exclusively for the business portion of the home and expenses which must be allocated to the portion of the home used for business, such as utilities, real estate taxes, insurance, mortgage interest, etc.

In addition, deductions for depreciation may be claimed on the portion of the home used for business.

For more information, refer to *Tax Information on Operating a Business in Your Home,* IRS Publication 587.

Depreciation

The law permits a homeowner to take regular tax deductions for the amount of annual depreciation of a portion of his or her home used for rental or business purposes. Depreciation deductions usually are computed on the *basis* at acquisition of the home and are spread systematically over its *useful life.*

Since land is not subject to physical deterioration, only the improvements (the building) may be depreciated. The improvements must therefore be allocated, as well as the portion of the improvements used for rental or business purposes.

Several methods can be used to compute annual depreciation deductions. The most common and simplest is the *Straight-Line* method. Under this method, equal annual depreciation deductions are computed by dividing the basis by the number of years of estimated useful life.

For example, if the basis for depreciation of the part of the home used for rental or business purposes is $10,000 and the estimated useful life of the property is 20 years, the annual depreciation deduction (assuming no allowance for salvage value is necessary) is $500 ($10,000 ÷ 20).

To determine which method of depreciation, in addition to Straight Line, is available, refer to IRS Publication 534, *Tax Information on Depreciation.*

Sale and Purchase of Another Home

Under Internal Revenue Code Section 1034, no gain is recognized if:

1. The taxpayer's principal personal residence is exchanged for another principal personal residence, provided the cost of the new residence equals or exceeds the Adjusted Sale Price of the old residence. (Adjusted sale price is the gross sale price, minus sales expenses, minus "fixing-up expenses." The cost of work performed to assist the sale, if performed within 90 days before the sale and paid within 30 days after the sale is called fixing-up expense.)
2. The old principal personal residence is sold and another residence is purchased and used as the taxpayer's principal personal residence

within 24 months before or after the sale of the old residence, provided the cost of the new residence equals or exceeds the Adjusted Sale Price of the old residence.

Any costs incurred prior to this period, such as purchase price of land upon which the taxpayer constructs a residence, may not be included in computing the cost of the new residence for qualifying purposes.

Gain is *recognized* (taxable) to the extent that the purchase price of the new residence is less than the sale price of the old residence.

If a sale and purchase of another home (also referred to as *rollover*) is contemplated, any portion of the home used for rental or business is not available for nonrecognition of gain under Section 1034, but must be treated as a taxable sale.

An exchange of a principal personal residence, or a sale and purchase, without recognition of gain can be repeated 24 months after the sale of the old residence.

Generally, a taxpayer is limited to only one rollover in a 24-month period with regard to nonrecognition of gain on the sale of a principal residence.

Figure 10.2 shows an example of how to compute the gain on sale of your old home and the tax basis of your new home.

Sale of Home by Persons 55 and Over

Under Internal Revenue Code Section 121, taxpayers 55 or older at the time they sell their principal residence may elect to exclude from their taxable income gain from such sale, provided that the taxpayer has owned and used the property as his or her principal personal residence for three out of the last five years preceding the sale. The amount of the gain excluded may not exceed $125,000.

Short temporary absences for vacation or other seasonal absences count as periods of use, even though the home may have been rented during such periods.

To be eligible, it is sufficient that either husband or wife meet the above requirements of age, ownership and use, as long as they are legally married at the time of sale and the property is held in joint tenancy or as community property.

Single persons owning a personal residence as joint tenants or as tenants in common, must both meet age, ownership and use requirements. Each joint tenant or tenant in common is fully exempt on his or her share of the profit up to the maximum of $125,000.

This tax exemption is available to a taxpayer and spouse only once during their lifetimes.

FIGURE 10.2   Computing Gain on Sale and Basis of a New Home

FORM H

Address of *home sold* _____ 23 Mountain Drive _____	*Closing* *date* _____ 1979 _____

Address of *new home* _____ 125 Pacific Avenue _____	*Closing* *date* _____ 1979 _____

1. Sales Price . . . . $ 130,000
2. Minus personal property included in price, if any . . . .   −$ 0
3. Net sales price (line 1 minus line 2). . . . . $ 130,000
4. Minus Selling Expenses (from Form F in Appendix C) . . . .   −$ 8,000
5. Amount Realized on Sale (line 3 minus line 4) . . . . $ 122,000
6. Minus Adjusted Basis of home sold (from Form E in Appendix C). . . . .   −$ 80,000
7. Gain realized on sale (line 5 less line 6) . . . . $ 42,000

8. Amount realized on sale (from line 5) . . . . $ 122,000
9. Minus Fixing-up Expenses (from Form G in Appendix C). . . . .   −$ 2,000
10. Adjusted Sales Price (line 8 less line 9). . . . . $ 120,000
11. Minus total Acquisition Cost of new home (from Form E in Appendix C)[†] . . .   −$ 170,000
12. Gain recognized (taxable) (line 10 minus line 11) . . . . $ 0

13. Gain Realized on Sale (from line 7) . . . . $ 42,000
14. Minus Gain Recognized (from line 12) . . . .   −$ 0
15. Deferred Gain (line 13 minus line 14) . . . . $ 42,000

16. Total Acquisition Cost of new home (from line 11) . . . . $ 170,000
17. Minus Deferred Gain (from line 15) . . . .   −$ 42,000
18. Basis of new home (line 16 minus line 17) . . . . $ 128,000

[†]If amount on line 11 is higher than line 10, Gain Recognized will be zero.

This form is included in Appendix C.

If the taxpayer or spouse already sold a personal residence and used the tax exemption prior to the present marriage, the exemption will not be available again.

If two taxpayers who separately owned personal residences and subsequently get married wish to sell both residences after marriage, the exemp-

FIGURE 10.3   Computing Gain on Sale and Basis of a New Home for Persons 55 and Over

FORM I

Address of   *Closing*
Home Sold _____   *Date* _____

Address of   *Closing*
New Home _____   *Date* _____

1. Sales Price	$	*210,000*
2. Minus personal property included in price, if any	−$	*10,000*
3. Net sales price (line 1 minus line 2).	$	*200,000*
4. Minus Selling Expenses	−$	*12,500*
5. Amount Realized on Sale (line 3 minus line 4)	$	*187,500*
6. Minus Adjusted Basis of home sold	−$	*50,000*
7. Gain realized on sale (line 5 minus line 6)	$	*137,500*
8. Minus Exemption	−$	*125,000*
9. Taxable gain on sale (line 7 less line 8)	$	*12,500*

10. Amount Realized on Sale (from line 5)	$	*187,500*
11. Minus Fixing-up Expenses	−$	*2,000*
12. Adjusted Sales Price (line 10 minus line 11)	$	*185,500*
13. Minus exemption	−$	*125,000*
14. Revised Adjusted Sales Price (line 12 minus line 13)	$	*60,000*

| 15. Minus Total Acquisition Cost of new home[†] . . . . | −$ | *90,000* |
| 16. Gain Recognized (taxable) (line 14 minus line 15). . . . . | $ | *0* |

17. Taxable Gain on sale (from line 9)	$	*37,500*
18. Minus Gain Recognized (from line 16)	−$	*0*
19. Deferred Gain (line 17 minus line 18)	$	*37,500*

20. Total Acquisition Cost of new home (from line 15)	$	*90,000*
21. Minus Deferred Gain (from line 19)	−$	*37,500*
22. Basis of new home (line 20 minus line 21).	$	*52,500*

[†]If amount on line 15 is higher than line 14, Gain Recognized on line 16 will be zero.

This form is included in Appendix C.

tion can only apply to one residence, provided age, ownership and use requirements are met. All requirements must be met by one spouse.

If a taxpayer elects the benefits of sections 121 and 1034 (a situation that might occur if the gain realized on the sale of a personal residence was in excess of $125,000), the basis of the new property would be determined by subtracting the deferred gain from the cost of the new residence. (See Figure 10.3.)

Installment Sales

The taxpayer's election to use the installment method under Internal Revenue Code Section 453, provides a way to spread tax on profit from the sale of an asset over a number of years. This avoids paying tax on the entire gain in the year of sale, which is usually the year in which title passes.

Payments during the year of sale would include the down payment (in whatever form) and the principal portion of installment payments received during the year.

If the buyer assumes an existing mortgage that exceeds the seller's basis, the difference between the outstanding balance of the mortgage and the seller's basis would be treated as a payment during the year of sale.

This method may or may not be to the advantage of a particular taxpayer. Sellers would be well advised to consult their tax counsel in this respect.

Example of Installment Sale Computation

Gross selling price	$100,000
Commission	5,000
Adjusted basis	65,000
Loan balance	40,000
Purchaser assumes the existing loan of	40,000
Seller takes back a second mortgage of	34,000
Down payment	26,000
Installment payments in the year of sale $1,500, of which $1,000 is interest and $500 is principal	
Down payment	26,000
Plus principal payments in year of sale	500
Initial payment	26,500

Gross selling price	$100,000
Minus commission	5,000
Net selling price	95,000
Minus Adjusted Basis	65,000
Realized gain	30,000
Gross selling price	$100,000
Minus mortgage assumed by purchaser	40,000
Contract price	60,000

Percentage of Initial Payment and of Principal portion of Installment Payments in subsequent years, which constitutes gain is realized gain divided by contract price:

$$\$30,000 \div \$60,000 = 50\%$$

Tax-Deductible Moving Expenses

Certain expenses connected with the move to a new principal place of employment are deductible. All employees, old or new, reimbursed or un-reimbursed, are treated alike and the self-employed are allowed comparable deductions as well.

Deductible expenses include cost of moving household goods and personal effects and the expense of traveling (including meals and lodging) from the old home to the new home of the taxpayer and members of his or her household. If traveling is done by car, expenses can either be itemized or by a standard deduction of $0.09 per mile plus tolls and parking.

The foregoing expenses are deductible only if the new principal place of work is at least 50 miles farther from the old residence than the old place of work was. This distance is measured by the shortest of the more commonly traveled routes between two points.

The taxpayer must be employed full time (not necessarily by one employer only) at the new location for a minimum of 39 weeks during the 12 months following the move. This test is waived if employment is terminated due to certain circumstances beyond his or her control. On a joint return the deduction is allowed if the husband or wife meet this 39-week test. The self-employed must work at the new location, either as a self-employed person or as an employee, for at least 78 weeks during the 24 months following the move, of which at least 39 weeks must be during the first 12 months.

Documentation of Moving Expenses

To substantiate tax deductions, the following expense records and dated receipts should be kept:

Mover's Documents

- Bill of lading
- Inventory
- Packing and unpacking certificate
- Weight certificate

Travel Expense Receipts

- Transportation costs (air, bus or train fares and automobile expenses)
- Meals
- Lodging

Use IRS Form 3903, "Moving Expense Adjustment." All reimbursements received in connection with the move must be included in the taxpayer's gross income for the year in which they were received. The employer must furnish a detailed breakdown of any reimbursements of moving expenses. Income tax and Social Security withholdings are required on reimbursements.

For more information, refer to the following publications, available free of charge from your local Internal Revenue Service office. They are published annually, so be sure to obtain the latest edition:

- *Tax Information on Moving Expenses,* IRS Publication 521
- *Rental Income and Royalty Income,* IRS Publication 527
- *Tax Information for Home Owners,* IRS Publication 530
- *Tax Information on Depreciation,* IRS Publication 534
- *Sale or Disposition of Assets,* IRS Publication 544
- *Property Converted to Business or Rental Property,* IRS Publication 551
- *Tax Information on Operating a Business in Your Home,* IRS Publication 587

CHAPTER ELEVEN

Financing and Refinancing

The majority of families in the United States own their own homes. This is made possible through a well-regulated credit system that allows a purchaser to acquire a home with an initial cash investment of as little as 10 percent or less of the purchase price.

The purpose of this chapter is to explain basic elements of real estate financing and terminology that can prove helpful to homeowners in the course of planning and negotiating the financing or refinancing of their homes.

The Secondary Mortgage Market

The process of financing or refinancing a home has become so complex that the importance of choosing a lending source, most beneficial to a homeowner's particular circumstances, cannot be overemphasized. To better understand the differences in home loans between lenders, it is important to comprehend the function of the secondary mortgage market and the control it exercises on the structure of most conventional loans available through lending institutions.

The secondary mortgage market is an investor market in which blocks of residential mortgage loans, originated by lending institutions, are purchased and assembled into mortgage pools for issuance of mortgage-backed securities. The main players among these so-called *poolers* are the Federal National Mortgage Association (nicknamed Fannie Mae) and the Federal Home Loan Mortgage Corporation (Freddie Mac).

Marketability of these mortgage-backed securities has been accomplished through standardization of mortgage instruments, terms and credit standards, brought about by Fannie Mae and Freddie Mac. Most lending institutions who originate residential mortgages sell their loans in the secondary market in order to free capital for new loan originations, although most continue to service the loans by collecting monthly payments. Lenders must adhere to strict underwriting guidelines to make their loans salable in the secondary market. These lenders are referred to as *conforming lenders* and the loans they originate are called *conforming loans.*

There are other lenders who keep loans in their portfolio, rather than selling them in the secondary market. Consequently, these so-called *portfolio lenders* do not need to observe the strict underwriting criteria required by the secondary market. They have more flexible lending rules and their loans are called *nonconforming loans.*

Lending Sources

Mortgage Companies

Mortgage companies, or mortgage bankers, now the largest force in residential lending, generally specialize in originating Federal Housing Administration (FHA), Veterans Administration (VA) and conventional loans. They usually obtain financing from commercial banks via lines of credit and sell their portfolios in the secondary market. Mortgage companies also represent large lenders as well as insurance companies and large pension funds, originating and servicing loans for these investors.

Savings Associations (Formerly Savings-and-Loan Associations)

Most savings associations, called thrifts, invest the majority of their assets in residential mortgages and home equity loans and generally adhere to underwriting guidelines of the secondary market.

The dominating market position thrifts once held in residential lending is now held by mortgage companies and commercial banks.

Savings Banks

Savings banks, traditionally located in the northeastern states, generally provide the same services as savings associations.

Commercial Banks

Commercial banks remain major participants in the mortgage market by supplying lines of credit to mortgage companies. Commercial banks have surpassed savings associations in market share of residential lending. Most banks sell the loans they originate in the secondary market. They tend to give preferential treatment to depositors, since customers' deposits constitute most of their assets. Traditionally, banks are a good source for office and apartment buildings, also for commercial construction loans.

Loan Underwriting

Underwriting a real estate loan is the process of evaluating the applicant as a credit risk and ascertaining that the property pledged as collateral is sufficient security for the mortgage.

The underwriting procedure includes the following steps:

1. Evaluation of the applicant's stable monthly income
2. Verification of liquid assets available for down payment, closing costs and reserves
3. Determination of the applicant's monthly financial obligations
4. Using income ratios to compare proposed housing expense with applicant's income
5. Evaluation of the applicant's credit history (credit report)
6. Valuation of the property pledged as collateral (appraisal)
7. The maximum loan for which the applicant qualifies (step 4) and the valuation of the property (step 6) establish the loan-to-value ratio (LTV)

Computerized Loan Origination

Computerized loan origination (CLO) has been in operation since 1986. The method consists of a computer terminal located in an agent's office (a real estate broker, mortgage broker or mortgage company). The agent assists a borrower answering questions on the computer screen, enabling the lender's underwriter to make an approval decision.

CLO agents are capable of offering loan comparison programs that allow a borrower to instantly see a lender's finance charges and make comparisons between fixed rate loans, ARMs and others.

Automated Underwriting System

Automated underwriting system is a new method that uses a computer to replace a human underwriter. Freddie Mac and Fannie Mae plan to introduce automated underwriting systems early in 1995 that could cut mortgage loan processing time to under ten days and save consumers $500 to $1,000 in the mortgage application process. The system allows a mortgage broker to enter a borrower's financial information into a computer and almost instantly find out if the customer qualifies and whether additional data are needed.

Types of Mortgages

Most home loans fall into one of three categories: conventional, government-guaranteed or insured, and various types of seller financing.

A conventional loan is any loan made by an institutional lender, which is not underwritten by an agent of the federal or a state government.

Government-guaranteed or insured loans include FHA and VA financing, plus financing by individual states.

The Federal Housing Administration (FHA), a division of the Department of Housing and Urban Development (HUD), insures residential mortgage loans against default and foreclosure and compensates approved lending institutions for losses resulting from borrower default.

The U.S. Department of Veterans Affairs (VA) guarantees loans made to eligible veterans for the purchase, improvement or refinance of single-family dwellings, condominium units or manufactured homes, to be owned and occupied by the veteran.

More in-depth information on all the financing options available to home-buyers, which is outside the scope of this book, is provided in the *Realty Bluebook,* Dearborn Financial Publishing, Inc.

Fixed-Rate Mortgages

A fixed-rate mortgage provides for repayment of the principal amount (the unpaid balance of a loan) over a specified number of years in equal monthly payments, including principal and interest. Interest is computed on the remaining principal balance at the end of each month. As the principal of the loan is reduced, the interest portion of the monthly payment decreases, while the principal payment increases each month.

Adjustable-Rate Mortgages

The concept of variable rate financing calls for the borrower to share with the lender the risks of a fluctuating economy.

An adjustable-rate mortgage (ARM) provides for interest rate adjustments tied to a reference index.

Although the terms of one ARM may vary widely from those of another, several characteristics are common to nearly any adjustable-rate financing plan.

Index This is an indicator of current economic conditions and is used to determine changes in the mortgage interest rate. The only two requirements a lender must meet in selecting an index are as follows:

1. The index must be beyond the control of the lender.
2. The index must be readily available to and verifiable by the public. Rate increases are at the option of the lender, while rate decreases are mandatory.

The variety of indexes used by lenders include One-Year Treasury Bill Rates, Federal Reserve Discount Rates and the Eleventh District Cost of Funds Index. Cost of Funds tend to fluctuate at a slower rate than Treasury bills.

Margin Also referred to as "spread" or "differential," the margin remains constant throughout the loan. It is a percentage added to the index rate, in order to arrive at the rate of interest. *A word of caution:* The initial interest rate is often a below-market "teaser rate," in effect for only a limited period of time, typically six or twelve months.

At each adjustment interval, the new interest rate is recalculated by adding the margin to the index rate. The margin varies with lender, type of index and market conditions.

Adjustment Interval This is the frequency for resetting the interest rate, the monthly payment amount, or both. A wide variety of ARM loans are on the market today, with adjustment intervals ranging from several months to a number of years and almost everything in between. Interest rate and payment adjustments may or may not be scheduled to change at the same time. For example, the interest rate on some plans changes more frequently than the monthly payment, which may reach the point where the monthly payments are not sufficient to cover the interest. The interest not covered by the payments is then added to the principal balance of the loan and accrues additional interest itself. This is called *negative amortization.*

Lenders restrict the amount of negative amortization by recasting the loan every few years, or whenever the loan balance has increased a certain percentage over and above the original loan amount. When a loan is recast, the monthly payment, regardless of any payment cap, is refigured based on the then remaining loan balance, the remaining term of the loan, and the interest rate then in effect. This can result in considerable payment increases.

As a result, it may be difficult to obtain secondary financing from lenders or sellers where the first mortgage is subject to negative amortization. In fact, where the first mortgage is subject to possible negative amortization, secondary financing is not acceptable by Fannie Mae, FHA or VA.

Cap Also referred to as the *ceiling,* a cap is a restriction on the periodic or lifetime change in interest rate or payment amount. A *periodic cap* limits the percentage of change at periodic or annual intervals. A *lifetime cap* sets a maximum on the percentage the interest rate can change from the initial rate over the entire term of the loan.

Biweekly Mortgages

A biweekly mortgage is a fixed-rate mortgage with monthly payments divided in half, payable every two weeks. Since there are 52 weeks in a year, the program results in 26 half-payments, or the equivalent of 13 monthly payments per year. As the following example shows, a homeowner with a 10 percent, 30-year, biweekly mortgage of $70,000 would save $53,771 in interest and pay off the balance in less than 21 years, compared to a fixed-rate 30-year mortgage.

Loan Amount	Term	Rate	Payment	Total Payments
$70,000	30 years	10%	$614.30	$221,148
$70,000	21 years	10%	$307.15	$167,376
Total interest savings				$ 53,771

Fifteen-Year Mortgages

Total interest charges on 15-year mortgages are considerably lower than those on 30-year loans. Furthermore, the rate of interest usually is slightly lower on 15-year loans.

The following example shows a homeowner's $85,748 savings in interest with a 15-year mortgage compared to a 30-year loan.

Loan Amount	Term	Rate	Monthly Payment	Total Payments
$70,000	30 years	10%	$614.30	$221,148
$70,000	15 years	10%	$752.22	$135,400
Total interest savings				$ 85,748

Reverse Mortgages

Originally offered in only a few areas reverse mortgages are now available nationwide. Senior homeowners can now get money from the equity in their homes through government-backed or privately insured reverse mortgages.

Under the Home Equity Conversion Insurance Program, insured by the FHA, the lender pays the borrower a single lump sum, a credit line on which to draw or monthly payments for as long as the person lives in his or her home. No repayment is required until the homeowner dies, sells the home or permanently moves. The program is available to homeowners at least 62 years old of all income levels, who own their home either free and clear or nearly so. For more information, call your local HUD field office.

Following are sample payment schedules for a reverse mortgage:

Cash Available from Federally Insured Reverse Mortgages

Home Value	$50,000	$100,000	$150,000
Age 70	$19,700	$44,000	$68,300
Age 75	23,100	50,600	78,100
Age 80	26,800	57,700	88,600

Amounts are based on national maximum at 7.25 percent interest; not available in all areas.
Source: National Center for Home Equity Conversion

The nonprofit National Center of Home Equity Conversion (NCHEC) has a list of participating lenders, *The Reverse Mortgage Locator,* which includes information on FHA and privately insured reverse mortgage options by state, including company names and phone numbers. Send $1 and a self-addressed, stamped business-size envelope to NCHEC, Suite 115, 7373 147th Street West, Apple Valley, MN 55124, 612-953-4474.

The National Center of Home Equity Conversion also publishes an excellent book on the subject, *Retirement Income on the House,* by Ken Scholen, 326 pages, $24.95.

For a free booklet on reverse mortgages, write to the American Association of Retired Persons, 601 E Street N.W., Washington, DC 20049, 202-434-2277.

Loan-to-Value Ratios

When evaluating a home loan, lenders use *loan-to-value ratios* (LTVs), which are determined by dividing the loan amount by the property value. For example, the LTV of a property appraised at $100,000, secured by a loan of $90,000, is 90 percent.

Loans with LTVs over 80 percent are referred to as high-ratio loans. Due to the risk involved, private mortgage insurance (PMI) is required for high-ratio loans.

A number of private mortgage insurance companies insure lending institutions against loss due to borrower default. The insurance covers the lender for the upper portion of the loan, typically 20 percent to 25 percent of the outstanding balance.

Qualifying Ratios

Lenders use two ratios to determine whether the borrower can reasonably be expected to meet expenses involved in home ownership. These two ratios are:

Ratio 1: Housing expense* expressed as a percentage of gross income**
Ratio 2: Total obligations*** expressed as a percentage of gross income

For example, suppose a prospective borrower wanted to know the maximum mortgage amount for which he or she can qualify, based on the following assumptions:

- Maximum allowable Ratio 1 = 28% of Gross income
- Maximum allowable Ratio 2 = 36% of Gross income
- Gross income = $3,500/month
- Taxes and insurance = $200/month
- Installment debt payments = $500/month
- Current interest rate of 30-year fixed-rate mortgages = 10%

Step A:	
Gross income	$3,500
Multiplied by Ratio 1	× 28%
Maximum housing expense under Ratio 1	$980 [A]

Step B:	
Maximum housing expense under Ratio 1	$980
Minus taxes and insurance	−$200
P&I payments under Ratio 1	$780 [B]

Step C:	
Gross income	$3,500
Multiplied by Ratio 2	× 36%
Maximum total obligations under Ratio 2	$1,260 [C]

Housing expense = the monthly payment for principal and interest (P&I), hazard insurance, real estate taxes and any mortgage insurance premium and homeowner's association dues.
**Gross income* = stable monthly income, reasonably expected to continue for at least three years.
***Total obligations* = the sum of housing expense and monthly payments on installment loans and revolving charge accounts extending beyond ten months, nonincome-producing real estate loans, alimony, child support, spousal maintenance and payments on all other debts of a continuing nature.

Step D:

Maximum total obligations under Ratio 2	$1,260
Minus debt payments	−500
Minus taxes and insurance	−200
P&I payments under Ratio 2	$560 [D]

Step E:

The lower amount of [B] or [D]	$560 [E]

Answer: The maximum 30-year, 10 percent interest loan, based on a monthly payment of $560, is **$63,812.** This can be determined easily by using a financial calculator.

Qualifying ratios are intended as guidelines and lenders may use a higher ratio if it can be justified by compensating factors. They vary between conventional, FHA and VA financing.

Seller Financing

Although seller financing is usually done to induce a sale by assisting the buyer in some way, under some circumstances it may be in the seller's best interest to take back a mortgage. For example, a seller may benefit from carrying the mortgage on his or her property to spread tax on profit from the sale over a number of years (see "Installment Sales" in Chapter 10) or a seller may prefer to carry a mortgage on the property in favor of investing money elsewhere.

Seller financing can take many different forms, including a purchase money (first or second) mortgage, a wraparound mortgage, a lease with option to purchase, or various degrees of seller-paid contributions, such as paying the buyer's moving expenses, closing costs and so on.

Purchase Money Mortgages

When a seller accepts a note for all or part of the purchase price, secured by a mortgage or deed of trust on the property, it is referred to as a purchase money mortgage.

Secondary seller financing generally is used to supplement a buyer's required cash for down payment, but also to help a buyer qualify for a new first loan from an institutional lender. Fannie Mae, FHA and VA impose certain requirements for secondary financing in conjunction with their new first loans, which are outlined in the following table.

Summary of Requirements for Second Loans in Conjunction with New First Loans

Conventional	*FHA*	*VA*
Sum of first and second may not exceed 90 percent of appraised value or price, whichever is less. The loan-to-value ratio of the first loan may not exceed 75 percent.	Sum of FHA and second mortgage may not exceed HUD's maximum mortgage amount for area. Secondary financing to obtain the required cash investment is prohibited.	Sum of VA and second mortgage may not exceed the amount of the VA Certificate of Reasonable Value (CRV).
The buyer must qualify for combined payments of first and second loans.	The buyer must qualify for combined payments of first and second loans.	The buyer must qualify for combined payments of first and second mortgages.
Minimum, five years, maximum, 30 years	No balloon payment before ten years.	
Regular scheduled payments may be amortized, interest-only, monthly, quarterly, etc. Balloon payment OK.	Any periodic payments made on account of the second mortgage must be made on a monthly basis in substantially the same amount.	The conditions of the second mortgage may not be more stringent than those of the VA loan.
For qualification purposes, payments on second mortgage are based on interest rate not less than 2 percent below market rate for seconds.		Interest rate on the second mortgage may not exceed the rate of the VA loan.
No negative amortization	No negative amortization	No negative amortization
No prepayment penalty	No Prepayment Penalty	No prepayment penalty

A seller who wants cash can sell his or her second mortgage to an investor. Second mortgages are negotiable instruments and have a cash value that is normally lower than the face value of the note. The difference between face value and cash value of the note is called the *discount*. Brokers can usually find private investors who buy such notes at a discount in order to realize a required return (yield) on their cash investment, provided the borrower's credit worthiness and his or her equity in the property (the difference between property value and total indebtedness) meet the investor's standards.

Wraparound Mortgages

The wraparound mortgage is a device that allows the seller to keep an existing low-interest first loan while making one larger loan to the buyer, secured by the wraparound mortgage. In addition to the amount of the existing first loan, the wrap includes the balance needed to purchase the home, referred to as the seller's equity. The device is normally used when the buyer has only a small down payment and institutional financing is difficult to obtain.

The concept of a wraparound is illustrated graphically in Figure 11.1. It shows a transaction in which a home is sold for $100,000 to a buyer who has only $10,000 cash for down payment and has difficulty in qualifying for financing from a lending institution. The home is encumbered by an existing low-interest mortgage with a balance of approximately $50,000. To assist the buyer, the seller proposes to finance the purchase with a wrap of $90,000.

FIGURE 11.1   Wraparound Mortgage

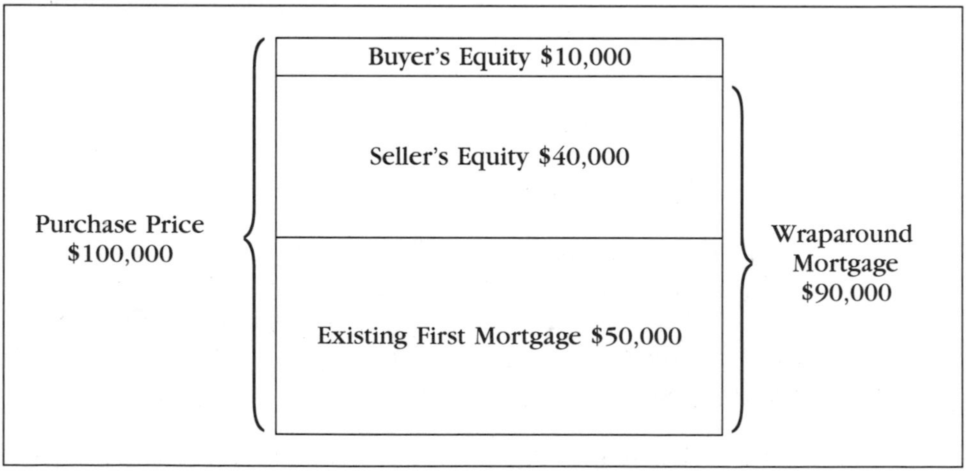

	Buyer's Equity $10,000
Purchase Price $100,000	Seller's Equity $40,000
	Existing First Mortgage $50,000

Wraparound Mortgage $90,000

The rate of interest of the existing first loan is usually several percentage points lower than that of the wrap, earning the seller a profit, as the following example demonstrates. Suppose that the existing first loan in Figure 11.1 carried a rate of interest of 7 percent and the wrap is written at 11 percent.

Seller collects 11% on $90,000	$ 9,900
Seller pays 7% on $50,000	−$ 3,500
Seller earns the difference	$ 6,400
Sale price	$100,000
Buyer's down payment	−$ 10,000
Existing loan balance	−$ 50,000
Seller's equity	$ 40,000

Seller's effective rate of return:
$$6,400 \div 40,000 = 16\%$$

The purchaser takes the property subject to the existing loan. This can only be done if the note secured by the existing mortgage does not contain an enforceable due-on-sale clause (see Glossary).

The wraparound mortgage includes the loan to the buyer and the existing mortgage of $50,000. The wrap is recorded as a lien junior to the existing mortgage(s).

The buyer may later assume the existing loan(s) by signing an assumption agreement with the lending institution. At such time the seller must reconvey the wraparound mortgage.

Wraparounds should only be prepared by legal counsel familiar with this type of financing.

Advantages of the wraparound mortgage include the following:

Advantages to the Buyer

- Can acquire larger property for same down payment
- Can purchase a property for which he or she could not qualify if using an institutional loan
- Saves points, appraisal and closing costs
- Saves time needed to shop and apply for new loan
- Is responsible for only one loan payment, rather than two or more

Advantages to the Seller

- Can earn a high rate of return

- Retains low interest of present financing, should it become necessary to repossess the property
- Can get a higher price for the property from the right buyer

Lease with Option To Purchase

A Lease with Option to Purchase is another tool sellers can use to induce a sale, where the buyer lacks sufficient funds for down payment and closing costs.

A Lease with Option to Purchase, also called Lease Option, entitles the lessee to purchase the leased property for a price and upon terms provided in the agreement, by exercising the option within a specified period of time (often a year). The lessee/buyer is referred to as the *optionee,* the lessor/seller as the *optionor.* The optionee pays the optionor an up-front, nonrefundable *option consideration,* which usually is applied toward the purchase price in the event the option to purchase is exercised. Lease Options generally provide that a portion of the rent is applied toward the purchase if the option is exercised, which is referred to as *rent credit.*

Consider the example of a seller who has a house on the market for $100,000. The buyer wants to buy the house, but does not have sufficient funds to qualify for a new loan. Instead of a purchase agreement, the seller and buyer enter into a Lease with Option to Purchase, which includes the following terms:

- Optionee pays optionor a nonrefundable option consideration of $4,000, which is to be applied toward the purchase price if the option to purchase is exercised.
- Optionee agrees to lease the property for 12 months, at which time he or she may exercise the option to purchase the property for $100,000.
- Optionee agrees further to pay rent of $800 per month, of which $400 is to be applied to the purchase price if the option is exercised.

Assume the optionee decides to exercise the option at the end of 12 months:

Agreed purchase price		$100,000
Option consideration	$4,000	
12 months' rent credit	$4,800	
Minus credits		($ 8,800)
Optionee pays		$ 91,200

Institutional lenders accept rent credits as part of the down payment, provided rental payments exceed the market rent and a valid lease/purchase agreement is in effect, a copy of which must be attached to the loan application.

Advantages to the Optionee

- Low cash requirement
- Partial rent credit applied toward down payment
- Purchase price locked in at today's prices
- Time to plan and prepare for finance of purchase
- May possibly sell the option, subject to the terms of the agreement

Advantages to the Optionor

- Monthly rent higher than market rent
- Top market value for property
- Optionee likely to treat the property like an owner
- Tax-free use of option consideration until the option expires or is exercised
- Continued tax deductions for expenses and depreciation during the option period

Refinancing a Home

Lenders' guidelines for refinancing are somewhat similar to purchase guidelines, with these differences:

- The maximum loan-to-value ratio for a refinance is often five to ten percent lower than for a purchase.
- Seasoning, or age of loan, is important and many lenders ask for at least one year and sometimes two years of seasoning.
- It is important to have an excellent payment history on the present mortgage, with no mortgage late payments reported.
- If the borrower is taking out cash, the lender will need to document the reason.

A general rule of thumb, when considering a refinance, is that the new interest rate should be approximately two percentage points lower than the current rate, and the borrower should plan to own the property for at least three more years. There are several situations where this might not apply, such as converting an ARM to a fixed-rate loan, retiring an existing lien, making repairs or improvements to the property, paying off a balloon payment, consolidating personal nondeductible interest loans into a home mortgage with tax-deductible interest, replacing a 30-year loan with a 15-year mortgage at a lower interest rate.

Premium Pricing

Lenders are allowed to pay discount points, closing costs and finance fees at time of closing. Recovery of these costs can be made through premium pricing of the loan, which means an increase in the interest rate or discount above the normal market rates.

Borrowers would be well advised to compare the cost of refinance loans by obtaining the annual percentage rate (APR) from lenders. The APR is the loan's interest rate adjusted for points, closing costs, finance fees and the term of the loan.

The following table shows the APR of a hypothetical $100,000 loan with varying terms, interest rates, points and finance charges.

Yrs	Rate	Pmts	Points	Finance Charges	APR
30	9%	805	1%	$4,000	9.58%
30	9.5	841	1	0	9.62
30	10	878	0	0	10.00
15	9%	1,014	1%	$4,000	9.89%
15	9.5	1,044	1	0	9.67
15	10	1,075	0	0	10.00

Streamline Refinancing

With streamline refinancing, no appraisal or credit approval is necessary. This can be particularly important if the market value of the property has declined since the loan was originated. It is available for refinancing FHA and VA loans, while certain portfolio lenders offer similar accommodations.

FHA The Federal Housing Administration provides rules for two types of refinances: Streamline Refinances and Cash-back Refinances.

1. Streamline refinances are designed to reduce interest on a current FHA mortgage and may not include cash back to the borrower. The term of the mortgage is the lesser of 30 years or the unexpired term of the mortgage, plus 12 years.
2. Cash-back refinances are permitted for owner-occupied principal residences that the borrower has owned for more than one year and

are limited to 85 percent of appraised value plus closing costs. Such refinancing is permitted for the purpose of retiring existing liens, making repairs and improvements to the property, paying off a mortgage subject to a balloon payment, paying a divorced spouse as a result of a court-ordered property settlement, paying heirs to settle an estate, or obtaining cash to finance family related expenditures, such as a college education.

VA The Veterans Administration allows two types of refinancing:

1. The Interest Rate Reduction Refinancing Loan (IRRRL), which permits restoration of used entitlement.
2. The refinance of an existing mortgage secured by a lien on a dwelling owned and occupied by the veteran.

Portfolio Loans Portfolio lenders, who keep loans in their portfolio, are more flexible in their lending rules than lenders who sell their loans in the secondary market. Loan applications with portfolio lenders tend to be less complex and cumbersome.

Glossary of Mortgage Financing Terms

accelerating a debt Calling the entire remaining balance of the mortgage due and payable immediately because of a default in one or more of the mortgage provisions

acquisition cost Sales price plus allowable closing costs

adjustable-rate mortgage (ARM) A mortgage that permits the lender to adjust the loan's interest rate periodically on the basis of movement in a specified index

adjustment interval The frequency for resetting the interest rate and/or monthly payment amount for an ARM

allowable closing costs Closing costs that may be financed in the mortgage, typically including title insurance, es-

crow, attorney, credit report, appraisal, loan origination and recording fees

amortization Gradual reduction of the mortgage debt through fixed installment payments scheduled over the term of the mortgage

annual percentage rate (APR) The interest rate adjusted for loan fees and term of the loan; used to compare loans

ARM *See* adjustable-rate mortgage

assumption A mortgage loan is assumed when a written assumption agreement is executed between the lender and the purchaser of the property as a result of a due-on-sale clause. Thus, the primary responsibility for repayment of the mortgage is placed upon the purchaser.

automatic loans   Loans that are automatically guaranteed without requiring specific prior VA approval

balloon payment   The remaining balance of a mortgage that must be paid in a lump sum at the end of the mortgage term; usually occurs with second mortgages

basis point   1/100th of 1 percent; for example, 7½ basis points equals .075

beneficiary   The lender in a deed of trust

bridge loan   A short-term loan obtained by a seller to finance the down payment on a new property while the old one is being sold. Also referred to as *swing loan* or *interim financing*

buydown   An arrangement wherein the property seller or the buyer deposits money into an account, to be released each month to reduce the mortgagor's monthly payments during the early years of a mortgage. The borrower's interest rate is "bought down" below the actual rate to help qualify the buyer, a technique often used by builders in periods of high interest rates

cap   A restriction, or ceiling, on the periodic or lifetime change in interest rate or payment amount of an ARM

cash out   A refinancing where the amount of money received from the new loan exceeds the total of the money needed to repay the old debt, closing costs and property improvements (if any)

ceiling   *See* cap

closing costs   Costs paid by the purchaser to close a transaction

conditional contract of sale   Also known as a land contract, a conditional contract of sale is an installment-type contract between buyer and seller, whereby the buyer obtains the right to occupy, but the seller retains legal title to the real property as security for repayment of the purchase price. During the term of the contract, the buyer has an equitable ownership interest in the property.

condominium   An individual ownership of a unit in a residential or commercial building and an undivided interest in the common areas of the project, including land, parking, recreational and parking areas, lobbies, stairs, elevators, mechanical equipment, exterior surfaces and so on

construction loan   A short-term loan to finance construction, setting aside funds for withdrawal as construction progresses

contract rate   *See* initial interest rate

conventional mortgage   A mortgage not insured or guaranteed by a government agency

convertible ARM   A type of ARM that includes an option for the mortgagor to change the mortgage to a fixed-rate mortgage on one of the early interest rate adjustment dates

certificate of reasonable value (CRV)   A certificate of value issued by the Department of Veterans Affairs

deed of trust   A deed of trust is a security instrument in which the borrower is called *trustor* and the lender is the *beneficiary.* The property is conveyed to the *trustee* (often a title company or bank) who holds title as security for repayment of the loan, for the benefit of the beneficiary.

deficiency judgment   A personal judgment created by court decree for the difference between the amount of the mortgage indebtedness and any lesser amount recovered from the foreclosure sale (the deficiency) against any person who is liable for the mortgage debt

discount   When a note is sold at a discount, its face value is reduced by the amount of the discount, which increases the yield

discount points   *See* points

due-on-sale clause   A provision in a mortgage allowing the lender to call the mortgage due and payable if ownership of the mortgaged property is transferred without the lender's permission

effective gross income   Used in FHA qualifying ratios, it is the applicant's monthly gross income from all sources that can be reasonably expected to continue for the first five years of the loan term

equitable ownership interest   *See* conditional contract of sale

Federal National Mortgage Association (FNMA)   Commonly referred to as Fannie Mae, FNMA purchases mortgages in the secondary mortgage market

Federal Housing Administration (FHA) Insures mortgages made by lending institutions on one to four residential units

Federal Home Loan Mortgage Corporation (FHLMC)   Commonly referred to as Freddie Mac, FHLMC is a congressionally chartered corporation that purchases mortgages in the secondary mortgage market

first mortgage   A mortgage that is the primary lien against a property

fixed-rate mortgage   A mortgage that provides for only one interest rate for the entire term of the mortgage

foreclosure   A procedure prescribed by law whereby real property, pledged as security for repayment of a debt, is sold to pay the debt in the event of default

high-ratio loan   A conventional mortgage with a loan-to-value ratio above 80 percent

homeowners' association   An association of owners that manages the affairs of a condominium or planned unit development

housing expense   Used in FHA qualifying ratios, includes principal, interest, real estate taxes, hazard insurance, utilities, home maintenance and special assessments

impound account   A trust account established to hold funds allocated for the payment of real estate taxes, insurance premiums and the like, as they are received each month and until such time as they are disbursed to pay the related bills; also called escrow account

income-to-debt ratios   Qualifying ratios used to determine a borrower's ability to meet the cost of home ownership. Two ratios are in use: (1) housing expense (loan payment, property tax, hazard insurance premium and homeowners' association dues) to gross income; and (2) total obligations (housing expense, monthly payments on revolving charge accounts, installment loans extending beyond ten months and other obligations of a continuing nature) to gross income. These ratios vary between conventional, FHA and VA financing.

index   This indicator of current economic conditions is used to determine changes in the mortgage interest rate. Lenders of ARMs may select from a variety of indexes, subject only to two require-ments: (1) The index must be beyond the control of the lender and (2) the index must be readily available to and verifiable by the public

initial interest rate   The initial interest rate of an ARM; also called *contract rate*

interim financing   A loan obtained by a seller to finance the down payment on a new property while the old one is being sold; also referred to as *bridge loan* or *swing loan*

junior lien   Any lien recorded subsequent to a prior lien (e.g., a second mortgage is junior to a first mortgage)

land contract   *See* conditional contract of sale

loan-to-value ratio   The relationship be-tween the loan amount and the lower of appraised value or sales price

lock-in   A mortgage is said to be locked in if it cannot be paid off or provides for a very high prepayment penalty. This may occur during the initial portion of the term, usually with insurance company loans

LTV   *See* loan-to-value ratio

margin   The percentage added to the in-dex rate, in order to arrive at the inter-est rate of an ARM

minimum cash investment   Used in FHA financing, minimum cash invest-ment is the difference between total acquisition costs and maximum loan amount

minimum documentation   Some lend-ers allow borrowers to furnish their own documentation in lieu of verifica-tions where the loan-to-value ratio is 75 percent or less

mortgage payment expense   Used in FHA financing; includes principal, inter-est, property taxes and hazard insur-ance (PITI), $\frac{1}{12}$ of the annual FHA mortgage insurance premium, and any homeowners' association dues

mortgage   A contract between a lender and borrower by which property is given as security for repayment of a note or bond; the borrower is called *mortgagor* and the lender the *mort-gagee*

negative amortization   An increase in the loan balance of an ARM resulting from loan payments being insufficient to cover the interest. This is usually caused by interest rate increases with-out a corresponding increase in monthly payments.

nonsupervised lenders   Lenders not un-der supervision of any government agency

nonconforming loan   A loan that does not conform to underwriting guidelines of the secondary mortgage market

open-end clause   An FHA loan may con-tain an open-end clause by which an outstanding balance may be increased by amounts advanced to the borrower for improvements, alterations or repairs to the property

or more   A term in a note that allows the borrower to pay more than the agreed monthly loan payments without incur-ring a prepayment penalty

origination fee   The fee charged by a lender to prepare loan documents and make credit checks, usually expressed as a percentage of the face value of the loan

planned unit development (PUD) A real estate project in which each individual owner has title to a unit and an undivided interest in the common areas of the project, including common land, streets and sidewalks, parking, recreational, social and storage areas, mechanical equipment and so on.

private mortgage insurance (PMI) Insures the lender against loss in the event of the borrower's default on a high ratio conventional mortgage

points Loan fees expressed as a percentage of the loan amount; one point equals 1 percent

portfolio lender A lender who retains loans in portfolio, rather than selling them in the secondary mortgage market

prepayment allowance or privilege A specified amount or percentage a borrower is allowed to pay in addition to the agreed monthly loan payments without incurring a prepayment penalty

prepayment penalty or fee A charge a borrower may be required to pay during the early years of the mortgage if he or she pays it in full or pays large sums to reduce the unpaid balance

PUD *See* planned unit development

qualifying ratios *See* income-debt ratios

recasting a loan Lenders restrict the amount of negative amortization by recasting the ARM whenever the loan balance has increased above the original loan amount; when a loan is recast, the monthly payment is refigured based on the then-remaining loan balance, term and interest rate in effect

recurring payment Payments on debts with more than six months remaining

redemption In the event the borrower defaults, the lender's remedy is foreclosure. The debtor has the right to redeem the property by making full payment of the mortgage debt any time after the obligation is due and before his right of redemption ends.

refinance The repayment of a debt from the proceeds of a new loan using the same property as security

Regulation Z Part of the Truth-in-Lending Act, Regulation Z covers every type of consumer credit and requires lenders extending credit to individuals, for personal, family and household uses, to fully disclose certain details of the proposed transaction to borrowers before obligating themselves to accept the loan

reinstatement The curing of a delinquency by paying all past-due payments to bring the mortgage to a current status

release of liability A formal agreement absolving a borrower from responsibility under a mortgage because another party has agreed to assume the mortgage obligation

real estate owned (REO) Property owned by lenders, usually acquired through foreclosure

residual income Used in VA underwriting, residual income refers to the income portion remaining for family support after deducting housing expense and family expenditures from gross income

Real Estate Settlement and Procedures Act (RESPA) Sets forth disclosure requirements for lenders who provide federally related loans, secured by one-to four-family residences, including purchase loans, refinancing, home equity loans and lines of credit

revolving debt An arrangement for credit in which the customer receives purchases or services on an ongoing basis being repaid at regular intervals, but not for a specified amount or term, such as charge accounts or credit cards

secondary mortgage market In the secondary mortgage market, lenders sell blocks of mortgages to investors in order to generate capital for new loans

security instrument A contract between lender and borrower by which property is given as security for repayment of a loan, evidenced by a note or bond. In some states, the mortgage is used as real property security instrument, in others the deed of trust.

"subject to" clause If the mortgage contains no due-on-sale clause, a buyer can take over the mortgage without the lender's permission. The buyer is then said to have taken the property "subject to" the mortgage.

substitution of entitlement Used in VA financing, this is a process whereby a veteran seller can have his or her entitlement restored if a veteran buying the home has sufficient entitlement and consents to substitute it for that of the seller

supervised lenders Lending institutions subject to supervision of an agency of the United States or of any state or territory

sweat equity By agreement with the builder, and upon approval by FHA or VA, a borrower may perform work for which he or she is considered qualified, on a dwelling under construction. The value of such work, as agreed upon by buyer and builder, referred to as "sweat equity," may be credited against the required down payment.

swing loan *See* interim financing

take-out loan A permanent mortgage to pay off a construction loan; also called *permanent loan*

teaser rate A term used with ARMs, indicating below-market initial interest rates in effect for a limited period (typically 6 or 12 months)

third party sale A foreclosure sale at which the successful purchaser of the property is someone other than the mortgagee or mortgagor or their representatives

title insurance A type of insurance that insures against defects in title not listed in the title report or abstract

total fixed payment Used in FHA qualifying ratios, total fixed payment includes mortgage payment expense plus all recurring obligations

trustee The third party in a deed of trust (usually a title company or bank) holding title to the property as security for repayment of the loan, for the benefit of the lender, called the beneficiary

trustor The borrower in a deed of trust

underwriting a loan Approving a loan

VA loan A mortgage guaranteed by the Department of Veterans Affairs

VA loan guaranty The VA guarantees a portion of VA loans to cover lending institutions against loss due to borrower default

verification of deposit (VOD) A document used to verify a loan applicant's bank balance

wraparound mortgage   A mortgage that is subordinate to an existing first mortgage, but yet includes not only the remaining balance of the underlying first mortgage to which it is subordinate, but also an additional amount to finance the balance of the purchase price. Also referred to as all-inclusive, overriding, overlapping or hold-harmless deed of trust. For more information, refer to "wraparound mortgages" in this chapter.

yield   Return on investment

CHAPTER
TWELVE

Selling a Home Profitably

To List or Not To List

Selling a house and carrying the transaction through to successful completion is no easy task. You can, of course, retain a professional to do the job or you can try to save the commission by making the sale yourself. Remember, though, the typical direct-from-owner buyer expects you to knock off the commission for his or her benefit and is likely to have experience in such negotiations.

Before you decide to go the "For Sale by Owner" route, you would be wise to ask yourself the questions in the following checklist. If most of your answers are "yes," by all means give it a whirl; however, if most of your answers are negative, list your home with the best broker you can find, often the broker through whom you purchased your home.

For Sale by Owner Checklist

Yes   No

❏   ❏   Do you have ample time to sell your house?

❏   ❏   Is your house easy to find?

❏   ❏   Is there a scarcity of your type of home for sale?

❏   ❏   Do you have the know-how to price your house at the highest figure that will attract buyers?

❏   ❏   Are you capable of running an effective advertising campaign?

❏   ❏   Do you have the time to answer phone calls at all hours, and to keep your house in top condition, ready for prospects at any time?

❏   ❏   Do you know how to show your house to its best advantage?

❏   ❏   Can you answer objections and criticisms without showing irritation?

❏   ❏   Can you tell a prospective buyer answering your ad by phone from a potential criminal using ads to get into homes, disguised as a homebuyer?

❏   ❏   Are you able to call back prospects without placing yourself in a poor bargaining position to negotiate an offer?

❏   ❏   Can you show prospects comparable properties, so they can see why yours is worth the money?

❏   ❏   Do you have the ability to bargain successfully for price, terms, moving date, etc.?

❏   ❏   Are you familiar with today's financing options and restrictions?

❏   ❏   Do you have an outlet for second mortgages?

❏   ❏   Do you have the professional skill necessary to draw up contracts?

❏   ❏   Can you handle all the details and paperwork required to close a transaction?

Choosing a Real Estate Broker

If you decide to list with a real estate firm, how can you choose one that will most likely do a first rate job for you? If your answer to most of the following questions is "yes," your selection is probably a good one.

Yes No

❏ ❏ Is the brokerage firm a member of the local board or association of REALTORS® or the local multiple listing service?

❏ ❏ Has the firm been in business long enough to be considered established?

❏ ❏ Does the firm have a reputation of integrity, aggressiveness and technical know-how?

❏ ❏ Does the firm have a proven record of selling homes in your neighborhood?

❏ ❏ Can the firm give your home maximum exposure to the market through its combined advertising program, existing contacts with buyers, contacts with large corporations transferring employees on a regular basis?

❏ ❏ Is the firm skilled in appraising homes in your neighborhood and in recommending the highest price range that will attract buyers? (Beware of real estate people who deliberately give unrealistically high appraisals in order to get listings.)

❏ ❏ Is the staff trained in screening lookers from qualified buyers?

❏ ❏ Is the firm well organized, so as to guide you through all the paperwork in closing the transaction?

❏ ❏ Does the agent have the know-how to advise you on what improvements would add value to the property in terms of sale price and which would not?

❏ ❏ Does the agent show genuine concern for your needs in terms of timing your move, financial requirements and other considerations?

❏ ❏ Is the agent knowledgeable in all available sources of financing?

❏ ❏ Have you talked to others who have done business with the brokerage firm and the agent?

The Real Estate Profession

Before being permitted to practice real estate brokerage, one must pass a state licensing examination and satisfy the authorities of one's integrity and competence. Real estate brokers and salespersons must adhere to strict standards in conducting their business or risk suspension or revocation of their license.

Not all licensed real estate brokers have affiliated themselves with the NATIONAL ASSOCIATION OF REALTORS® (NAR), thereby earning the title of REALTOR®, a registered trademark. Every REALTOR® has pledged to observe a strict code of ethics promulgated by NAR and adopted by all local boards or associations of REALTORS®, to govern real estate practices by their members. The organization also provides highly specialized continuing education, constantly striving for increased competence among its members.

Another, smaller group of brokers promoting high professional standards is the National Association of Real Estate Brokers, whose members have the copyrighted designation of REALTIST®.

The majority of real estate brokers are ethical and courteous professional people. In the event that you, as property owner or purchaser, should experience unprofessional conduct on the part of a REALTOR®, you may complain to the local board or association of REALTORS®, which is interested in maintaining the good name of the profession. In the event of suspected unlawful conduct you have of course the option of seeking legal counsel or filing a complaint with the state or local authority in charge of supervising real estate licensees, or both.

Types of Listings

Exclusive Listing

In this type of listing, you grant one broker the exclusive authorization and right to sell your property. Even if you produce the buyer yourself, the broker is entitled to the commission under this type of contract.

The advantage of this type of listing is that the broker agrees to make a diligent effort to produce the sale because he or she is guaranteed a return. As your agent, the broker is also committed to represent your interests.

Multiple Listing

This is an exclusive listing with a broker who places the listing with a multiple listing service, which authorizes other brokers to show the property, and, if one succeeds in selling the property, to split the commission.

In addition to the advantages of an exclusive listing, a multiple listing affords maximum exposure to the market. Your primary multiple listing agent (with whom you sign the listing contract) will represent you in all negotiations. The drawback is that the seller may be held liable for misrepresentations or lack of disclosures by any of the multiple listing brokers.

Exclusive Agency Listing

In this type of listing, you authorize one broker exclusively to sell your property for a certain commission unless you find a buyer and make the sale yourself. You must be careful not to advertise different prices for the same house. No other brokers have the right to sell your property, except by permission of the listing broker who would then split the commission.

The advantage of the exclusive agency listing is that you deal with one broker only who represents your interest and you retain the right to make the sale yourself.

A drawback is that the broker may not devote as much effort to marketing the property as he or she would with an exclusive listing.

Open Listing

In an open listing, you list your house with as many brokers as you like and pay a commission only to the one who makes the sale. You pay no commission if you produce the buyer yourself. One drawback of this is that brokers may not spend much effort or money with so little chance of profit. Remember: Everyone's job is no one's job.

Preparing Your Home To Sell

"Fixing-up expenses" can reduce the amount on which you pay capital gain tax, if the work is performed within 90 days before the agreement to sell and paid within 30 days after the date escrow is closed.

Certain improvements add value to a home in terms of sale price; others do not. In preparing your home for the market, avoid expensive improvements, such as adding rooms, remodeling kitchens or installing new carpets or draperies. They may not suit the buyer's needs or taste. A possible exception may be where a remodeled kitchen would bring your home up to the standard of comparable properties in the area.

Suggested Improvements

❑ Fresh paint, both inside and outside, invariably increases the salability of your house. Use neutral colors that appeal to most people and are easy to decorate with. Fill holes and cracks. Wash fingerprints off doors.
❑ Replace stained or torn wallpaper.
❑ Remove unsightly stains from kitchen and bathroom counters, fixtures, etc.
❑ Replace worn kitchen and bathroom floor coverings.

❑ Shampoo carpets.
❑ Replace missing or broken door and cupboard hardware.
❑ Use soap to lubricate sticky windows and drawers.
❑ Oil creaking door hinges.
❑ Repair broken shutters, storm windows, windows and shower doors.
❑ Repair clogged plumbing lines, leaky faucets and leaks underneath sinks.
❑ Fix creaky floors.
❑ Make sure all mechanical systems and appliances are in good working condition. Make repairs where needed.
❑ Replacing a worn out water heater, an inadequate or hazardous heating system, etc., although expensive, will usually pay for itself in commanding a better sale price.
❑ Repair the roof if needed, fix leaks and replace loose or missing shingles. Replace worn and leaky rain gutters and downspouts.
❑ After fixing roof, paint ceilings that show water marks from leaks.
❑ Fix and paint fence if needed.
❑ Repair potholes in blacktop and large cracks in concrete.
❑ Remove oil stains from garage floor and driveway.

Remodeling To Assist the Sale

Remodeling may assist the sale if it is the type of improvement generally found in neighboring homes, but beware of overimprovement. Remodeling your property beyond the level of homes in your area is generally a waste of money.

When deciding whether to remodel, consider also the following study by the National Association of Remodeling Industry that compares average remodeling costs with average resale values.

Remodeling Job	Average Job Cost	Average Resale Value	Cost Recouped
Minor kitchen remodeling	$ 6,234	$ 6,551	104%
Bath addition	10,552	10,020	95
Major kitchen remodeling	19,261	18,021	94
Bath remodeling	7,207	6,109	85
Family room addition	28,455	24,069	85
Master bedroom suite	22,060	18,320	83
Attic bedroom	21,904	17,715	81
Deck addition	5,731	4,456	78
Replace windows	7,315	5,289	72
Replace siding	9,052	6,403	71
Sun space addition	24,929	17,416	70

Pest Control Inspection

Government financing and many private lending institutions require an inspection report by a licensed pest control operator and most purchase offers are subject to termite and dry rot damage repaired at seller's expense. This is a bad time to be hit with an unexpected expense that could run into a great deal of money. It is therefore advisable to have the house inspected before putting it on the market and to find out the cost of any repair work in advance. (See Chapter 9.)

Fixtures

A fixture is personal property converted into real property when it is permanently nailed, bolted, screwed, plastered, cemented or built into a structure or attached to the land. Therefore, fixtures go with the property when it is sold.

Fixtures usually include trees, shrubs and plants (except potted plants), fences, built-in appliances, drapery hardware, wall-to-wall carpets, light fixtures, chandeliers, television antennae and the like.

To determine whether a personal property has been converted into a fixture consider the method of attachment. If the item is permanently attached so it cannot be removed without damaging the property, it is a fixture. But if it can be removed easily, it remains personal property. For example, draperies attached to drapery hardware are personal property because they can be removed easily. The drapery hardware is a fixture because it is permanently attached to the wall.

If you wish to keep a particular fixture, replace it with something comparable before putting your house on the market, or at least specify in the written contract that the fixture is not included in the sale.

The Right Asking Price

Establishing the right price range is a critical consideration in marketing real property. Overpricing, as well as underpricing, can be detrimental to the sale.

Many sellers tend to price their house far above market value for a number of reasons: sentimental attachment, expensive improvements made over the years (not always appreciated by prospective buyers), false rumors of high priced sales in the neighborhood, and often unrealistic opinions of well meaning friends.

An overpriced house discourages serious buyers and real estate salespeople. It usually remains on the market too long, causing people to wonder if something is wrong with the house.

On the other hand, unfamiliarity with the market may cause a seller to underprice the home, only to find it snapped up by a speculator for quick resale at a profit.

Determining Market Value of Your Home

Market Comparison For the purpose of establishing a price at which to buy or sell a home, market comparison is the method relied upon most by professional appraisers.

One compares actual sale prices, not asking prices, of similar homes sold recently in the same neighborhood. Such homes must be comparable in location, age, size and quality. Because no two homes are exactly alike, adjustments need to be made for differences in the following:

- Physical condition (some homes are maintained better than others)
- Additions (bedrooms, recreation rooms, bathrooms and so on)
- Unusual features (a spectacular view, lovely setting, swimming pool, mechanical convenience features, expensive carpets and draperies, modernized kitchen)
- Personal property included in the price (refrigerator, washer, dryer, furnishings and the like)
- Favorable financing terms (An extremely low down payment or an assumable low interest loan would command a higher price.)
- Seller's urgency to sell (A quick sale forced by unusual circumstances may account for an abnormally low selling price.)
- Discounted overimprovements (A $40,000 game room added to a $60,000 house, located in a $60,000 neighborhood, may not add $40,000 value to the house in terms of sale price.)

Perhaps the best source for collecting data for a market comparison is personal research over a period of time before putting your home on the market. Look at comparable homes for sale in your neighborhood, making notes on how they differ from yours. Note the asking price and the date the house went on the market. When the house is sold, complete your notes with the date of sale, sale price and financing terms. Be sure to obtain price and terms from a reliable source. Your multiple listing broker will generally be glad to give such information after the sale is closed.

The market data thus collected on three or more comparable homes must now be compared to derive a market value for your own home. By making upward and downward adjustments, a common denominator is established for a reasonable comparison.

FHA or VA Appraisals In many localities houses have been selling at or close to FHA or VA appraised values.

Assessed Value Homes in most areas are reassessed periodically to reflect their fair market value. Ask to see the appraisal of your property at the tax assessor's office or an equivalent county office. Also ask what comparable sales were used to establish the assessed value.

Real Estate Appraisers The Federal Appraiser Law, effective January 1, 1993, requires all states to license or certify any appraiser who works on loans of $250,000 or more that are involved with federally regulated lending institutions. A federal law also requires lenders to notify residential loan applicants that they can obtain the results of an appraisal if they paid for it. State laws may have more stringent provisions.

Property Information Sheet

A property information sheet containing the following data is of considerable use in marketing your home, regardless of whether you list your home with a broker.

Location

❑ Street address
❑ Nearest cross-street
❑ District, subdistrict and tract
❑ Public transportation
❑ Shopping facilities
❑ Schools (grade, junior high, college, parochial)
❑ Houses of worship
❑ Nearest hospital
❑ Fire and police station
❑ Recreational facilities

Grounds and Site Information

❑ Lot size
❑ View, setting and so on

- ❑ Zoning
- ❑ Lawn sprinkler system
- ❑ Pool
- ❑ Description and condition of grounds, fences and so on
- ❑ Patio, lanai and so on

Structural Information

- ❑ Age of house
- ❑ Architectural style
- ❑ Attached or detached garage
- ❑ Type and quality of construction
- ❑ Name of builder
- ❑ Exterior finish
- ❑ Number of stories or levels
- ❑ Type of roof
- ❑ Basement, crawl space, slab floors
- ❑ Garage, number of cars
- ❑ Storage
- ❑ Wired for 220 volt?
- ❑ Copper water lines?
- ❑ Type of heating and cooling
- ❑ Insulation, weather stripping
- ❑ Type of flooring, carpeting
- ❑ Storm windows and doors?

Floor Plan

- ❑ Square footage of living space
- ❑ Number and size of bedrooms
- ❑ Number of bathrooms
- ❑ Living room size
- ❑ Fireplace
- ❑ Dining room size, separate or combination?
- ❑ Breakfast room
- ❑ Family room
- ❑ Kitchen—gas or electric, built-in appliances
- ❑ Laundry room
- ❑ Workshop
- ❑ Unusual extras
- ❑ Personal property included, if any

Assumable Existing Loans

- ❏ Loan balances of first and second loans, if any
- ❏ Monthly payments (taxes and insurance, if included)
- ❏ Lender, loan number, assumption fee, if any
- ❏ Interest rate
- ❏ Due date and balloon payment of second loan, if any

Loan Commitments

- ❏ Lender
- ❏ Amount, term, interest, monthly payments, loan fee

Property Disclosure Statements

Non-disclosure of certain property defects has been the subject of an ever increasing number of legal actions brought by buyers since the 1980s. For the protection of homebuyers, sellers and brokers, most states have enacted laws requiring sellers to provide buyers with a written statement disclosing any known defects of the property.

Showing Your House to Its Best Advantage

- ❏ Keep the lawn mowed and edged, hedges trimmed, the yard tidy and the pool sparkling.
- ❏ Keep walks and steps free of ice, snow, leaves, toys and debris.
- ❏ Leave porch lights on when showing the house at night.
- ❏ Greet prospects in a friendly, but businesslike manner.
- ❏ Keep the house well ventilated, fresh smelling and avoid cooking odors.
- ❏ Empty ashtrays and avoid smoking while your house is shown.
- ❏ Let enough light in each room, open draperies to show view, if any.
- ❏ Place flowers and touches of greenery throughout the house.
- ❏ Keep the temperature at a comfortable level.
- ❏ Have a crackling fire on a chilly winter day.
- ❏ Avoid distractions, play soft music, turn off TV, keep children and toys out of the way and pets outside.
- ❏ Stay out of the way of the real estate salesperson—let him or her do the selling—or leave the house if at all possible.
- ❏ Keep kitchen spotless, no dirty dishes, keep counters clean.
- ❏ Keep bathrooms clean and tidy.
- ❏ Keep closets and storage spaces clean and uncluttered.

❑ Keep garage, workshop, basement and attic tidy.
❑ Keep windows and mirrors clean.
❑ Keep floors scrubbed and vacuumed.

The Sale

A contract for the sale of real property must be in writing in order to be legally enforceable. The drafting of such a contract or filling in the necessary terms and conditions on printed contract forms should not be attempted by a person without considerable training. Instruction for writing such a contract, with the many variables required by different states, is beyond the scope of this book. Real estate attorneys, or qualified licensed real estate persons are trained to protect the parties' interests in drafting this important document.

The following provisions in a contract are of particular importance to a seller:

1. The amount of deposit the seller is entitled to keep if the buyer defaults should be specified. (Do not accept a postdated check, nor a check that, to your knowledge, is not covered by sufficient funds at the time you accept it.)
2. The buyer should be allowed a limited time to qualify for a mortgage loan or release the seller from the contract.
3. In the event the seller is to take back a second mortgage, the buyer should have a sufficient amount of cash invested to make a foreclosure unattractive. (For more information on seller financing, see Chapter 11.)
4. Specify who is to pay which part of the closing costs.
5. Specify the closing date and the date on which the seller must give possession to the buyer. You may need a short time between the closing and the moving date. The buyers should be reasonably compensated for the days that you occupy their property.
6. Beware of agreeing to pay for damage caused by termites and dry rot before you know the cost of such repairs. (The best solution is usually to have your house inspected before putting it on the market.)
7. The contract should specify any personal property included in the sale and any fixtures not included.
8. If you have agreed to make certain repairs, the contract should specify them.
9. If the offer is made by husband or wife alone, both can subsequently appear on the title. However, both names should not appear on the contract as purchasers, unless both are present to sign, as such an agreement would be incomplete.

In the event the price, or any other conditions of the offer, are unacceptable, you have the choice to make a counteroffer or you may flatly reject the offer. The latter choice has the advantage that you do not disclose the price you are ultimately willing to accept. Once you have made a counteroffer, you can no longer decide to accept the original offer at a later date, should you change your mind.

CHAPTER
THIRTEEN

Moving to a
New Residence

Major portions of this chapter are reprinted courtesy of United Van Lines, Fenton, Missouri, from their copyrighted publication, *Pre-Planned Moving Guide.*

Things You Should Know about Moving

In Search of a New Residence

❏ Subscribe to the Sunday edition of the new area's local newspaper in advance of your move. It usually contains a large real estate section, which can be very helpful in giving you some idea of the type of housing available in the new city, as well as other useful information.

❏ Arrange for a house-hunting trip to your new city. Unless you have a real estate broker who is a member of a national referral organization, ask friends, your banker or the local board or association of REALTORS® in your new locality to recommend a reputable broker. (See Chapter 12.)

❏ When looking for a new home, take along a tape measure and a list of the exact dimensions of each of your major appliances and other large pieces of furniture. Measure the areas provided for them to be sure your appliances and furniture will fit.

❏ Establish credit in the new city. Ask your banker for a referral to a correspondent bank and to act as a credit reference.

Preplanning Your Move

❏ Plan the move as early as possible. If you are able to move at any time of the year, don't wait until summer, the peak moving season. Consider also that the first and last few days of the month are extra busy.

❏ If you plan to sell your house, get it on the market as soon as possible. (See Chapter 12.) If renting, give your landlord timely notice of your moving date.

❏ Keep a record of all expenses related to the move, some of which may be tax deductible. (See Chapter 10.)

❏ Fill out the Personal Household Inventory for each room, using the handy form in Appendix D. This is important for establishing the amount of declared valuation for the shipment and as a permanent inventory for insurance purposes. List, as nearly as possible, the year of purchase and original cost of each item. Attach any invoices or records of purchase to the completed inventory.

❏ Prepare a separate high-value inventory if the shipment will contain articles of "extraordinary" value. In the moving industry, items worth $100 per pound are considered articles of extraordinary value. The following list includes items that might fall into this category:
  • antiques
  • art collections

- cameras
- china collections
- computer equipment
- crystal
- figurines
- firearms
- furs
- jewelry
- manuscripts
- oriental rugs
- silver
- stones or gems
- tapestries
- TVs or stereos

Estimate of Moving Costs

The Interstate Commerce Commission (ICC) requires strict compliance with provisions set forth in tariffs governing all costs of moving and services performed by moving companies. At the time the agent gives you the estimated cost of service (nonbinding) or a binding estimate, you acknowledge receiving a copy of the *Annual Carrier's Performance Report* (OCP-101) and the booklet, *Your Rights and Responsibilities When You Move* (OCP-100), both required by the ICC.

Unless you have been given a binding estimate where a firm cost is established in advance, the exact cost of a move cannot be determined until after the shipment has been loaded on the van and weighed. The weight on which charges are based is calculated by weighing the van before and after loading.

The total cost of the move will include transportation charges, any charges for declared valuation, plus charges for any extra services performed at your request. All of these charges are based on tariff rate schedules.

Unless other billing arrangements are made in advance, payment is required upon delivery in cash or by traveler's check, money order or cashier's check. Personal checks are not accepted. If you choose to use a major credit card, authorization must be obtained from the agent of origin prior to loading.

Carrier Liability

Basic carrier liability for loss or damage to each article in the shipment is 60 cents per pound. This basic liability level is provided at no charge.

In general, the household goods moving industry provides programs for providing higher amounts of carrier liability for an additional charge. These programs are frequently identified as "declared valuation."

Articles worth more than $100 per pound are considered articles of "extraordinary or unusual" value. To ensure that such articles are not limited to minimal liability, you need to notify your agent before packing and complete and sign a high-value inventory form.

Valuation is not insurance; it is simply a tariff-based level of motor carrier liability. If you desire the kinds of additional protection afforded by insurance coverage, check with your insurance agent or broker.

Owner's Responsibility

It is the owner's responsibility to see that all mechanical and electrical equipment and appliances are properly serviced for shipping prior to the arrival of the moving van. For safe moving, have these items prepared by a licensed or properly trained technician. This service may be performed by a technician of your choice or by qualified personnel of the moving company. If the owner has failed to have an item serviced, the van operator may load and haul it, but will mark the inventory sheet, "Not Serviced—Loaded at Owner's Risk." For more information, request a free booklet, *Moving Appliances and Other Home Furnishings,* from United Van Lines.

Six to Eight Weeks before Moving Day

Working with the Mover

❑ Have the moving company conduct a household goods survey in order to furnish you with a written estimate, although the final cost will depend on the actual weight of your household goods after they are loaded on the van.

❑ Before the agent arrives, tour your house from attic to basement. Include the garage, patio and storage shed.

❑ Decide what to move and what to discard. Remember the cost of moving an item may be greater than the cost of replacing it.

❑ Decide whether you want to do any of the packing or have it done by the moving company's experienced personnel.

❑ Show the agent everything that is to be moved. Specify articles that are to be packed so the estimate will include these charges. Any items that are later added to the shipment will add to the cost estimate.

Transfer of Personal Records

❏ Arrange for closing or transfer of charge accounts.

❏ Check personal insurance policies to see whether moving is covered. Transfer fire, theft and other personal property insurance to ensure coverage at the new home.

❏ Obtain W-2 forms from your former employer or arrange to have them forwarded.

❏ Obtain transcripts of the children's school records and credentials from school authorities or secure transcripts of school records, if you prefer to take them along.

❏ Gather medical and dental records including vaccination data, medical and lens prescriptions, dates of last examinations, history of past illnesses and so on.

❏ Ask your doctor and dentist to recommend colleagues in the new city. Be sure to check current telephone numbers and addresses of physicians, dentist and hospital, which will help when transferring your records.

❏ Obtain letters of introduction from your church, organization, club, business associates, etc.

❏ Transfer, sell or resign memberships in clubs or associations.

❏ Report your move to any lending agency with which you do business. A lender's permission may be required to move personal property in which the lender has an interest.

Four to Six Weeks before Moving Day

Planning Your Packing

❏ If you plan to do the packing yourself, start collecting suitable containers. You can purchase specialized containers from most moving companies, such as:
  - Wardrobe containers
  - Small cartons for heavy items (books, record albums, tools)
  - Medium-sized cartons for bulkier but not so heavy items (towels, linens, small appliances)
  - Large cartons for bulky items (pillows, blankets, stuffed toys)
  - Special dish and glassware containers

❏ Collect other packing materials:
  - White paper, tissue paper, paper towels or unprinted paper
  - Newspapers for outer wrapping
  - Tape or strong twine for sealing packed cartons

- Scissors or sharp knife (keep out of children's reach)
- Felt marker for labeling cartons
- Notebook and pencil for listing contents of cartons
- Labels or stickers available from your moving company

For more information, request a free booklet, *Doing Your Own Packing,* from United Van Lines.

❏ Set goals and deadlines to ensure that all packing is completed by moving day. You may want to pack one room per week. Use the Moving Planner in Appendix D.

❏ Attach a list of contents to each carton.

❏ Separate and mark goods that will go into storage.

❏ Consider having a garage sale to dispose of unwanted items. For special tips, request a free booklet, *Pre-Planning a Garage Sale,* from United Van Lines.

❏ If you donate clothing or household goods to charitable organizations, get receipts showing their approximate value for tax deductions. Remember, the cost of moving an item may be greater than replacing it.

❏ Begin to use up large supplies of canned goods and frozen foods. Buy only what will be used before moving.

Places To Notify of Impending Address Change

Utilities

- Electric
- Gas
- Water
- Telephone
- Fuel
- Trash removal

Professional Services

- Doctor
- Dentist
- Accountant
- Lawyer
- Real estate broker
- Stock broker

Insurance Agents

- Life
- Health

- Fire
- Auto
- Boat

Established Business Accounts

- Credit cards
- Finance companies
- Banks
- Department stores
- Diaper service
- Water softener service
- Dairy
- Drug store

Government and Public Offices

- Veterans Administration
- Motor Vehicle Department
- Social Security Administration
- Federal and state income tax bureaus

Publications

- Newspapers
- Magazines
- Professional and trade
- Fraternal

Credit Card Companies

- Bank cards
- Oil companies
- Store cards
- Other cards

Miscellaneous

- Relatives and friends
- Business associates
- Book and record clubs
- Schools and colleges
- Church
- Landlord, if you are a tenant
- Tenants, if you are a landlord

Two to Three Weeks before Moving Day

❑ Let the post office know your moving date and new address. If you do
not have a permanent address by the time you move, the post office
will hold your mail and forward it upon written instructions from you.
    First-class mail is forwarded free of charge for one year. Magazines
and newspapers are forwarded for 60 days and parcel post for one year
if you indicate you will pay any extra postage due.

❑ Phone the local business office of the telephone company. They can
make arrangements for service in your new home and, on request, give
out your new number when your present number is called.

❑ Contact the utility companies in the new city to establish credit so
there will be no delay in service. Some moving companies offer assis-
tance in obtaining their addresses:
  • Electric
  • Gas
  • Water
  • Fuel
  • Cable TV
If possible, arrange to have utilities connected before your arrival.

❑ Make family travel plans. Reserve air or rail transportation and hotel
accommodations as needed.

❑ Have your car prepared for the trip—tires, brakes, lubrication, oil
change, tune-up—as needed.

❑ Dispose of flammables such as fireworks, cleaning fluids, matches, acids,
pressure cans or paint thinner.

❑ Drain oil and fuel from your power mower and other machinery.
Discard partly used cans of oil, paint, syrup or any other substance that
may leak.

❑ Carefully tape-seal and place in individual waterproof bags any jars of
liquids or semiliquids you do not wish to discard.

❑ Have rugs cleaned that are to be moved. Leave them rolled and wrapped
when they are returned from the cleaners.

❑ If draperies are to be moved, have them cleaned and ready for
alterations that might be needed in your new home.

❑ Collect items that are being cleaned, stored or repaired (clothing, furs,
shoes, watches). Empty your locker at the club, bowling alley and so on.

❑ Return library books and anything borrowed from friends or neighbors.
Also collect things you may have loaned.

❑ Decide what to do with your house plants. Request a free booklet,
Moving with House Plants, from United Van Lines.

❏ Set a date with a reliable service person to prepare your appliances for shipment, preferably the day before the move. Depending on the appliance, pre- as well as postservice may be needed for refrigerator, freezer, range, washer, dryer, grandfather clock, CD changers and others. For more information, request a free booklet, *Moving Appliances and other Furnishings,* from United Van Lines.

❏ Pianos and organs need to be prepared for moving by a specialized technician.

❏ Make arrangements to have utilities disconnected on moving day:
  • Electric
  • Gas
  • Water
  • Fuel
  • Cable TV
  Plan to keep your telephone in service through moving day in case last minute calls are necessary.

❏ Take pets to the veterinarian. Most states require health certificates and rabies inoculations. Make sure identification and rabies tags are securely attached to the pet's collar.

❏ Arrange for transportation of pets if going by air. For more information, request a free booklet, *Moving with Pets,* from United Van Lines.

Three Days before Moving Day

Instant Aid Box

Pack a box for instant needs on arrival. Mark the box "To Be Loaded Last and Unloaded First." Package each group of items separately in labeled paper bags. Here are some suggestions.

Cleaning

  • Powdered detergent
  • Sponge
  • Paper towels
  • Dish towels
  • Dish cloth
  • Kitchen cleanser
  • Window cleaner
  • Scouring pads

Kitchen

- Paper plates, cups, napkins
- Plastic knives, forks, spoons
- Small saucepan
- Serving spoons
- Aluminum foil

Snacks

- Easy-to-open cans of pudding
- Dry soup mix
- Sandwich spreads
- Jars of cheese
- Package of crackers
- Boxes of dry cereals
- Instant coffee, tea, chocolate
- Instant creamer, sugar, salt

Bathroom

- Towels and face cloths
- Toilet tissue
- Facial tissue
- Soap, hand lotion, deodorant
- Toothbrushes and toothpaste

Miscellaneous

- Cellular telephone
- Light bulbs
- Flashlight
- Hammer, screwdriver, pliers, assorted nails and screws
- Shelf paper
- Trash bags and ties

Children

- Coloring books and crayons
- A favorite toy or two
- Reading materials
- Puzzles

Last-Minute Packing

❏ Complete the "Take-with-Me Inventory" checklist in Appendix D.

❏ Check contents of drawers. Remove all spillables or breakables. Soft goods such as blankets, pillows, blouses, shirts and lingerie may be left in drawers.

❏ Pin clothing to hangers if it is to be moved in wardrobe cartons to keep it from slipping off.

❏ Remove items left in the attic or other storage areas.

❏ Empty the refrigerator and freezer so they can dry at least 24 hours before moving. Be careful not to overlook the defrost water pan. Failure to have the appliances completely dry can lead to mildew and unpleasant odor. For more information, request a free booklet, *Moving Appliances and Other Home Furnishings,* from United Van Lines.

❏ Be sure the water is emptied from your steam iron.

❏ Launder all soiled clothing prior to the day the appliance service technician is expected.

❏ Take the telephone directory with you for contacting former doctors, dentists, suppliers, etc., and for preparing holiday card lists.

❏ Pack suitcases for the trip to the new home. Put in extra clothing for emergencies.

❏ Consider packing a picnic lunch to eat while traveling. Take along snacks such as fruit and cookies for the children. Include towelettes for a quick cleanup.

❏ Arrange for a babysitter for moving day, or have older children look after the younger ones.

The Day before Moving Day

Packing

❏ If you are doing your own packing, it must be completed the day prior to loading.

❏ When household goods are professionally packed, the packing usually is done the day before the actual move. Plan to be at home during the packing process to answer questions.

❏ Be on hand when the service person arrives to prepare appliances for shipment.

❏ Point out to the packers any extra fragile items.

❏ Place a big "Do Not Load" label on any item you do not want packed.

❏ Place a "Load Last" label on cartons needed first when you arrive.

❏ In the event items of extraordinary value are to be included in the shipment, remind packers to leave open cartons containing high-value items for the van operator's inspection. Be sure you have filled in and signed the High-Value Inventory form for the packers.

❏ Take valuables with you, including stamp collections or other items of extraordinary value. Check with your local bank or post office for alternate methods of transporting valuables. Check to see if your homeowner's insurance covers valuable items after.you leave your old address.

❏ Unplug all television sets 24 hours prior to moving to prevent internal damage to sets.

❏ Be sure water is emptied from your steam iron.

❏ Collect things to be packed together.

❏ Have dishes washed and dried and leave them in normal storage cabinets for packers to remove.

❏ Leave pictures and mirrors on walls.

❏ Remove items permanently attached, such as drapery rods, towel bars, chandeliers, can openers and the like.

❏ Leave beds assembled, but disassemble water beds according to manufacturer's instructions.

❏ When the movers finish packing, be sure to sign the Certificate of Packing, verifying the number of containers they packed.

❏ Inform the police department of your move.

Moving Day

❏ Be on hand when the movers arrive. Otherwise, it is important to let the agent know to whom you have given authority to take your place. Be sure this person knows exactly what to do. Remember the person may be asked to sign documents obligating you to charges.

❏ Accompany the van operator through the house inspecting and tagging each piece of furniture with an identifying number. These numbers, along with a description of your goods and their condition at the time of loading, will appear on the inventory.

❏ Be sure the condition of each item is recorded and the van operator has a clear understanding about what is to be loaded last.

❏ It is your responsibility to see that all of your goods are loaded, so remain on the premises until loading is completed. After making a final tour of the house to be sure no items have been overlooked, check and sign the inventory. Get your copy and keep it in a safe place.

❑ Approve and sign the combination Bill of Lading and Freight Bill. It states the terms and conditions under which your goods are moved and is also your receipt for the shipment. You will need to sign and date the Extraordinary (Unusual) Value Article Declaration box on the Bill of Lading, if applicable to your shipment.

❑ Check to see the van operator has the exact destination address. Be specific as to where and how you can be reached pending the arrival of your household goods.

❑ Leave the phone connected throughout the moving day. After the van leaves and you finish last-minute calls, pack your phone in one of your suitcases.

❑ Leave a note listing your new address in a conspicuous place in the house so the new occupants will be able to forward any of your mail inadvertently delivered to them.

❑ *Take a last look around:*
- Water shut off?
- Furnace shut off?
- Air-conditioning shut off?
- Light switches turned off?
- All utilities arranged for disconnection?
- Windows shut and locked?
- Have you left anything?

❑ Lock the house and leave the keys with a responsible person or in a prearranged location.

At Destination

❑ Contact the destination agent whose name appears on the Bill of Lading as soon as possible and indicate where and how you can be reached.

❑ Make sure the house is ready for occupancy before the van arrives.

❑ If you have not already done so, contact the utility companies and make necessary arrangements for service. Ask if any of them provides free appliance connection service.

❑ Make arrangements for reinstallation of appliances.

❑ Be on hand to accept delivery of your household goods. Otherwise authorize an adult as your representative to accept delivery and pay the charges for you. Inform the agent of the person so authorized.

❏ The van operator will contact you or the destination agent 24 hours prior to expected arrival time. On the day of delivery, the van operator will attempt to contact you by phone and make an appearance at the residence if unable to reach you. If no one appears to accept the shipment within the free waiting time, the goods will be placed in storage at the owner's expense. One hour of free time is allowed at destination if the shipment is traveling less than 200 miles; two hours of free time are allowed if the shipment is traveling 200 miles or more. (No free waiting time is allowed at origin.)

❏ The van operator is obligated by law to receive payment *before* unloading the goods. Payment is required in cash, traveler's check, money order or cashier's check, unless other billing arrangements have been made in advance. Personal checks are not accepted. Payment by major credit card must be authorized with the agent of origin prior to loading.

❏ Check your household goods as they are unloaded. If there is a change in the condition of the property from that noted on the inventory at the time of loading or if any items are missing, note any damage and/or missing items on the van operator's copy of the inventory sheet. *By signing the inventory sheet, you are acknowledging receipt of all items listed.*

❏ Personally report any loss or damage to the moving company agent at destination immediately.

❏ You must file the claim yourself; the van operator cannot do it for you. Claims must be received by the moving company agent within nine months from date of delivery.

❏ To save time and confusion, place a floor plan of your new home at the entrance the movers will use, indicating where each piece of furniture should go.

❏ When unloading, each piece of furniture will be placed as you direct, including the laying of rugs and setting up of bed frames, box springs and mattresses. However, appliances and fixtures will not be installed. At your request and additional cost, the agent may arrange for this service and for refilling of water bed mattresses.

❏ To prevent possible damage, television sets, other electronic equipment and certain major appliances should not be used for 24 hours after delivery, allowing them time to adjust to room temperature.

❏ If you have paid for unpacking, you are entitled to unpacking service and removal of the cartons. If you decide to unpack at your convenience after having ordered unpacking service, remember to annotate the Bill of Lading accordingly.

Getting Settled

❏ If you have not already done so, contact the utility companies and make necessary arrangements for service. Ask if any of them provides free appliance connection service.

❏ Make arrangements for reinstallation of appliances.

❏ Keep all documents pertaining to your move in a safe place. You will need them for verification of moving expenses and for filing your income tax returns. For more information on tax-deductible moving expenses, see Chapter 10.

❏ Check with the post office for any mail being held and ask for delivery to start.

❏ Check state and local requirements for auto registration and operator's license.

❏ Have your medical and dental records transferred after selecting a family physician and dentist.

❏ You may want to select an attorney and discuss laws pertaining to your destination state, county and/or city. Be sure to cover such matters as wills, transfers of property and investments, insurance regulations, inheritance laws, taxes and the like. Most laws affect a family as soon as residence in the new state and city is established.

❏ Register to vote.

❏ Locate the selected schools. Take the children, introduce yourself and register them.

Consumer Materials

The following booklets can be obtained free of charge from United Van Lines.

- *Moving Appliances and Other Home Furnishings*
- *Doing Your Own Packing*
- *Pre-Planning a Garage Sale*
- *Moving with Pets*
- *Moving with House Plants*

Facts about the city to which you are moving are available as well. Contact your local United Van Lines agent or phone or write:

United Van Lines, Inc.
One United Drive
Fenton, MO 63026
314-326-3100

Appendix A

Real Estate Computations and Conversions

Monthly Payment To Amortize a Loan of $1,000

Factors to Compute Monthly Interest

Monthly Payment To Amortize a Loan of $1,000

The following table shows monthly payments for loans of $1,000. To find the payment for a loan of any amount, multiply the number found in the table by the loan amount and divide by 1,000.

Example: What is the monthly payment necessary to amortize a $90,000 loan at 8½ percent interest per year over a 30-year term?

Answer: On the page containing terms of 30 years and 8.500% interest, locate the point of intersection of the 30-year column and the line for 8.500 percent interest. The number at that point of intersection is 7.6891, which is the monthly payment for a $1,000 loan at 8½ percent for 30 years. To find the monthly payment for a $90,000 loan at 8½ percent: 7.6891 × 90 = $692.02.

MONTHLY PAYMENT TO AMORTIZE A LOAN OF $1,000

Term of Loan

Interest Rate	1 Year	2 Years	3 Years	4 Years	5 Years	6 Years	7 Years	8 Years
6.000%	86.0664	44.3206	30.4219	23.4850	19.3328	16.5729	14.6086	13.1414
6.125%	86.1239	44.3770	30.4786	23.5424	19.3910	16.6320	14.6686	13.2024
6.250%	86.1814	44.4333	30.5353	23.5998	19.4493	16.6912	14.7287	13.2635
6.375%	86.2389	44.4898	30.5921	23.6573	19.5077	16.7505	14.7890	13.3248
6.500%	86.2964	44.5463	30.6490	23.7150	19.5661	16.8099	14.8494	13.3862
6.625%	86.3540	44.6028	30.7059	23.7726	19.6248	16.8695	14.9100	13.4479
6.750%	86.4115	44.6593	30.7629	23.8304	19.6835	16.9292	14.9708	13.5096
6.875%	86.4691	44.7159	30.8200	23.8883	19.7423	16.9890	15.0316	13.5716
7.000%	86.5267	44.7726	30.8771	23.9462	19.8012	17.0490	15.0927	13.6337
7.125%	86.5844	44.8293	30.9343	24.0043	19.8602	17.1091	15.1539	13.6960
7.250%	86.6420	44.8860	30.9915	24.0624	19.9194	17.1693	15.2152	13.7585
7.375%	86.6997	44.9428	31.0488	24.1206	19.9786	17.2296	15.2767	13.8211
7.500%	86.7574	44.9996	31.1062	24.1789	20.0379	17.2901	15.3383	13.8839
7.625%	86.8151	45.0565	31.1637	24.2373	20.0974	17.3507	15.4000	13.9468
7.750%	86.8729	45.1134	31.2212	24.2957	20.1570	17.4114	15.4620	14.0099
7.875%	86.9306	45.1703	31.2787	24.3543	20.2166	17.4723	15.5240	14.0732
8.000%	86.9884	45.2273	31.3364	24.4129	20.2764	17.5332	15.5862	14.1367
8.125%	87.0462	45.2843	31.3941	24.4716	20.3363	17.5943	15.6486	14.2003
8.250%	87.1041	45.3414	31.4518	24.5304	20.3963	17.6556	15.7111	14.2641
8.375%	87.1619	45.3985	31.5096	24.5893	20.4563	17.7169	15.7737	14.3280
8.500%	87.2198	45.4557	31.5675	24.6483	20.5165	17.7784	15.8365	14.3921
8.625%	87.2777	45.5129	31.6255	24.7074	20.5768	17.8400	15.8994	14.4564
8.750%	87.3356	45.5701	31.6835	24.7665	20.6372	17.9017	15.9625	14.5208
8.875%	87.3935	45.6274	31.7416	24.8257	20.6977	17.9636	16.0257	14.5854
9.000%	87.4515	45.6847	31.7997	24.8850	20.7584	18.0255	16.0891	14.6502
9.125%	87.5095	45.7421	31.8579	24.9444	20.8191	18.0876	16.1526	14.7151
9.250%	87.5675	45.7995	31.9162	25.0039	20.8799	18.1499	16.2162	14.7802
9.375%	87.6255	45.8570	31.9745	25.0635	20.9408	18.2122	16.2800	14.8455
9.500%	87.6835	45.9145	32.0329	25.1231	21.0019	18.2747	16.3440	14.9109
9.625%	87.7416	45.9720	32.0914	25.1829	21.0630	18.3373	16.4081	14.9765
9.750%	87.7997	46.0296	32.1499	25.2427	21.1242	18.4000	16.4723	15.0422
9.875%	87.8578	46.0873	32.2085	25.3026	21.1856	18.4629	16.5367	15.1081
10.000%	87.9159	46.1449	32.2672	25.3626	21.2470	18.5258	16.6012	15.1742
10.125%	87.9740	46.2026	32.3259	25.4227	21.3086	18.5889	16.6658	15.2404
10.250%	88.0322	46.2604	32.3847	25.4828	21.3703	18.6522	16.7306	15.3068
10.375%	88.0904	46.3182	32.4435	25.5431	21.4320	18.7155	16.7956	15.3733
10.500%	88.1486	46.3760	32.5024	25.6034	21.4939	18.7790	16.8607	15.4400
10.625%	88.2068	46.4339	32.5614	25.6638	21.5559	18.8426	16.9259	15.5069
10.750%	88.2651	46.4919	32.6205	25.7243	21.6180	18.9063	16.9913	15.5739
10.875%	88.3234	46.5498	32.6796	25.7849	21.6801	18.9701	17.0568	15.6411

MONTHLY PAYMENT TO AMORTIZE A LOAN OF $1,000

Term of Loan

Interest Rate	9 Years	10 Years	11 Years	12 Years	13 Years	14 Years	15 Years	16 Years
6.000%	12.0057	11.1021	10.3670	9.7585	9.2472	8.8124	8.4386	8.1144
6.125%	12.0677	11.1649	10.4309	9.8233	9.3130	8.8791	8.5062	8.1830
6.250%	12.1298	11.2280	10.4949	9.8884	9.3790	8.9461	8.5742	8.2519
6.375%	12.1920	11.2913	10.5592	9.9537	9.4453	9.0134	8.6425	8.3212
6.500%	12.2545	11.3548	10.6238	10.0192	9.5119	9.0810	8.7111	8.3908
6.625%	12.3172	11.4185	10.6885	10.0850	9.5787	9.1488	8.7799	8.4606
6.750%	12.3800	11.4824	10.7535	10.1510	9.6458	9.2169	8.8491	8.5308
6.875%	12.4431	11.5465	10.8187	10.2173	9.7131	9.2853	8.9185	8.6013
7.000%	12.5063	11.6108	10.8841	10.2838	9.7807	9.3540	8.9883	8.6721
7.125%	12.5697	11.6754	10.9497	10.3506	9.8486	9.4230	9.0583	8.7432
7.250%	12.6333	11.7401	11.0156	10.4176	9.9167	9.4922	9.1286	8.8146
7.375%	12.6971	11.8050	11.0817	10.4848	9.9851	9.5617	9.1992	8.8863
7.500%	12.7610	11.8702	11.1480	10.5523	10.0537	9.6314	9.2701	8.9583
7.625%	12.8252	11.9355	11.2145	10.6200	10.1226	9.7015	9.3413	9.0306
7.750%	12.8895	12.0011	11.2813	10.6879	10.1917	9.7718	9.4128	9.1032
7.875%	12.9540	12.0668	11.3483	10.7561	10.2611	9.8423	9.4845	9.1761
8.000%	13.0187	12.1328	11.4154	10.8245	10.3307	9.9132	9.5565	9.2493
8.125%	13.0836	12.1989	11.4829	10.8932	10.4006	9.9843	9.6288	9.3227
8.250%	13.1487	12.2653	11.5505	10.9621	10.4708	10.0557	9.7014	9.3965
8.375%	13.2139	12.3318	11.6183	11.0312	10.5412	10.1273	9.7743	9.4706
8.500%	13.2794	12.3986	11.6864	11.1006	10.6118	10.1992	9.8474	9.5449
8.625%	13.3450	12.4655	11.7547	11.1701	10.6827	10.2713	9.9208	9.6195
8.750%	13.4108	12.5327	11.8232	11.2400	10.7538	10.3438	9.9945	9.6945
8.875%	13.4767	12.6000	11.8919	11.3100	10.8252	10.4164	10.0684	9.7697
9.000%	13.5429	12.6676	11.9608	11.3803	10.8968	10.4894	10.1427	9.8452
9.125%	13.6093	12.7353	12.0299	11.4508	10.9687	10.5626	10.2172	9.9209
9.250%	13.6758	12.8033	12.0993	11.5216	11.0408	10.6360	10.2919	9.9970
9.375%	13.7425	12.8714	12.1689	11.5925	11.1131	10.7097	10.3670	10.0733
9.500%	13.8094	12.9398	12.2386	11.6637	11.1857	10.7837	10.4422	10.1499
9.625%	13.8764	13.0083	12.3086	11.7352	11.2586	10.8579	10.5178	10.2268
9.750%	13.9437	13.0770	12.3788	11.8068	11.3316	10.9324	10.5936	10.3039
9.875%	14.0111	13.1460	12.4493	11.8787	11.4049	11.0071	10.6697	10.3813
10.000%	14.0787	13.2151	12.5199	11.9508	11.4785	11.0820	10.7461	10.4590
10.125%	14.1465	13.2844	12.5907	12.0231	11.5523	11.1572	10.8227	10.5370
10.250%	14.2144	13.3539	12.6618	12.0957	11.6263	11.2327	10.8995	10.6152
10.375%	14.2826	13.4236	12.7330	12.1684	11.7005	11.3084	10.9766	10.6937
10.500%	14.3509	13.4935	12.8045	12.2414	11.7750	11.3843	11.0540	10.7724
10.625%	14.4193	13.5636	12.8761	12.3146	11.8497	11.4605	11.1316	10.8514
10.750%	14.4880	13.6339	12.9480	12.3880	11.9247	11.5370	11.2095	10.9307
10.875%	14.5568	13.7043	13.0201	12.4617	11.9999	11.6136	11.2876	11.0102

MONTHLY PAYMENT TO AMORTIZE A LOAN OF $1,000

Term of Loan

Interest Rate	17 Years	18 Years	19 Years	20 Years	21 Years	22 Years	23 Years	24 Years
6.000%	7.8310	7.5816	7.3608	7.1643	6.9886	6.8307	6.6885	6.5598
6.125%	7.9006	7.6521	7.4322	7.2366	7.0618	6.9048	6.7634	6.6356
6.250%	7.9705	7.7229	7.5040	7.3093	7.1353	6.9793	6.8387	6.7118
6.375%	8.0407	7.7941	7.5761	7.3823	7.2093	7.0541	6.9145	6.7884
6.500%	8.1112	7.8656	7.6486	7.4557	7.2836	7.1294	6.9906	6.8654
6.625%	8.1821	7.9375	7.7214	7.5295	7.3583	7.2050	7.0672	6.9429
6.750%	8.2533	8.0096	7.7945	7.6036	7.4334	7.2811	7.1441	7.0207
6.875%	8.3248	8.0822	7.8681	7.6781	7.5089	7.3575	7.2215	7.0990
7.000%	8.3966	8.1550	7.9419	7.7530	7.5847	7.4342	7.2992	7.1776
7.125%	8.4688	8.2282	8.0161	7.8282	7.6609	7.5114	7.3773	7.2566
7.250%	8.5412	8.3017	8.0907	7.9038	7.7375	7.5889	7.4558	7.3361
7.375%	8.6140	8.3756	8.1656	7.9797	7.8144	7.6668	7.5347	7.4159
7.500%	8.6871	8.4497	8.2408	8.0559	7.8917	7.7451	7.6139	7.4960
7.625%	8.7605	8.5242	8.3163	8.1325	7.9693	7.8237	7.6935	7.5766
7.750%	8.8342	8.5990	8.3922	8.2095	8.0473	7.9027	7.7735	7.6576
7.875%	8.9082	8.6742	8.4685	8.2868	8.1256	7.9821	7.8538	7.7389
8.000%	8.9826	8.7496	8.5450	8.3644	8.2043	8.0618	7.9345	7.8205
8.125%	9.0572	8.8254	8.6219	8.4424	8.2833	8.1418	8.0156	7.9026
8.250%	9.1321	8.9015	8.6991	8.5207	8.3627	8.2222	8.0970	7.9850
8.375%	9.2074	8.9779	8.7766	8.5993	8.4424	8.3030	8.1788	8.0677
8.500%	9.2829	9.0546	8.8545	8.6782	8.5224	8.3841	8.2609	8.1508
8.625%	9.3588	9.1316	8.9326	8.7575	8.6028	8.4655	8.3433	8.2343
8.750%	9.4349	9.2089	9.0111	8.8371	8.6834	8.5472	8.4261	8.3181
8.875%	9.5113	9.2865	9.0899	8.9170	8.7645	8.6293	8.5092	8.4022
9.000%	9.5880	9.3644	9.1690	8.9973	8.8458	8.7117	8.5927	8.4866
9.125%	9.6650	9.4427	9.2484	9.0778	8.9275	8.7945	8.6765	8.5714
9.250%	9.7423	9.5212	9.3281	9.1587	9.0094	8.8775	8.7606	8.6566
9.375%	9.8199	9.6000	9.4081	9.2398	9.0917	8.9609	8.8450	8.7420
9.500%	9.8978	9.6791	9.4884	9.3213	9.1743	9.0446	8.9297	8.8277
9.625%	9.9760	9.7585	9.5690	9.4031	9.2573	9.1286	9.0148	8.9138
9.750%	10.0544	9.8382	9.6499	9.4852	9.3405	9.2129	9.1002	9.0002
9.875%	10.1331	9.9182	9.7311	9.5675	9.4240	9.2975	9.1858	9.0869
10.000%	10.2121	9.9984	9.8126	9.6502	9.5078	9.3825	9.2718	9.1739
10.125%	10.2914	10.0790	9.8944	9.7332	9.5919	9.4677	9.3581	9.2612
10.250%	10.3709	10.1598	9.9764	9.8164	9.6763	9.5532	9.4447	9.3488
10.375%	10.4507	10.2409	10.0588	9.9000	9.7610	9.6390	9.5315	9.4366
10.500%	10.5308	10.3223	10.1414	9.9838	9.8460	9.7251	9.6187	9.5248
10.625%	10.6112	10.4039	10.2243	10.0679	9.9312	9.8114	9.7061	9.6133
10.750%	10.6918	10.4858	10.3075	10.1523	10.0168	9.8981	9.7938	9.7020
10.875%	10.7727	10.5680	10.3909	10.2370	10.1026	9.9850	9.8818	9.7910

MONTHLY PAYMENT TO AMORTIZE A LOAN OF $1,000

Term of Loan

Interest Rate	25 Years	26 Years	27 Years	28 Years	29 Years	30 Years	35 Years	40 Years
6.000%	6.4430	6.3368	6.2399	6.1512	6.0700	5.9955	5.7019	5.5021
6.125%	6.5196	6.4142	6.3181	6.2303	6.1499	6.0761	5.7861	5.5895
6.250%	6.5967	6.4921	6.3968	6.3098	6.2302	6.1572	5.8708	5.6774
6.375%	6.6742	6.5704	6.4760	6.3898	6.3109	6.2387	5.9559	5.7657
6.500%	6.7521	6.6492	6.5555	6.4702	6.3921	6.3207	6.0415	5.8546
6.625%	6.8304	6.7284	6.6356	6.5510	6.4738	6.4031	6.1276	5.9438
6.750%	6.9091	6.8079	6.7160	6.6323	6.5558	6.4860	6.2142	6.0336
6.875%	6.9883	6.8880	6.7969	6.7140	6.6384	6.5693	6.3011	6.1237
7.000%	7.0678	6.9684	6.8781	6.7961	6.7213	6.6530	6.3886	6.2143
7.125%	7.1477	7.0492	6.9598	6.8786	6.8047	6.7372	6.4764	6.3053
7.250%	7.2281	7.1304	7.0419	6.9616	6.8884	6.8218	6.5647	6.3967
7.375%	7.3088	7.2121	7.1244	7.0449	6.9726	6.9068	6.6533	6.4885
7.500%	7.3899	7.2941	7.2073	7.1287	7.0572	6.9921	6.7424	6.5807
7.625%	7.4714	7.3765	7.2906	7.2128	7.1422	7.0779	6.8319	6.6733
7.750%	7.5533	7.4593	7.3743	7.2974	7.2276	7.1641	6.9218	6.7662
7.875%	7.6355	7.5424	7.4584	7.3823	7.3133	7.2507	7.0120	6.8595
8.000%	7.7182	7.6260	7.5428	7.4676	7.3995	7.3376	7.1026	6.9531
8.125%	7.8012	7.7099	7.6276	7.5533	7.4860	7.4250	7.1936	7.0471
8.250%	7.8845	7.7942	7.7128	7.6393	7.5729	7.5127	7.2849	7.1414
8.375%	7.9682	7.8788	7.7983	7.7257	7.6601	7.6007	7.3766	7.2360
8.500%	8.0523	7.9638	7.8842	7.8125	7.7477	7.6891	7.4686	7.3309
8.625%	8.1367	8.0491	7.9705	7.8996	7.8357	7.7779	7.5610	7.4262
8.750%	8.2214	8.1348	8.0570	7.9871	7.9240	7.8670	7.6536	7.5217
8.875%	8.3065	8.2209	8.1440	8.0749	8.0126	7.9564	7.7466	7.6175
9.000%	8.3920	8.3072	8.2313	8.1630	8.1016	8.0462	7.8399	7.7136
9.125%	8.4777	8.3939	8.3189	8.2515	8.1909	8.1363	7.9335	7.8100
9.250%	8.5638	8.4810	8.4068	8.3403	8.2805	8.2268	8.0274	7.9066
9.375%	8.6502	8.5683	8.4950	8.4294	8.3705	8.3175	8.1216	8.0035
9.500%	8.7370	8.6560	8.5836	8.5188	8.4607	8.4085	8.2161	8.1006
9.625%	8.8240	8.7440	8.6725	8.6086	8.5513	8.4999	8.3109	8.1980
9.750%	8.9114	8.8323	8.7617	8.6986	8.6421	8.5915	8.4059	8.2956
9.875%	8.9990	8.9209	8.8512	8.7890	8.7333	8.6835	8.5012	8.3934
10.000%	9.0870	9.0098	8.9410	8.8796	8.8248	8.7757	8.5967	8.4915
10.125%	9.1753	9.0990	9.0311	8.9705	8.9165	8.8682	8.6925	8.5897
10.250%	9.2638	9.1885	9.1214	9.0618	9.0085	8.9610	8.7886	8.6882
10.375%	9.3527	9.2782	9.2121	9.1533	9.1008	9.0541	8.8848	8.7868
10.500%	9.4418	9.3683	9.3030	9.2450	9.1934	9.1474	8.9813	8.8857
10.625%	9.5312	9.4586	9.3943	9.3371	9.2862	9.2410	9.0781	8.9847
10.750%	9.6209	9.5492	9.4857	9.4294	9.3793	9.3348	9.1750	9.0840
10.875%	9.7109	9.6401	9.5775	9.5220	9.4727	9.4289	9.2722	9.1834

MONTHLY PAYMENT TO AMORTIZE A LOAN OF $1,000

Term of Loan

Interest Rate	1 Year	2 Years	3 Years	4 Years	5 Years	6 Years	7 Years	8 Years
11.000%	88.3817	46.6078	32.7387	25.8455	21.7424	19.0341	17.1224	15.7084
11.125%	88.4400	46.6659	32.7979	25.9063	21.8048	19.0982	17.1882	15.7759
11.250%	88.4983	46.7240	32.8572	25.9671	21.8673	19.1624	17.2542	15.8436
11.375%	88.5567	46.7821	32.9166	26.0280	21.9299	19.2267	17.3202	15.9114
11.500%	88.6151	46.8403	32.9760	26.0890	21.9926	19.2912	17.3865	15.9794
11.625%	88.6735	46.8985	33.0355	26.1501	22.0554	19.3557	17.4528	16.0475
11.750%	88.7319	46.9568	33.0950	26.2113	22.1183	19.4204	17.5193	16.1158
11.875%	88.7903	47.0151	33.1546	26.2725	22.1813	19.4853	17.5860	16.1842
12.000%	88.8488	47.0735	33.2143	26.3338	22.2444	19.5502	17.6527	16.2528
12.125%	88.9073	47.1319	33.2740	26.3953	22.3077	19.6153	17.7197	16.3216
12.250%	88.9658	47.1903	33.3338	26.4568	22.3710	19.6804	17.7867	16.3905
12.375%	89.0243	47.2488	33.3937	26.5183	22.4344	19.7457	17.8539	16.4596
12.500%	89.0829	47.3073	33.4536	26.5800	22.4979	19.8112	17.9212	16.5288
12.625%	89.1414	47.3659	33.5136	26.6417	22.5616	19.8767	17.9887	16.5982
12.750%	89.2000	47.4245	33.5737	26.7036	22.6253	19.9424	18.0563	16.6677
12.875%	89.2586	47.4831	33.6338	26.7655	22.6891	20.0082	18.1241	16.7374
13.000%	89.3173	47.5418	33.6940	26.8275	22.7531	20.0741	18.1920	16.8073
13.125%	89.3759	47.6006	33.7542	26.8896	22.8171	20.1401	18.2600	16.8773
13.250%	89.4346	47.6593	33.8145	26.9517	22.8813	20.2063	18.3282	16.9474
13.375%	89.4933	47.7182	33.8749	27.0140	22.9455	20.2726	18.3965	17.0177
13.500%	89.5520	47.7770	33.9353	27.0763	23.0098	20.3390	18.4649	17.0882
13.625%	89.6108	47.8359	33.9958	27.1387	23.0743	20.4055	18.5335	17.1588
13.750%	89.6695	47.8949	34.0563	27.2012	23.1388	20.4721	18.6022	17.2295
13.875%	89.7283	47.9539	34.1169	27.2638	23.2035	20.5389	18.6710	17.3004
14.000%	89.7871	48.0129	34.1776	27.3265	23.2683	20.6057	18.7400	17.3715
14.125%	89.8459	48.0720	34.2384	27.3892	23.3331	20.6727	18.8091	17.4427
14.250%	89.9048	48.1311	34.2992	27.4520	23.3981	20.7398	18.8784	17.5141
14.375%	89.9637	48.1902	34.3600	27.5150	23.4631	20.8071	18.9478	17.5856
14.500%	90.0225	48.2494	34.4210	27.5780	23.5283	20.8744	19.0173	17.6573
14.625%	90.0815	48.3087	34.4820	27.6410	23.5935	20.9419	19.0870	17.7291
14.750%	90.1404	48.3680	34.5430	27.7042	23.6589	21.0095	19.1568	17.8010
14.875%	90.1993	48.4273	34.6041	27.7674	23.7244	21.0772	19.2267	17.8731
15.000%	90.2583	48.4866	34.6653	27.8307	23.7899	21.1450	19.2968	17.9454
15.125%	90.3173	48.5461	34.7266	27.8942	23.8556	21.2130	19.3670	18.0178
15.250%	90.3763	48.6055	34.7879	27.9576	23.9214	21.2810	19.4373	18.0904
15.375%	90.4354	48.6650	34.8492	28.0212	23.9872	21.3492	19.5077	18.1631
15.500%	90.4944	48.7245	34.9107	28.0849	24.0532	21.4175	19.5783	18.2359
15.625%	90.5535	48.7841	34.9722	28.1486	24.1193	21.4859	19.6491	18.3089
15.750%	90.6126	48.8437	35.0337	28.2124	24.1854	21.5544	19.7199	18.3821
15.875%	90.6717	48.9034	35.0954	28.2763	24.2517	21.6231	19.7909	18.4554

MONTHLY PAYMENT TO AMORTIZE A LOAN OF $1,000

Term of Loan

Interest Rate	9 Years	10 Years	11 Years	12 Years	13 Years	14 Years	15 Years	16 Years
11.000%	14.6259	13.7750	13.0923	12.5356	12.0753	11.6905	11.3660	11.0900
11.125%	14.6950	13.8459	13.1648	12.6096	12.1509	11.7677	11.4446	11.1700
11.250%	14.7644	13.9169	13.2375	12.6839	12.2268	11.8451	11.5234	11.2503
11.375%	14.8339	13.9881	13.3104	12.7584	12.3029	11.9227	11.6026	11.3309
11.500%	14.9037	14.0595	13.3835	12.8332	12.3792	12.0006	11.6819	11.4116
11.625%	14.9735	14.1312	13.4568	12.9081	12.4557	12.0786	11.7615	11.4927
11.750%	15.0436	14.2029	13.5303	12.9833	12.5325	12.1570	11.8413	11.5740
11.875%	15.1138	14.2749	13.6040	13.0586	12.6095	12.2355	11.9214	11.6555
12.000%	15.1842	14.3471	13.6779	13.1342	12.6867	12.3143	12.0017	11.7373
12.125%	15.2548	14.4194	13.7520	13.2100	12.7641	12.3933	12.0822	11.8193
12.250%	15.3256	14.4920	13.8263	13.2860	12.8417	12.4725	12.1630	11.9015
12.375%	15.3965	14.5647	13.9007	13.3622	12.9196	12.5520	12.2440	11.9840
12.500%	15.4676	14.6376	13.9754	13.4386	12.9977	12.6317	12.3252	12.0667
12.625%	15.5388	14.7107	14.0503	13.5152	13.0760	12.7116	12.4067	12.1496
12.750%	15.6102	14.7840	14.1254	13.5920	13.1545	12.7917	12.4884	12.2328
12.875%	15.6818	14.8574	14.2006	13.6690	13.2332	12.8721	12.5703	12.3162
13.000%	15.7536	14.9311	14.2761	13.7463	13.3121	12.9526	12.6524	12.3999
13.125%	15.8255	15.0049	14.3518	13.8237	13.3912	13.0334	12.7348	12.4837
13.250%	15.8976	15.0789	14.4276	13.9013	13.4706	13.1144	12.8174	12.5678
13.375%	15.9699	15.1531	14.5036	13.9791	13.5502	13.1956	12.9002	12.6521
13.500%	16.0423	15.2274	14.5799	14.0572	13.6299	13.2771	12.9832	12.7367
13.625%	16.1149	15.3020	14.6563	14.1354	13.7099	13.3587	13.0664	12.8214
13.750%	16.1877	15.3767	14.7329	14.2138	13.7901	13.4406	13.1499	12.9064
13.875%	16.2606	15.4516	14.8097	14.2925	13.8704	13.5226	13.2335	12.9916
14.000%	16.3337	15.5266	14.8867	14.3713	13.9510	13.6049	13.3174	13.0770
14.125%	16.4070	15.6019	14.9638	14.4503	14.0318	13.6874	13.4015	13.1626
14.250%	16.4804	15.6773	15.0412	14.5295	14.1128	13.7701	13.4858	13.2484
14.375%	16.5540	15.7529	15.1187	14.6089	14.1940	13.8529	13.5703	13.3345
14.500%	16.6277	15.8287	15.1964	14.6885	14.2754	13.9360	13.6550	13.4207
14.625%	16.7016	15.9046	15.2743	14.7683	14.3570	14.0193	13.7399	13.5071
14.750%	16.7757	15.9807	15.3524	14.8483	14.4387	14.1028	13.8250	13.5938
14.875%	16.8499	16.0570	15.4307	14.9284	14.5207	14.1865	13.9104	13.6806
15.000%	16.9243	16.1335	15.5091	15.0088	14.6029	14.2704	13.9959	13.7677
15.125%	16.9989	16.2101	15.5878	15.0893	14.6852	14.3545	14.0816	13.8549
15.250%	17.0736	16.2869	15.6666	15.1700	14.7678	14.4388	14.1675	13.9424
15.375%	17.1485	16.3639	15.7456	15.2509	14.8505	14.5232	14.2536	14.0300
15.500%	17.2235	16.4411	15.8247	15.3320	14.9335	14.6079	14.3399	14.1179
15.625%	17.2987	16.5184	15.9041	15.4133	15.0166	14.6928	14.4264	14.2059
15.750%	17.3741	16.5958	15.9836	15.4948	15.0999	14.7778	14.5131	14.2941
15.875%	17.4496	16.6735	16.0633	15.5764	15.1834	14.8630	14.5999	14.3825

MONTHLY PAYMENT TO AMORTIZE A LOAN OF $1,000

Term of Loan

Interest Rate	17 Years	18 Years	19 Years	20 Years	21 Years	22 Years	23 Years	24 Years
11.000%	10.8538	10.6505	10.4746	10.3219	10.1887	10.0722	9.9701	9.8803
11.125%	10.9352	10.7332	10.5586	10.4071	10.2751	10.1597	10.0586	9.9698
11.250%	11.0169	10.8162	10.6429	10.4926	10.3617	10.2475	10.1474	10.0596
11.375%	11.0988	10.8994	10.7274	10.5783	10.4486	10.3355	10.2365	10.1497
11.500%	11.1810	10.9830	10.8122	10.6643	10.5358	10.4237	10.3258	10.2400
11.625%	11.2634	11.0667	10.8972	10.7506	10.6232	10.5123	10.4154	10.3306
11.750%	11.3461	11.1507	10.9825	10.8371	10.7109	10.6011	10.5052	10.4214
11.875%	11.4290	11.2350	11.0681	10.9238	10.7988	10.6901	10.5953	10.5125
12.000%	11.5122	11.3195	11.1539	11.0109	10.8870	10.7794	10.6856	10.6038
12.125%	11.5956	11.4043	11.2399	11.0981	10.9754	10.8689	10.7762	10.6954
12.250%	11.6792	11.4893	11.3262	11.1856	11.0641	10.9587	10.8670	10.7872
12.375%	11.7631	11.5745	11.4127	11.2734	11.1530	11.0487	10.9581	10.8792
12.500%	11.8473	11.6600	11.4995	11.3614	11.2422	11.1390	11.0494	10.9714
12.625%	11.9316	11.7457	11.5865	11.4496	11.3316	11.2294	11.1409	11.0639
12.750%	12.0162	11.8317	11.6738	11.5381	11.4212	11.3202	11.2326	11.1566
12.875%	12.1011	11.9179	11.7613	11.6268	11.5111	11.4111	11.3246	11.2495
13.000%	12.1861	12.0043	11.8490	11.7158	11.6011	11.5023	11.4168	11.3427
13.125%	12.2714	12.0910	11.9369	11.8049	11.6915	11.5937	11.5092	11.4360
13.250%	12.3570	12.1779	12.0251	11.8943	11.7820	11.6853	11.6018	11.5296
13.375%	12.4427	12.2650	12.1135	11.9839	11.8727	11.7771	11.6946	11.6233
13.500%	12.5287	12.3523	12.2021	12.0737	11.9637	11.8691	11.7876	11.7173
13.625%	12.6149	12.4399	12.2910	12.1638	12.0549	11.9613	11.8808	11.8114
13.750%	12.7013	12.5276	12.3800	12.2541	12.1463	12.0538	11.9743	11.9058
13.875%	12.7879	12.6156	12.4693	12.3445	12.2379	12.1464	12.0679	12.0003
14.000%	12.8748	12.7038	12.5588	12.4352	12.3297	12.2393	12.1617	12.0950
14.125%	12.9618	12.7922	12.6485	12.5261	12.4217	12.3323	12.2557	12.1900
14.250%	13.0491	12.8809	12.7384	12.6172	12.5139	12.4256	12.3500	12.2851
14.375%	13.1366	12.9697	12.8285	12.7085	12.6063	12.5190	12.4443	12.3803
14.500%	13.2242	13.0587	12.9188	12.8000	12.6989	12.6126	12.5389	12.4758
14.625%	13.3121	13.1480	13.0093	12.8917	12.7917	12.7065	12.6337	12.5714
14.750%	13.4002	13.2374	13.1000	12.9836	12.8847	12.8004	12.7286	12.6672
14.875%	13.4885	13.3271	13.1909	13.0756	12.9778	12.8946	12.8237	12.7632
15.000%	13.5770	13.4169	13.2820	13.1679	13.0712	12.9890	12.9190	12.8593
15.125%	13.6657	13.5069	13.3733	13.2603	13.1647	13.0835	13.0144	12.9556
15.250%	13.7546	13.5972	13.4647	13.3530	13.2584	13.1782	13.1100	13.0520
15.375%	13.8437	13.6876	13.5564	13.4458	13.3523	13.2731	13.2058	13.1486
15.500%	13.9329	13.7782	13.6483	13.5388	13.4464	13.3681	13.3018	13.2454
15.625%	14.0224	13.8690	13.7403	13.6320	13.5406	13.4633	13.3979	13.3423
15.750%	14.1120	13.9600	13.8325	13.7253	13.6350	13.5587	13.4941	13.4394
15.875%	14.2019	14.0511	13.9249	13.8189	13.7296	13.6542	13.5905	13.5366

MONTHLY PAYMENT TO AMORTIZE A LOAN OF $1,000

Term of Loan

Interest Rate	25 Years	26 Years	27 Years	28 Years	29 Years	30 Years	35 Years	40 Years
11.000%	9.8011	9.7313	9.6695	9.6148	9.5663	9.5232	9.3696	9.2829
11.125%	9.8916	9.8227	9.7618	9.7079	9.6601	9.6178	9.4672	9.3827
11.250%	9.9824	9.9143	9.8543	9.8012	9.7542	9.7126	9.5649	9.4826
11.375%	10.0734	10.0063	9.9471	9.8948	9.8486	9.8077	9.6629	9.5826
11.500%	10.1647	10.0984	10.0401	9.9886	9.9431	9.9029	9.7611	9.6828
11.625%	10.2562	10.1909	10.1333	10.0826	10.0379	9.9984	9.8594	9.7832
11.750%	10.3480	10.2835	10.2268	10.1769	10.1329	10.0941	9.9579	9.8836
11.875%	10.4400	10.3764	10.3205	10.2714	10.2281	10.1900	10.0566	9.9843
12.000%	10.5322	10.4695	10.4145	10.3661	10.3236	10.2861	10.1555	10.0850
12.125%	10.6247	10.5629	10.5087	10.4611	10.4192	10.3824	10.2545	10.1859
12.250%	10.7174	10.6565	10.6030	10.5562	10.5151	10.4790	10.3537	10.2869
12.375%	10.8104	10.7503	10.6977	10.6516	10.6112	10.5757	10.4531	10.3880
12.500%	10.9035	10.8443	10.7925	10.7471	10.7074	10.6726	10.5525	10.4892
12.625%	10.9969	10.9385	10.8875	10.8429	10.8039	10.7697	10.6522	10.5905
12.750%	11.0905	11.0329	10.9827	10.9388	10.9005	10.8669	10.7520	10.6920
12.875%	11.1843	11.1276	11.0781	11.0350	10.9973	10.9644	10.8519	10.7935
13.000%	11.2784	11.2224	11.1738	11.1313	11.0943	11.0620	10.9519	10.8951
13.125%	11.3726	11.3175	11.2696	11.2279	11.1915	11.1598	11.0521	10.9969
13.250%	11.4670	11.4127	11.3656	11.3246	11.2888	11.2577	11.1524	11.0987
13.375%	11.5616	11.5082	11.4618	11.4214	11.3864	11.3558	11.2529	11.2006
13.500%	11.6564	11.6038	11.5581	11.5185	11.4841	11.4541	11.3534	11.3026
13.625%	11.7515	11.6996	11.6547	11.6157	11.5819	11.5525	11.4541	11.4047
13.750%	11.8467	11.7956	11.7514	11.7131	11.6799	11.6511	11.5549	11.5069
13.875%	11.9420	11.8917	11.8483	11.8107	11.7781	11.7498	11.6557	11.6091
14.000%	12.0376	11.9881	11.9453	11.9084	11.8764	11.8487	11.7567	11.7114
14.125%	12.1334	12.0846	12.0425	12.0062	11.9749	11.9477	11.8578	11.8138
14.250%	12.2293	12.1813	12.1399	12.1043	12.0735	12.0469	11.9590	11.9162
14.375%	12.3254	12.2781	12.2375	12.2024	12.1722	12.1461	12.0603	12.0187
14.500%	12.4216	12.3751	12.3351	12.3007	12.2711	12.2456	12.1617	12.1213
14.625%	12.5181	12.4723	12.4330	12.3992	12.3701	12.3451	12.2632	12.2240
14.750%	12.6146	12.5696	12.5310	12.4978	12.4693	12.4448	12.3647	12.3267
14.875%	12.7114	12.6671	12.6291	12.5965	12.5686	12.5445	12.4664	12.4294
15.000%	12.8083	12.7647	12.7274	12.6954	12.6680	12.6444	12.5681	12.5322
15.125%	12.9054	12.8625	12.8258	12.7944	12.7675	12.7445	12.6699	12.6351
15.250%	13.0026	12.9604	12.9243	12.8935	12.8672	12.8446	12.7718	12.7380
15.375%	13.0999	13.0584	13.0230	12.9928	12.9669	12.9448	12.8738	12.8410
15.500%	13.1975	13.1566	13.1218	13.0922	13.0668	13.0452	12.9758	12.9440
15.625%	13.2951	13.2550	13.2208	13.1916	13.1668	13.1456	13.0780	13.0471
15.750%	13.3929	13.3534	13.3198	13.2913	13.2669	13.2462	13.1801	13.1502
15.875%	13.4908	13.4520	13.4190	13.3910	13.3671	13.3468	13.2824	13.2533

Factors To Compute Monthly Interest

Annual Interest %	Monthly Interest %	Annual Interest %	Monthly Interest %	Annual Interest %	Monthly Interest %
6	0.5000	11	0.9167	16	1.333
6¼	0.5208	11¼	0.9375	16¼	1.354
6½	0.5417	11½	0.9583	16½	1.375
6¾	0.5625	11¾	0.9792	16¾	1.396
7	0.5833	12	1.0000	17	1.417
7¼	0.6042	12¼	1.0208	17¼	1.438
7½	0.6250	12½	1.0417	17½	1.458
7¾	0.6458	12¾	1.0625	17¾	1.479
8	0.6667	13	1.0833	18	1.500
8¼	0.6875	13¼	1.1042	18¼	1.521
8½	0.7083	13½	1.1250	18½	1.542
8¾	0.7292	13¾	1.1458	18¾	1.563
9	0.7500	14	1.1667	19	1.583
9¼	0.7708	14¼	1.1875	19¼	1.604
9½	0.7917	14½	1.2083	19½	1.625
9¾	0.8125	14¾	1.2292	19¾	1.646
10	0.8333	15	1.2500	20	1.667
10¼	0.8542	15¼	1.2708	20¼	1.688
10½	0.8750	15½	1.2917	20½	1.708
10¾	0.8958	15¾	1.3125	20¾	1.729

Example:

Loan Balance $19,866.66

Interest 10%/year or 0.8333/month

Monthly Payment $300.00

Interest: 0.8333 × 19,866.66 .... (165.55)

Payment Toward Principal 134.45

New Loan Balance $19,732.21

Monthly Payment $300.00

Interest: 0.8333 × 19,732.21 .... (164.43)

Payment Toward Principal 135.57

New Loan Balance $19,596.64

Appendix B

Measurements and Conversions

Measurements

Square Footage Formulas

Metric Measurements and Conversions

Measurements

Computing Square Feet

Square Feet	Acres	Square Feet	Acres	Square Feet	Acres	Square Feet	Acres
1,742,400	40	217,800	5	26,136	0.6	3,049.2	0.07
1,306,800	30	174,240	4	21,780	0.5	2,613.6	0.06
871,200	20	130,680	3	17,424	0.4	2,178	0.05
435,600	10	87,120	2	13,068	0.3	1,742.4	0.04
392,040	9	43,560	1	8,712	0.2	1,306.8	0.03
348,480	8	39,204	0.9	4,356	0.1	871.2	0.02
304,920	7	34,848	0.8	3,920.4	0.09	435.6	0.01
261,360	6	30,492	0.7	3,484.8	0.08		

Number of Various Lots per Acre

For the purpose of subdivision, the number of lots per acre given below must be adjusted to allow for streets and other dedications.

Lot Size	Approximate Number of Lots per Acre	Lot Size	Approximate Number of Lots per Acre	Lot Size	Approximate Number of Lots per Acre	Lot Size	Approximate Number of Lots per Acre
25 × 100	17.42	30 × 100	14.52	50 × 100	8.71	100 × 100	4.35
25 × 120	14.52	30 × 120	12.1	50 × 120	7.26	100 × 120	3.63

Widths Times Depths Equaling One Acre

1 Acre Equals		1 Acre Equals		1 Acre Equals	
Length	Width	Length	Width	Length	Width
16.5 ft.	2640.0 ft.	66.0 ft.	660.0 ft.	132.00 ft.	330.00 ft.
33.0	1320.0	75.0	580.8	150.00	290.40
50.0	871.2	100.0	435.6	208.71	208.71

Price Per Acre Produced by Certain Prices Per Square Foot

Cents Per Square Foot	$ Per Acre	Cents Per Square Foot	$ Per Acre	Cents Per Square Foot	$ Per Acre	Cents Per Square Foot	$ Per Acre
1¢	$ 435.60	9¢	$ 3,920.40	30¢	$13,068	70¢	$30,492
2	871.20	10	4,356.00	35	15,246	75	32,670
3	1,306.80	12	5,227.20	40	17,424	80	34,848
4	1,742.40	14	6,098.40	45	19,602	85	37,026
5	2,178.00	16	6,969.60	50	21,780	90	39,204
6	2,613.60	18	7,840.80	55	23,958	95	41,382
7	3,049.20	20	8,712.00	60	26,136	100	43,560
8	3,484.80	25	10,890.00	65	28,314		

1 link = 7.92 inches
1 rod = 16½ feet
5½ yards = 25 links
1 chain = 66 feet = 4 rods = 100 links
1 furlong = 660 feet = 40 rods
1 mile = 8 furlongs = 320 rods = 80 chains = 5,280 feet
1 square mile = 1 section = 640 acres
1 township = 36 sections or square miles
1 square rod = 272¼ square feet = 30¼ square yards
1 acre = 43,560 square feet
1 acre = 160 square rods
1 acre is about 208¾ feet square
1 acre is 8 rods × 20 rods (or any two numbers of rods whose product is 160)

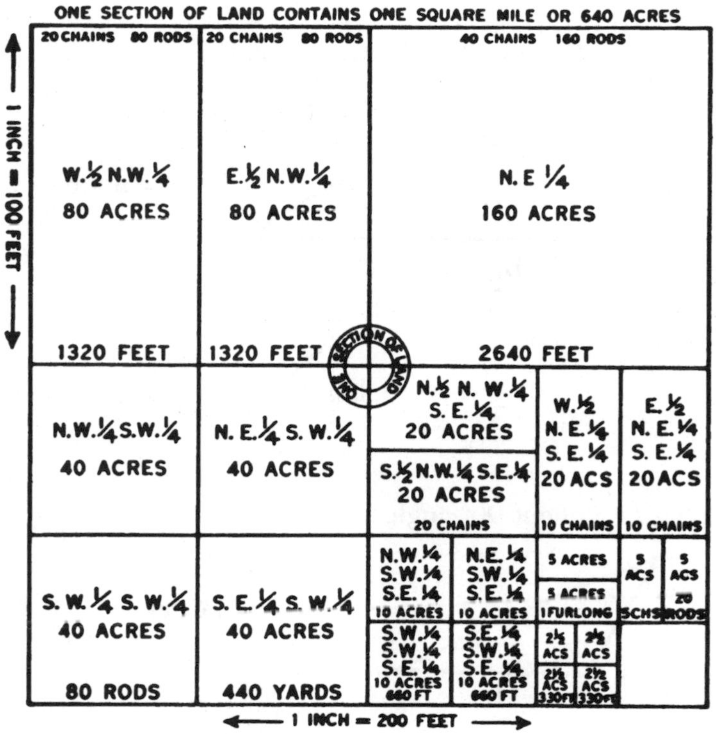

ONE SECTION OF LAND CONTAINS ONE SQUARE MILE OR 640 ACRES

20 CHAINS 80 RODS	20 CHAINS 80 RODS	40 CHAINS 160 RODS

1 INCH = 100 FEET

W.½ N.W.¼ 80 ACRES	E.½ N.W.¼ 80 ACRES	N.E ¼ 160 ACRES
1320 FEET	1320 FEET	2640 FEET

SECTION OF LAND

N.W.¼ S.W.¼ 40 ACRES	N.E.¼ S.W.¼ 40 ACRES	N.½ N. W.¼ S.E.¼ 20 ACRES	W.½ N.E.¼ S.E.¼ 20 ACS	E.½ N.E.¼ S.E.¼ 20 ACS
		S.½ N.W.¼ S.E.¼ 20 ACRES		
		20 CHAINS	10 CHAINS	10 CHAINS

S.W.¼ S.W.¼ 40 ACRES	S.E.¼ S.W.¼ 40 ACRES	N.W.¼ S.W.¼ S.E.¼ 10 ACRES	N.E.¼ S.W.¼ S.E.¼ 10 ACRES	5 ACRES	5 ACS	5 ACS
				5 ACRES	5	20
		S.W.¼ S.W.¼ S.E.¼ 2½ ACS	S.E.¼ S.W.¼ S.E.¼ 2½ ACS	1 FURLONG	5CHS	RODS
80 RODS	440 YARDS	S.W.¼ S.E.¼ S.E.¼ 2½ ACS 330ft	S.E.¼ S.E.¼ S.E.¼ 2½ ACS 330ft			

1 INCH = 200 FEET

Square Footage Formulas

a = area   b = base   h = height

① Squares

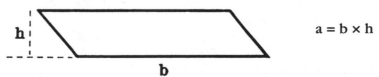

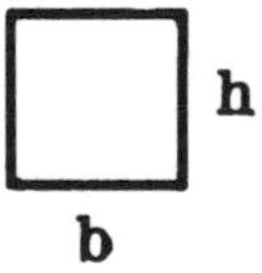

a = b × h

② Rectangles

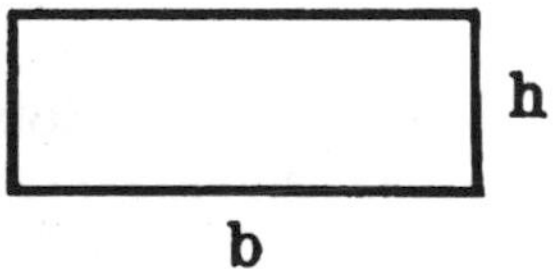

a = b × h

③ Parallelograms
(four-sided figures with parallel opposite sides)

a = b × h

④ Trapezoid
(four-sided figure with only two parallel sides)

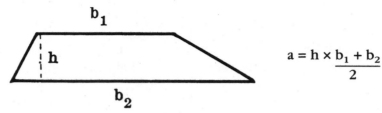

$$a = h \times \frac{b_1 + b_2}{2}$$

⑤ Triangles with 90° angle

$$a = \tfrac{1}{2}(b \times h)$$

⑥ Triangles without 90° angle

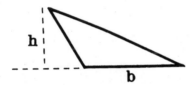

$$a = \tfrac{1}{2}(b \times h)$$

⑦ Circle
R = radius

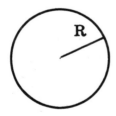

$a = R^2 \times 3.1416$
If radius is 14 feet,
$a = 14 \times 14 \times 3.1416 = 615.75$

⑧ Segment of circle

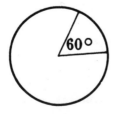

Since there are 360° in a
circle, the area of a 60°
section is $\frac{60}{360}$, or $\frac{1}{6}$
of the entire circle.

⑨ Segment of circle
If the radius and length of an arc are given:

$$a = \text{length of arc} \times \tfrac{1}{2}\text{ radius}$$

Metric Measurements and Conversions

Distance
km = kilometer   cm = centimeter
m = meter   mm = millimeter
dm = decimeter

	km	**m**	**dm**	**cm**	**mm**	**mile**	**yard**	**foot**	**inch**
1 km	1	1,000	10,000	100,000	1,000,000	0.6214	1,093.64	3280.9	
1 m	$\frac{1}{1,000}$	1	10	100	1,000	0.00062	1.0936	3.2809	39.371
1 dm	$\frac{1}{10,000}$	$\frac{1}{10}$	1	10	100		0.1094	0.3281	3.9371
1 cm		$\frac{1}{100}$	$\frac{1}{10}$	1	10		0.0109	0.0328	0.3937
1 mm		$\frac{1}{1,000}$	$\frac{1}{100}$	$\frac{1}{10}$	1			0.0033	0.0394
1 mile	1.6093	1609.33				1	1,760	5,280	63,360
1 yard		0.9144	9.1438	91.438	914.38		1	3	36
1 foot		0.3048	3.0479	30.479	304.79		$\frac{1}{3}$	1	12
1 inch		0.0254	0.254	2.54	25.4		0.0277	0.0833	1

Volume
1 cubic yard = 0.7646 cubic meters   1 cubic meter = 1.308 cubic yards
1 cubic foot = 0.0283 cubic meters   1 cubic meter = 35.34 cubic feet

Liquid Volume
10 milliliters = 1 centiliter = 0.338 fluid ounce
10 centiliters = 1 deciliter = 0.845 liquid gill
10 deciliters = 1 liter = 1.0567 liquid quarts
10 liters = 1 dekaliter = 2.6417 liquid gallons
10 dekaliters = 1 hectoliter = 2.8375 U.S. bushels
10 hectoliters = 1 kiloliter = 28.375 U.S. bushels
                     (or stere)

Weight
kg = kilogram   g = gram
1 kg = 1,000 grams
1 kg = 2.205 pounds   1 pound = 0.4536 kg
1 g = 0.0353 ounce   1 ounce = 28.35 g

Distance Conversions

Inches	Centimeters	Centimeters	Inches	Feet	Meters	Meters	Feet
1	2.54	1	.3937	1	.3048	1	3.281
2	5.08	2	.7874	2	.6096	2	6.562
3	7.62	3	1.181	3	.9144	3	9.843
4	10.16	4	1.575	4	1.219	4	13.12
5	12.70	5	1.969	5	1.524	5	16.40
6	15.24	6	2.362	6	1.829	6	19.69
7	17.78	7	2.756	7	2.133	7	22.97
8	20.32	8	3.150	8	2.438	8	26.25
9	22.86	9	3.543	9	2.743	9	29.53
10	25.40	10	3.937	10	3.048	10	32.81
20	50.80	20	7.874	20	6.096	20	65.62
30	76.20	30	11.81	30	9.144	30	98.43
40	101.6	40	15.75	40	12.19	40	131.2
50	127.0	50	19.69	50	15.24	50	164.0
60	152.4	60	23.62	60	18.29	60	196.9
70	177.8	70	27.56	70	21.33	70	229.7
80	203.2	80	31.50	80	24.38	80	262.5
90	228.6	90	35.43	90	27.43	90	295.3
100	254.0	100	39.37	100	30.48	100	328.1
200	508.0	200	78.74	200	60.96	200	656.2
300	762.0	300	118.1	300	91.44	300	984.3
400	1,016	400	157.5	400	121.9	400	1,312
500	1,270	500	196.9	500	152.4	500	1,640
600	1,524	600	236.2	600	182.9	600	1,969
700	1,778	700	275.6	700	213.3	700	2,297
800	2,032	800	315.0	800	243.8	800	2,625
900	2,286	900	354.3	900	274.3	900	2,953
1,000	2,540	1,000	393.7	1,000	304.8	1,000	3,281

Yards	Meters	Meters	Yards	Miles	Kilometers	Kilometers	Miles
1	.9144	1	1.094	1	1.609	1	.6214
2	1.829	2	2.188	2	3.218	2	1.243
3	2.743	3	3.282	3	4.828	3	1.864
4	3.658	4	4.376	4	6.437	4	2.486
5	4.572	5	5.470	5	8.047	5	3.107
6	5.486	6	6.564	6	9.656	6	3.728
7	6.401	7	7.658	7	11.27	7	4.350
8	7.315	8	8.752	8	12.87	8	4.971
9	8.230	9	9.846	9	14.48	9	5.592
10	9.144	10	10.94	10	16.09	10	6.214
20	18.29	20	21.88	20	32.18	20	12.43
30	27.43	30	32.82	30	48.28	30	18.64
40	36.58	40	43.76	40	64.37	40	24.86
50	45.72	50	54.70	50	80.47	50	31.07
60	54.86	60	65.64	60	96.56	60	37.28
70	64.01	70	76.58	70	112.7	70	43.50
80	73.15	80	87.52	80	128.7	80	49.71
90	82.30	90	98.46	90	144.8	90	55.92
100	91.44	100	109.4	100	160.9	100	62.14
200	182.9	200	218.8	200	321.8	200	124.3
300	274.3	300	328.2	300	482.8	300	186.4
400	365.8	400	437.6	400	643.7	400	248.6
500	457.2	500	547.0	500	804.7	500	310.7
600	548.6	600	656.4	600	965.6	600	372.8
700	640.1	700	765.8	700	1,127	700	435.0
800	731.5	800	875.2	800	1,287	800	497.1
900	823.0	900	984.6	900	1,448	900	559.2
1,000	914.4	1,000	1,094	1,000	1,609	1,000	621.4

Fractional Equivalents

Fractional Inches	Decimal Inches	Millimeters	Fractional Inches	Decimal Inches	Millimeters
1/16	.0625	1.587	9/16	.5625	14.287
1/8	.1250	3.175	5/8	.6250	15.875
3/16	.1875	4.762	11/16	.6875	17.462
1/4	.2500	6.350	3/4	.7500	19.050
5/16	.3125	7.937	13/16	.8125	20.637
3/8	.3750	9.525	7/8	.8750	22.225
7/16	.4375	11.112	15/16	.9375	23.812
1/2	.5000	12.700	1	1	25.400

Area Conversions

Square Inches	Square Centimeters	Square Centimeters	Square Inches	Square Yards	Square Meters	Square Meters	Square Yards
1	6.452	1	.1550	1	.8361	1	1.196
2	12.90	2	.3100	2	1.672	2	2.392
3	19.36	3	.4650	3	2.508	3	3.588
4	25.81	4	.6200	4	3.344	4	4.784
5	32.26	5	.7750	5	4.181	5	5.980
6	38.71	6	.9300	6	5.017	6	7.176
7	45.16	7	1.085	7	5.853	7	8.372
8	51.62	8	1.240	8	6.689	8	9.568
9	58.07	9	1.395	9	7.525	9	10.76
10	64.52	10	1.550	10	8.361	10	11.96
20	129.0	20	3.100	20	16.72	20	23.92
30	193.6	30	4.650	30	25.08	30	35.88
40	258.1	40	6.200	40	33.44	40	47.84
50	322.6	50	7.750	50	41.81	50	59.80
60	387.1	60	9.300	60	50.17	60	71.76
70	451.6	70	10.85	70	58.53	70	83.72
80	516.2	80	12.40	80	66.89	80	95.68
90	580.7	90	13.95	90	75.25	90	107.6
100	645.2	100	15.50	100	83.61	100	119.6
200	1,290	200	31.00	200	167.2	200	239.2
300	1,936	300	46.50	300	250.8	300	358.8
400	2,581	400	62.00	400	334.4	400	478.4

Square Inches	Square Centimeters	Square Centimeters	Square Inches	Square Yards	Square Meters	Square Meters	Square Yards
500	3,226	500	77.50	500	418.1	500	598.0
600	3,871	600	93.00	600	501.7	600	717.6
700	4,516	700	108.5	700	585.3	700	837.2
800	5,162	800	124.0	800	668.9	800	956.8
900	5,807	900	139.5	900	752.5	900	1,076
1,000	6,452	1,000	155.0	1,000	836.1	1,000	1,196

Area

1 square mile = 2.59 square kilometers
1 acre = 4068.8 square meters
1 square yard = 0.836 square meters
1 square foot = 0.0929 square meters = 929 square centimeters

Temperature

°F	°C	°F	°C	°C	°F	°C	°F
−10	−23.0	90	32.2	−20	− 4	40	104
0	−17.8	100	37.8	−10	14	50	122
10	−12.2	110	43	0	32	60	140
20	− 6.7	120	49	5	41	80	176
30	− 1.1	130	54	10	50	100	212
40	4.4	150	66	15	59	120	248
50	10	200	93	20	68	150	302
60	15.6	300	149	25	77	180	356
70	21.1	400	204	30	86	200	392
80	26.7	500	260	35	95	250	482

Appendix C
Homeowner's Records

Home Purchase Information

Home Sales Information

Directory of Professional Advisers

Directory of Technicians and Suppliers

Maintenance of House and Equipment

Capital Home Improvements (Tax Form A)

Noncompensated Casualty Losses in Excess of $100 (Tax Form B)

Depreciation Schedule of Portion of Home Used for Rental or
  Business (Tax Form C)

Maintenance Expenses for Portion of Home Used for Rental or
  Business (Tax Form C-1)

Depreciation Schedule of Furniture and Equipment Used for Rental
  or Business (Tax Form D)

Tax Basis (Tax Form E)

Selling Expenses (Tax Form F)

Fixing-Up Expenses (Tax Form G)

Computing Gain on Sale and Basis of a New Home (Tax Form H)

Computing Gain on Sale and Basis of a New Home for Persons 55
  and Older (Tax Form I)

Tax-Deductible Moving Expenses (Tax Form J)

Suggested System for Filing Documents and Records

Home Purchase Information

Property Purchased _____

Legal Description _____

_____ Tax Assessor's Number _____

Date of Agreement   Date of Recordation
To Purchase _____   of Deed _____

Title Held By _____

Form of Ownership _____

	Name	Reference Number	Address	Phone	Fax
Real Estate Firm					
Salesperson					
Escrow Holder					
Title or Abstract Company					
Attorney					
First Loan					
Second Loan					
Third Loan					
Termite Company					
Home Protection Company					
Insurance Company					
Insurance Agent					
Seller					

Home Sales Information

Property Sold _____

Date of Agreement
To Sell _____

Date of Recordation
of Deed _____

	Name	Reference Number	Address	Phone	Fax
Real Estate Firm					
Salesperson					
Escrow Holder					
Title or Abstract Company					
Attorney					
First Loan					
Second Loan					
Third Loan					
Termite Company					
Home Protection Company					
Insurance Company					
Insurance Agent					
Buyer					

_____

_____

_____

_____

Directory of Professional Advisers

(Real Estate Brokers, Attorneys, Insurance Brokers, Accountants, etc.)

Profession	Name	Address	Phone	Fax

Directory of Technicians and Suppliers

Trade or Business	Name	Address	Phone	Fax

Maintenance of House and Equipment

Description of Work	Anticipated Life	Date of Repairs	Repairs Made By	Cost

Tax Form A
Capital Home Improvements

Refer to Chapter 10 under the heading "Capital Improvements."

Description of Work	Date	Check Number	Contractor	Invoice Number	Cost
Examples: structural, carpentry, storage, plumbing, electrical, security systems, insulation, etc.					

Tax Form B
Noncompensated Casualty Losses in Excess of $100

Refer to Chapter 10 under the heading "Casualty Losses."

Date Loss Occurred	Description of Loss	Amount

Tax Form C
Depreciation Schedule
of Portion of Home Used for Rental or Business

Refer to Chapter 10 under the headings "Rental Use of Home," "Business Use of Home" and "Depreciation."

Refer to

- IRS Publication 527 "Rental Income and Royalty Income"
- IRS Publication 587 "Operating a Business in Your Home"
- IRS Publication 534 "Tax Information on Depreciation"
- *Consult your tax adviser*

Description of Area Used for ☐ Rental, ☐ Business: _____

_____

_____

_____

Proportionate Cost of Area Used for Rental or Business $_____

Estimated Useful Life _____ Years. Depreciation Method _____

Tax Year	Amount Depreciated	Tax Year	Amount Depreciated	Tax Year	Amount Depreciated	Tax Year	Amount Depreciated

Tax Form C-1
Maintenance Expenses
for Portion of Home Used for Rental or Business

Date	Description of Expense	Cost

Tax Form D
Depreciation Schedule
of Furniture and Equipment Used for Rental or Business

Items Depreciated:					
Date Acquired					
Cost Basis					
Useful Life					
Depreciation Method					
Tax Year	*Amount Depreciated*	*Amount Depreciated*	*Amount Depreciated*	*Amount Depreciated*	*Amount Depreciated*

Tax Form E
Tax Basis

Property
Address _____

Date of
Purchase _____

Purchase Price . . . . $_____

Less: Personal Property Included in Price, if Any . . . . −$_____

Net Purchase Price . . . . $_____

Plus: Nondeductible Acquisition Costs*

_____ $_____

_____ $_____

_____ $_____

_____ $_____

_____ $_____

_____ $_____

_____ $_____

+$_____

Total Acquisition Cost of Home . . . . $_____

Minus: Deferred Gains from Previous Transactions . . . . −$_____

Tax Basis of Home. . . . . $_____

Plus: Capital Improvements (Form A)

_____ $_____

_____ $_____

_____ $_____

_____ $_____

_____ $_____

_____ $_____

+$_____

Less: Noncompensated Casualty Losses in Excess of $100 (Form B). . . . . −$_____

Less: Depreciation Deductions for Rental or Business Use of Home (Form C). . . . . . −$_____

Adjusted Tax Basis of Home. . . . . $_____

Examples include appraisal fees, credit reports, inspection fees, title fees, attorney fees, mortgage insurance premiums.

Tax Form F
Selling Expenses

Selling expenses are deducted from the selling price, thus reducing the amount realized from sale of the property. Examples: commission, advertising cost, title or abstract fee, legal fee, escrow fee, discount points, transfer tax, recording fee, notary fee, appraisal fee, reconveyance fee, forwarding fee, statement fee.

(*Prepayment Penalties* are considered interest and as such deductible against ordinary income).

Address of
Home Sold _____

Closing
Date _____

Description	Amount

Tax Form G
Fixing-Up Expenses

Fixing-up expenses are the cost of work to assist the sale, if performed within 90 days prior to the agreement of sale and paid within 30 days after closing. While fixing-up expenses cannot be deducted against ordinary income nor do they have any effect on the tax basis of the property, they do reduce the taxable (recognized) gain upon sale of the home. Examples include repairs, painting, cleaning and servicing of lawn and trees. (Any minor improvements should be added to the basis as capital improvements.)

Address of
Home Sold _____   *Closing*
                                                         Date _____

Date of Agreement To Sell _____   *Date of Closing* _____

Description of Work	Date Performed	Date Paid	Check Number	Performed By	Cost

Tax Form H
Computing Gain on Sale and Basis of a New Home

Refer to Chapter 10 under the heading "Sale and Purchase of Another Home."

Address of
Home Sold _____   *Closing*
Date _____

Address of
New Home _____   *Closing*
Date _____

1. Sales price. . . . . $_____

2. Minus personal property included in price, if any. . . . .   −$_____

3. Net sales price (line 1 minus line 2) . . . . $_____

4. Minus selling expenses (from Form F). . . . .   −$_____

5. Amount realized on sale (line 3 minus line 4). . . . . $_____

6. Minus adjusted basis of home sold (from Form E).   −$_____

7. Gain realized on sale (line 5 minus line 6) . . . . $_____

8. Amount realized on sale (from line 5) . . . . $_____

9. Minus fixing-up expenses (from Form G). . . . .   −$_____

10. Adjusted sales price (line 8 less line 9) . . . . $_____

11. Minus total acquisition cost of new home (from Form E)* . . . .   −$_____

12. Gain recognized (taxable) (line 10 minus line 11). . . . . $_____

13. Gain realized on sale (from line 7). . . . . $_____

14. Minus gain recognized (from line 12) . . . .   −$_____

15. Deferred gain (line 13 minus line 14) . . . . $_____

16. Total acquisition cost of new home (from line 11) . . . . $_____

17. Minus deferred gain (from line 15) . . . .   −$_____

18. Basis of new home (line 16 minus line 17). . . . . $_____

If amount on line 11 is higher than line 10, gain recognized will be zero.

Tax Form I
Computing Gain on Sale and Basis of a New Home
for Persons 55 and Older

Refer to Chapter 10 under the heading "Sale by Person 55 and Over."

Address of
Home Sold _____   *Closing*
                                                               Date _____

Address of
New Home _____   *Closing*
                                                               Date _____

1. Sales price. . . . . $_____

2. Minus personal property included in price, if any.   −$_____

3. Net sales price (line 1 minus line 2) . . . . $_____

4. Minus selling expenses (from Form F).   −$_____

5. Amount realized on sale (line 3 minus line 4). . . . . $_____

6. Minus adjusted basis of home sold (from Form E). . . . .   −$_____

7. Gain realized on sale (line 5 minus line 6) . . . . $_____

8. Minus exemption. . . . .   −$_____

9. Taxable gain on sale (line 7 minus line 8). . . . . $_____

10. Amount realized on sale (from line 5) . . . . $_____

11. Minus fixing-up expenses (from Form G). . . . .   −$_____

12. Adjusted sales price (line 10 minus line 11). . . . . $_____

13. Minus exemption. . . . .   −$_____

14. Revised adjusted sales price (line 12 minus line 13) . . . . $_____

15. Minus total acquisition cost of new home (from Form E)*. . . . .   −$_____

16. Gain recognized (taxable) (line 14 minus line 15). . . . . $_____

17. Taxable gain on sale (from line 9) . . . . $_____

18. Minus gain recognized (from line 16) . . . .   −$_____

19. Deferred gain (line 17 minus line 18) . . . . $_____

20. Total acquisition cost of new home (from line 15) . . . . $_____

21. Minus deferred gain (from line 19) . . . .   −$_____

22. Basis of new home (line 20 minus line 21). . . . . $_____

If amount on line 14 is higher than line 15, gain recognized on line 16 will be zero.

Tax Form J
Tax-Deductible Moving Expenses

Refer to Chapter 10 under the heading "Tax-Deductible Moving Expenses."

Date	Nature of Expense	Paid To	Amount	Check Number

Suggested System for Filing Documents and Records

There are many vital housing-related documents that should not only be kept in a safe place (see Chapter 3), but should also be filed in a manner that allows for quick retrieval when needed.

Hanging folders are among the more efficient systems for filing documents. They are readily available in office supply stores, as are inexpensive storage boxes for hanging folders. Three-ring binders with vinyl jackets are especially useful for filing operating instructions and warranties for equipment and appliances.

The following *main headings* are suggested titles for file folders to hold such documents as are listed under each heading.

Home Purchase Documents

Home purchase information form (p. 206)
Previously filled-in home inspection checklists
Financing data and loan commitments
Agreement to purchase
Preliminary title report
Pest control report
Other inspection reports (roof, built-in appliances, etc.)
Closing (settlement) statement
Recorded deed*
Copy of note and trust deed or mortgage*
Title insurance policy or abstract information*
Homeowner's insurance policy*
Home protection certificate or HOW warranty*
Bill of sale for personal property
Other receipts of acquisition costs

Home Sale Documents

Listing agreement
Agreement to sell
Pest control report
Closing statement
Note and recorded trust deed or mortgage, if taken back by seller
Receipts or canceled checks of "fixing-up expenses"
Other receipts of selling expenses
Home sales information form (p. 207)

Deductible Moving and House-Hunting Expenses

Receipts, canceled checks and other documentation
Tax Form J (p. 221)
(See Chapter 10.)

Capital Home Improvements

Receipts, canceled checks, bills, contracts, drawings
Tax Form A (p. 211)
(See chapter 10.)

Expenses for Portion of Home Used for Rental or Business

Receipts and canceled checks
Tax Forms C and C-1 (pp. 213 and 214)
(See Chapter 10.)

Other Deductible Housing Costs

Receipts and canceled checks
(See chapter 10.)

Copies of Federal and State Income Tax Returns

Inventory of Household and Personal Property*

Forms on pages 241 and 242 in Appendix D
Inventory lists, receipts for new acquisitions, and photographs or video
recordings

These documents may be kept in a fireproof safe or in a safe deposit box.

Appendix D

Homeowner's Checklists

Home and Equipment Maintenance Checklist

Checklist of Security Routines

Fire Prevention Checklist

Earthquake Checklist

Babysitter Information and Safety Checklist

The Moving Planner

Personal Household Inventory

Take-With-Me Inventory

Home and Equipment Maintenance Checklist

☑ Done   ■ Spring   ● Fall   ◆ As Required

Foundations, Basement, Crawlspace and Garage

☐	■			Check foundation walls and floors for large cracks.
☐	■			Check for signs of termite infestation.
☐	■			Check grading to assure water drains away from house.
☐	■	●		Make sure downspouts empty into drainage system or onto splash blocks directing water away from house.
☐	■		◆	Check for signs of excessive moisture or leakage following wet weather.
☐	■			Check vent screens for damage.
☐	■			Make sure clothes dryer is vented to outside.
☐	■			Check garage door hardware and lubricate moving parts.

Doors and Windows

☐	■		Check doors, windows and trim for finish failure.
☐	■		Check glazed openings for loose putty.
☐	■	●	Check for broken glass and damaged screens.
☐	■		Clean screens.
☐	■	●	Check hardware and lubricate moving parts.
☐		●	Check weatherstripping for damage and tightness of fit.
☐	■	●	Check caulking at doors, windows and all other openings and joints between wood and masonry.
☐		●	Check for condensation inside storm windows.
☐		●	Install storm windows and doors.

Building Exterior

☐	■		Check masonry for cracks and loose joints.
☐	■		Check painted surfaces for paint failure.
☐	■		Check siding and trim for damage and decay.
☐	■	●	Check all trim for tightness of fit.
☐	■		Keep vines away from walls.
☐	■		Check wooden decks, porches, patios and stairs for signs of termites, decay and wood-soil contact. Clear any accumulated debris.

Roof, Gutters, Downspouts

□	■	●		Check for damaged, loose or missing shingles.
□	■			Check for blisters, cracks and delaminated spots on flat roofs.
□	■			Check underside of roof where accessible for water stains, dampness and termite infestation.
□	■			Check for damaged flashing at roof penetrations, roof ridge and roof edge.
□	■			Check for sagging roof ridge.
□	■			Check masonry chimneys for cracks.
□	■			Check fascias and soffits for paint failure and decay.
□	■			Check for damaged or sagging gutters, downspouts, hangers and strainers.
□	■	●		Clean gutter strainers, gutters and downspouts.
□	■			Check damper and soot build-up inside fireplace flue.
□	■			Check antenna guy wires and supports. (*Caution:* Keep antenna away from power lines; keep TV antenna grounded.)
□	■			Evaluate gutters, downspouts and other sheet metal for repainting or replacement.
□	■			Evaluate roof for future replacement.
□	■	●		Check vents and louvers for bird nests, etc.

Interior Surfaces

□	■			Check all painted and natural finished surfaces for dirt, finish failure, damp spots, mildew, discolorations and cracks and bulges caused by leaks or condensation.
□	■			Check all joints in ceramic tile, laminated plastic and similar surfaces.
□	■			Check caulking around bathtubs, showers, sinks and toilet base.

Floors

□	■			Check for wear and damage, particularly where one floor material joins another (i.e., wood-tile or wood-carpet).
□	■			On hardwood floors, remove old wax and apply new wax.
□	■			Nail down creaking floor boards and replace damaged floor tiles.

Plumbing System

□			◆	Check for drips and leaks around and under sinks, toilets, showers, bathtubs and lavatories.
□			◆	Check faucets, hosebibbs and toilet valves for leakage.
□			◆	Check for signs of excessive rust in water supply pipes.

☐	■			Check for faulty or leaky lawn sprinkler valves.
☐	■			Lubricate well water pump.
☐	■			Have water from private well checked for safety.
☐	■			Check build-up of scum and sludge in septic tank.
☐	■			Check water heater for signs of leaks.
☐	■			Check water heater for signs of excessive mineral deposits and rust.
☐	■			Test operation of sump pump by pouring two buckets of water into sump.
☐	■			Flush out floor drains with hose.
☐		●		Turn off irrigation system and drain exposed pipes.
☐		●		In sub-freezing climates insulate water pipe between meter and house, as well as pipes in basement and attic.
☐			♦	Check last few water bills for sudden jump in usage.

Electrical System

Always follow safety precautions. Reread "Electrical Safety" section of Chapter 5.

☐	■	●		Check condition of lamp cords, extension cords, plugs and outlets. Replace at first sign of wear or damage.
☐	■	●		Check areas where wiring is exposed. Replace at first sign of wear or damage.
☐			♦	If fuses blow or circuit breakers trip frequently, contact an electrician to determine cause and make necessary repairs.
☐			♦	If an appliance sparks, stalls, overheats, smells burnt or if you experience a slight tingling shock from handling or touching it, disconnect the appliance immediately and have it repaired.
☐			♦	Replace all darkened light bulbs.
☐			♦	Fluorescent tubes that flicker or have darkened ends should be replaced. A long delay in starting is a sign the starter needs to be replaced. A humming sound indicates that the ballast needs to be remounted or replaced.
☐	■	●		Clean glass or plastic diffusers and shields of light fixtures.

Heating System

☐		●	♦	Clean or change filter (every two or three months during winter).
☐	■	●		Dust around furnace, air grille and ducts.
☐		●		Lubricate fan and motor bearings.
☐		●		Inspect fan belt tension.
☐	■	●		Check radiator shutoff valve for leakage (hot water and steam systems).
☐	■	●		Check oil storage tank for leakage (oil furnaces).

| □ | | ● | | Have system checked by service professional. |
| □ | | ● | | Have a chimney sweep clean fireplace and chimney. |

Cooling System

□	■		♦	Clean or change filter (every two or three months during summer).
□	■			Lubricate fan and motor bearings.
□	■			Inspect fan belt tension.
□	■			Clean and service humidifier and or dehumidifier.
□	■			Keep garden debris clear of condensing unit.
□	■			Keep air flow unobstructed by draperies and furniture.

Safety Equipment

Smoke Detectors

| □ | | | ♦ | Test regularly, in accordance with manufacturer's recommendations. |

Fire Extinguishers

□	■			Have extinguishers inspected annually by authorized fire extinguisher service agency.
□			♦	Have extinguisher recharged after each use, even the slightest discharge.
□			♦	Check gauge regularly to see if extinguisher is fully charged.
□			♦	Check for rust spots and nozzle obstructions.

Appliances

□	■	●		For *gas ranges,* clean burners as needed.
□			♦	For *electric ranges,* check coils of top elements. If they fail to get red hot throughout when turned on high, the element, switch or wiring may be faulty. Call a service contractor.
□	■	●		Vacuum dust from the refrigerator's condensing unit.
□	■	●		Degrease all parts of the range hood regularly, and remove filters and wash with detergent.
□			♦	Clean and oil electric motors as needed. Check belts.

Grounds and Yard

□		●		Drain outside water lines and hoses before freeze.
□	■	●		Clean area wells, window wells and storm drains.
□	■			Check driveways and walks for cracks and soil erosion.

☐	■			Check fences for loose posts, loose nails, faulty hinges and gate locks, paint failure, decay and termites.
☐	■			Check all outbuildings for decay and termites.
☐	■			Check retaining walls for cracks caused by water build-up.
☐	■			Unplug drain holes in retaining walls.
☐	■	●		Clean and repair out-of-season equipment.
☐	■			Spray trees for insects.
☐	■			Feed and prune trees, shrubs and plants.
☐	■	●		Keep foundations clear of debris, leaves and soil build-up.

Checklist of Security Routines

When You Leave Your Home

During the Day

❑ Check all your windows and doors before you leave. Someone in the family probably left a window open.

❑ Lock the door from the garage to the kitchen or house. An intruder can simply pry open the garage door or enter the garage through a side door or window and have free access to the house.

❑ Bring in the morning newspaper if it is still outside.

❑ Lock your deadbolt lock. Don't get lazy and revert to using only the key-in-knob lock.

❑ Turn on your burglar alarm, if you have one. Remember, daytime burglaries are increasing faster than nighttime burglaries.

❑ Try to arrange with a neighbor to pick up your mail (if you don't have a mail slot in the door). Mail in the box is one of the best clues to an empty house. Burglars know that the average person scoops up the mail just after it arrives.

❑ Make absolutely certain that you have closed and locked your garage door.

❑ Don't leave notes telling anyone you are not at home.

❑ As a fire safety measure, make certain all burners and heating elements not thermostatically controlled are turned off (stove, oven, broiler, hot plate, portable heater, etc.).

❑ When valet-parking your car at a concert, dance, charity event, etc., remove the registration materials from the car, so the attendant cannot find out where the occupants live. A dishonest attendant could easily read the registration address and pass it on to a burglar who could be robbing the household while the owners are at the function.

At Night

❑ Try to leave as many "at home" signs as you can think of.

❑ Use your timers to come on first in the living areas, then in the sleeping areas. Don't leave the bedroom lights on all night. Use a timer so your bedroom light goes off at your usual bedtime.

❑ Leave a radio playing, put it on the same timer. Don't leave a television set on, as this can create a fire hazard.

❏ Double-check your windows and door deadbolts to see that they are secure.

❏ Turn on your yard and porch lights, or let them come on with timers or photo cells.

❏ Set your burglar alarm.

❏ Make sure your garage is locked.

Vacations

❏ Try to have your house maintain a "lived-in" look during your vacation.

❏ Have your inside lights on timers; lights left on all day will stand out.

❏ Have a radio on a timer.

❏ If you have a burglar alarm, see that a trusted neighbor, your private patrol or the police have a key to the alarm, if the shut-off is outside. If the shut-off is inside, provide the same person with a house key, so he or she can enter in case of an alarm. Make sure your neighbor has a key or the combination to the alarm locker, the phone number of the central station and the security code, to avoid having authorities respond if not necessary.

❏ Put as many valuables as possible in safekeeping, in your safe deposit box, with a friend, at the office and so on.

❏ Cancel deliveries of newspapers, milk and so on.

❏ Ask a neighbor to put rubbish and advertising materials in your trash container each collection day. This takes a really good friend!

❏ Ask the post office to hold your mail, submit a temporary change of address or ask a neighbor to pick up your mail each day.

❏ Make arrangements to have your lawn mowed and walks and drives shoveled in case of snow. A few footprints in the snow would help too.

❏ Notify the police department or private police patrol of the dates of your departure and return. Give them a description and the license numbers of all cars that will be parked near the house or have reason to be there for short periods.

❏ If you have a second car, leave it parked in the driveway. If neighbors are going to be looking after your house, ask them to vary the position of your car from day to day.

❏ Do not leave house keys outside, no matter how well you have hidden them.

❏ If possible, avoid loading your car for a vacation in daylight in plain view.

❏ Discuss your vacation plans as little as possible in public. Don't publicize your plans in local newspapers.

Fire Prevention Checklist

Escaping a Fire

Most fire casualties are caused not by flames but by intake of smoke, poisonous gases and superheated air (up to 1,000°F). If a fire breaks out in your home, do the following:

❑ Stay low to the floor. This will give you the best chance of getting out of smoke-filled rooms and hallways. Hot gases and smoke collect near the ceiling first, then move toward the floor as the smoke layer gets thicker. *The best air is near the floor.*

❑ Never rise straight up from bed. You may thrust your head into a layer of toxic gases or superheated air, which could kill you with one breath. Always roll out of bed.

❑ Sleep with your bedroom doors closed. This prevents rapid movement of gases and shuts off potential drafts of air currents, which could spread the fire more rapidly throughout the house.

❑ As you approach a door, feel it first. If the door is hot, don't open it! If the door is not hot to the touch, brace your feet against the door and open it just an inch or so. If warm air comes through the crack, don't go out the door. While no flames may be present, toxic gases, often under pressure, could engulf you as soon as you open the door.

❑ Always close the door before opening a window. This prevents smoke and fire from being drawn into the room.

❑ Stuff blankets or wet towels against the bottom of the door to keep out smoke while awaiting rescue.

Escape Plans   Most fires spread by 100 percent every 60 seconds so that survival may depend upon rapid evacuation. For your best chance at a rapid evacuation, practice the following:

❑ Conduct fire drills at regular intervals, first using regular escape routes, then alternate routes. Since most fires occur after people have retired for the night, it is best to accustom your family to holding fire drills after dark.

❑ Make sure that everyone in your household recognizes the importance of getting out immediately if they even suspect the existence of a fire.

❑ Work out a way to communicate in case of fire (banging on walls, shouting, using intercom systems, fire alarm system and so on), and make sure everyone knows it.

❏ Make sure everyone knows that life safety is the first consideration and that no actions (even calling the fire department) should be taken until after everyone has been alerted of the fire's presence.

❏ Make sure every person in your household knows the ways to get out in case of fire. There should be more than one way out. Use folding escape ladders for second-floor windows.

❏ Make sure all windows and doors needed for emergency escape can be opened easily from the inside.

❏ Designate a meeting place outside the house, so nobody will go back inside looking for someone who is safe outside. Watch your children; don't let them reenter the house to rescue a pet or stuffed animal.

❏ Make sure everyone in your household knows the location of a nearby telephone or street fire alarm box, which fire department to call and to tell the firemen if anyone is trapped inside the building.

❏ Ensure that everyone in your household knows the four points of information to give in an emergency phone call:
   1. Tell exactly where it happened, then repeat it.
   2. Tell what has happened.
   3. Tell who you are.
   4. Tell what kind of help is needed.

❏ Make special plans to evacuate elderly and disabled persons.

❏ Teach small children to first close their bedroom doors in case of fire and then wait by an open window until someone can reach them from outside.

❏ Make it a regular practice to let babysitters know what to do in case of fire. (See babysitter instruction form in Appendix D.)

Earthquake Checklist

Disaster Preparation Guidelines

❑ Have the following basic emergency supplies in a designated place:
- Portable radio (with extra batteries)
- Several flashlights (with extra batteries)
- First aid kit
- Medications used by family members
- Water (several gallons for each family member)
- Small bottle of chlorine bleach to purify drinking water
- Food (canned foods and powdered milk for at least one week's meals)
- Alternate means of cooking, like barbecue or camp stove
- Clothing, sleeping bags and blankets

❑ Keep valuable documents in bank safety deposit.

❑ Have fire extinguishers in operating condition.

❑ Tie water heater with metal straps.

❑ Know the location of your electric circuit breaker or fuse box. Practice turning off the power to make sure you can do it in an emergency.

❑ Know the location of the main water shut-off valve.

❑ Have pipe wrenches and crescent wrenches on hand (for turning off water; and—if necessary—gas.)

❑ Know where gas, electric and water main shutoffs are. If in doubt, ask your water, power and gas companies. The main gas shut-off valve is located next to your gas meter on the inlet pipe. Use a wrench and give it a quarter-turn in either direction so that it runs crosswise on the pipe. The line is now closed. *Note:* Turn off gas only if there is a hiss that sounds like escaping gas or if there is a smell of rotten eggs, or you see evidence of pipe damage. *Do not relight gas pilot!* Call the utility company to turn gas back on.

Preparing the Home for Quakes

❑ Bolt existing sill plates to the concrete foundation to prevent house from slipping off its foundation. Drill hole through sill plate and into concrete, insert and set ⅝″ steel expansion bolt; secure bolt with washer and nut.

❑ Reinforce frame walls in basement or crawl space to prevent walls from collapsing. Nail ½″ exterior structural grade plywood to studs, using eight-penny nails every 3″ around edges.

❑ Secure water heater to wall to prevent fire and water damage from broken gas line caused by falling water heater. Appropriate straps are available at most hardware stores. Make sure to use flexible gas pipe connection between gas pipe and water heater.

❑ Secure bookshelves and heavy furniture to walls.

❑ Store heavy objects on lower shelves.

❑ Keep fire extinguishers near appliances.

❑ Place beds away from windows and heavy objects.

During an Earthquake

Keep calm. Panic kills. The motion is frightening, but unless it shakes something down on top of you, it is harmless.

❑ If you are indoors, stay there. Get under a desk or a table, or in a doorway. Stay clear of windows, glass doors and mirrors. The greatest hazard from falling objects is just outside doorways and close to outer walls. Stay inside!

❑ If you are outside, get into the open, away from buildings and power lines. Stay there until the shaking stops.

❑ If you are driving a car, pull over to side of road, stop the car, but stay inside. Avoid overpasses, bridges and power lines.

After an Earthquake

Injuries

❑ Check for injuries. If anyone has stopped breathing, give mouth-to-mouth rescue breathing. (See "Rescue Breathing" section in Chapter 5.)

❑ Stop any bleeding injury by applying direct pressure over the site of the wound.

❑ Do not attempt to move seriously injured persons unless they are in immediate danger of further injury.

❑ Cover injured persons with blankets to keep them warm. Be reassuring and calm.

Safety Check

❑ Check for safety. Check your home for fire or fire hazards.

❑ Check utility lines and appliances for damage.

❑ If a gas leak exists, open windows and shut off the main gas valve. Leave building and report leakage to authorities. Do not search for a leak with a match. Do not turn on the gas again; let the gas company restore service.

❏ Shut off electrical power at the control box if there is any damage to your house wiring.

❏ Do not use lighters or open flame appliances until you are certain that no gas leak exists.

❏ Do not operate electrical switches or appliances if gas leaks are suspected. Sparks can ignite gas from broken lines.

❏ Do not touch downed power lines or objects touched by them, or by electrical wiring of any kind.

❏ Check to see that sewage lines are intact before using your toilet. *Note:* The toilet tank (not the bowl) can be a source of emergency water supply if water is cut off. Don't waste it.

❏ Check your chimney for cracks and damage. Approach chimneys with caution. They may topple. *Caution:* Using a damaged chimney invites fire. When in doubt, don't use it.

❏ Check closets and cupboards. Open doors cautiously. Beware of falling objects tumbling off shelves.

Food and Water

❏ Check your food supply. If the water supply is shut off, emergency water supplies may be all around you, in water heaters, toilet tanks (again, not the bowl), melted ice cubes and in canned vegetables.

❏ Do not eat or drink anything from open containers near shattered glass. Liquids may be strained through a clean handkerchief or cloth if danger of glass contamination exists. Water may be disinfected with household chlorine bleach. Use the following proportions:

Clear Water	Chlorine Bleach
1 quart	2 drops
1 gallon	8 drops
5 gallons	½ teaspoon

Mix thoroughly and let stand 30 minutes.

❏ If the power is off, check your freezer and plan meals to use up food that will spoil quickly.

❏ Use outdoor charcoal broilers for emergency cooking.

Cooperate with Public Safety Efforts

❏ *Do not:* Use lighters, candles, open flame appliances or smoke until you are sure there are no gas leaks.

❏ *Do not:* Operate electrical switches or appliances, including telephones, if you suspect a gas leak. The appliances may create a spark that could ignite the leaking gas.

❏ *Do not:* Use your telephone except to report medical, fire or violent crime emergencies. If lines are blocked, it may be easier to call out of the disaster area during emergencies.

❏ Turn on your portable radio for instructions and news reports.

❏ *Do not:* Go sightseeing immediately afterwards, especially in beach and waterfront areas where seismic waves could strike.

❏ Keep streets clear for emergency vehicles.

❏ Be prepared for aftershocks. Most of these are smaller than the main quake, but some may be large enough to do additional damage.

❏ Cooperate with public safety officials. Don't go into damaged areas unless your help is requested.

❏ Informed and cooperative citizens can help minimize damage and injury.

❏ Stay calm and lend a hand to others.

Babysitter Information and Safety Checklist

Name of Family _____ Phone _____

Address _____

Phone Where Parents Can Be Reached _____

_____

Names of Children	Ages	Special Medical Needs
_____	_____	_____
_____	_____	_____
_____	_____	_____
_____	_____	_____
_____	_____	_____
_____	_____	_____
_____	_____	_____

Time To Eat _____ _____ _____ Time To Bed _____

Emergency Telephone Numbers

Doctor _____ Phone _____

Hospital _____ Phone _____

Poison Control Center _____ Phone _____

Fire Department _____ Phone _____

Police _____ Phone _____

Ambulance _____ Phone _____

Taxi _____ Phone _____

Neighbors _____ Phone _____

_____ Phone _____

_____ Phone _____

_____ Phone _____

Babysitter Information and Safety Checklist Dos and Don'ts

Important Instructions to the Babysitter

❏ Lock all doors after parents leave.

❏ Never allow a stranger to enter, even if the caller insists he or she is a friend, relative or neighbor. Giving an explanation or apology to the injured party the following day is far more desirable than taking the chance of letting a potential criminal into the house.

❏ Do not hesitate to call police if any unusual activity occurs.

❏ If you receive telephone calls from unidentified callers, do not give out information of any kind. Never leave the impression you and the children are alone in the house.

❏ Leave the telephone line free in case the parents need to call home.

What To Say in Emergency Telephone Calls

❏ 1. *Tell where it happened.* Give exact location and repeat.

❏ 2. *Tell what has happened.* Is the house on fire? Is someone trapped inside? Is someone bleeding badly? Has someone swallowed poison—what kind of poison?

❏ 3. *Give your name.* Say you are the babysitter.

❏ 4. *Tell what kind of help is needed.*

What To Do in Case of Poisoning

❏ 1. *Read the label* of the substance swallowed.

❏ 2. *Phone* the doctor, poison control center or emergency room of a hospital.

❏ 3. Check label for antidote and administer *only* at the direction of a doctor or the poison control center.

❏ 4. If you take the child to the doctor or hospital, take the poison container with you.

Fire Safety

❏ Be sure you know the location of fire extinguishers, fuse box and flash light.

❏ Be sure you know emergency escape routes (windows, garage roof, ladders).

In Case of Fire

❏ Get everyone out of the house fast, even before calling the fire department.

❑ Be sure you and the children know a designated meeting place outside the house, so no one will go back inside looking for someone who is safe outside.

❑ Don't let children reenter the house to rescue a pet or stuffed animal.

❑ Phone the fire department from a neighbor's house.

❑ If you are trapped inside a room, keep the door closed, then open the window. Stuff towels or other material against bottom of door to keep out smoke. Escape through window or wait for help from outside.

❑ Never open doors that feel hot or warm to the touch.

❑ Never throw water on a flaming electrical appliance. You must unplug it first, or turn off the main switch at the fuse box.

❑ If you smell gas, open a window, get everyone out of the house. Don't switch on lights, don't strike a match, to avoid an explosion. Call fire department or gas company from a neighbor's house.

If Clothing Catches Fire

❑ If it is your own clothing—don't run, it fans the flames. Lie down, roll over and over. Remove the clothing if you can do so without pulling it over your head. Act fast.

❑ If it is someone else's clothing—don't let the person run. Get the victim on the ground—grab and push if necessary. Roll the victim over and over. Use anything handy to smother the flames—a rug, coat, blanket, drapes, towel, bedspread or jacket. Don't wrap the victim's face, only the body. Try to remove burning clothing, but don't pull it over the victim's head.

The Moving Planner

Use this handy calendar to help plan your move.

Six Weeks Before Moving　　　Month _____

Sunday	Date	Monday	Date	Tuesday	Date	Wednesday	Date	Thursday	Date	Friday	Date	Saturday	Date

Five Weeks Before Moving　　　Month _____

Sunday	Date	Monday	Date	Tuesday	Date	Wednesday	Date	Thursday	Date	Friday	Date	Saturday	Date

Four Weeks Before Moving　　　Month _____

Sunday	Date	Monday	Date	Tuesday	Date	Wednesday	Date	Thursday	Date	Friday	Date	Saturday	Date

Three Weeks Before Moving　　　Month _____

Sunday	Date	Monday	Date	Tuesday	Date	Wednesday	Date	Thursday	Date	Friday	Date	Saturday	Date

Two Weeks Before Moving   Month _____

Sunday	Date	Monday	Date	Tuesday	Date	Wednesday	Date	Thursday	Date	Friday	Date	Saturday	Date

One Week Before Moving   Month _____

Sunday	Date	Monday	Date	Tuesday	Date	Wednesday	Date	Thursday	Date	Friday	Date	Saturday	Date

Moving Week   Month _____

Sunday	Date	Monday	Date	Tuesday	Date	Wednesday	Date	Thursday	Date	Friday	Date	Saturday	Date

After the Move   Month _____

Sunday	Date	Monday	Date	Tuesday	Date	Wednesday	Date	Thursday	Date	Friday	Date	Saturday	Date

Personal Household Inventory

Prior to packing day, prepare your personal household inventory, listing all items in each room of your home. Remember to note the number of items in the space provided, e.g. Living Room [2] end tables.

Living Room	Year of Purchase	Orig. Cost	Present Value

Family Room/Den	Year of Purchase	Orig. Cost	Present Value

Bedrooms	Year of Purchase	Orig. Cost	Present Value

Dining Room	Year of Purchase	Orig. Cost	Present Value

Personal Household Inventory

Kitchen/Pantry/Breakfast Room

	Year of Purchase	Orig. Cost	Present Value

Bathroom/Hall Closets

Basement/Utility Room/Attic/Storage

	Year of Purchase	Orig. Cost	Present Value

Garage/Yard/Porch/Recreation Equipment

Miscellaneous

Take-With-Me Inventory

Important Papers
- ☐ Automobile ownership records
- ☐ Children's school records
- ☐ Insurance policies
- ☐ Medical and dental records
- ☐ Other records
- ☐ _____
- ☐ _____
- ☐ _____
- ☐ _____

For the Trip
- ☐ Suitcases (clothing)
- ☐ Sunglasses
- ☐ Credit cards
- ☐ Duplicate keys
- ☐ Baby's equipment
- ☐ _____
- ☐ _____
- ☐ _____
- ☐ _____
- ☐ _____
- ☐ Travel toys for children
- ☐ _____
- ☐ _____
- ☐ _____
- ☐ _____
- ☐ _____
- ☐ Picnic lunch or snacks
- ☐ Canned/bottled water
- ☐ Paper towels
- ☐ Pre-moistened towels or damp washcloth in plastic bag
- ☐ Pillows and a blanket
- ☐ Pet food/dishes
- ☐ _____
- ☐ _____
- ☐ _____
- ☐ _____
- ☐ _____

Valuables
- ☐ Coin or stamp collection
- ☐ Currency
- ☐ Furs
- ☐ Jewelry
- ☐ Silver
- ☐ Irreplaceable photos, slides or videotapes
- ☐ _____
- ☐ _____
- ☐ _____
- ☐ _____
- ☐ _____

In the Car
- ☐ Emergency tools
- ☐ Aerosol tire inflator
- ☐ First-aid kit
- ☐ Flashlight
- ☐ Fire extinguisher
- ☐ Litter basket
- ☐ Road maps and compass
- ☐ Driver's license
- ☐ Car registration certificate
- ☐ Insurance identification cards
- ☐ _____
- ☐ _____
- ☐ _____
- ☐ _____
- ☐ _____

Miscellaneous
- ☐ "Instant Aid" box
- ☐ Camera and film
- ☐ Telephone answering machine (so van operator can alert you of delivery)
- ☐ _____
- ☐ _____
- ☐ _____
- ☐ _____
- ☐ _____

Index